THE GIRL
ON THE
VELVET SWING

ALSO BY SIMON BAATZ

Venerate the Plough: A History of the Philadelphia
Society for Promoting Agriculture, 1785–1985

Knowledge, Culture, and Science in the Metropolis:
The New York Academy of Sciences, 1817–2017

For the Thrill of It: Leopold, Loeb, and the Murder
That Shocked Jazz Age Chicago

THE GIRL
ON THE
VELVET SWING

SEX, MURDER, AND MADNESS
AT THE DAWN OF THE
TWENTIETH CENTURY

SIMON BAATZ

MULHOLLAND BOOKS
LITTLE, BROWN AND COMPANY
NEW YORK   BOSTON   LONDON

Mulholland Books / Little, Brown and Company
Hachette Book Group
1290 Avenue of the Americas, New York, NY 10104
mulhollandbooks.com

First Edition: January 2018

Mulholland Books is an imprint of Little, Brown and Company, a division of Hachette Book Group, Inc. The Mulholland Books name and logo are trademarks of Hachette Book Group, Inc.

The publisher is not responsible for websites (or their content) that are not owned by the publisher.

The Hachette Speakers Bureau provides a wide range of authors for speaking events. To find out more, go to hachettespeakersbureau.com or call (866) 376-6591.

ISBN 978-0-316-39665-3
LCCN 2017942372

10 9 8 7 6 5 4 3 2 1

LSC-H

Printed in the United States of America

CONTENTS

THE GIRL
ON THE
VELVET SWING

1

FIRST ENCOUNTER

EDNA GOODRICH SETTLED INTO HER SEAT AS THE HORSE PULLED away from the curb. The coachman flicked his whip, pulling gently on the reins to steer the chestnut-brown mare into the street. The lunch hour traffic had dispersed, and Thirty-eighth Street was now almost deserted. The horse cantered eastward, toward Broadway.

Goodrich glanced at the young girl seated beside her. Evelyn Nesbit was leaning forward slightly, looking straight ahead, clutching the hat on her head with her right hand and holding the handrail with her left. Edna Goodrich, smugly satisfied at her success, settled herself more comfortably in her seat as the hansom slowed at the approach to Broadway.[1]

The carriage, suddenly stuck in the congestion of wagons and carts that crawled south along Broadway, almost came to a stop. The girl released the grip on her hat and turned to interrogate her companion.

Who was Stanford White? she asked. Why had Edna pestered her so insistently to accept his invitation? Since Evelyn's first appearance on the stage, six weeks previously, dozens of men had tried to attract her attention. They sent her flowers; they shouted her name from the stalls; some waited for her at the stage door. What, she inquired, was so special about Stanford White that they should spend an afternoon fighting the traffic to get across town to visit him?

Edna Goodrich, amused that Evelyn remained unaware of Stanford White's existence, patted the girl's hand reassuringly. White, she replied, was a great man, perhaps the greatest man in New York. He was the architect who had designed so many of the city's most famous buildings, the man responsible for Madison Square Garden on Twenty-sixth Street, the man who had built the Washington Square Arch on Fifth Avenue. He knew everyone, and everyone knew Stanford White. And because he was friendly with so many actors and directors— he had designed the Players' Club on Gramercy Park— Stanford White was influential among theater folk. "He can make you," Edna confided to Evelyn, her voice full of meaning, "anything you wish to be on the stage."[2]

Edna Goodrich was feeling pleased with herself. Stanford White had mentioned to her, several weeks earlier, the photographs of Evelyn that he had seen in the *New York World*. Who was this new girl? he asked. How could he meet her? Goodrich, one of the singers in the *Florodora* sextet, had become acquainted with Evelyn at the end of June after the manager of the company, John Fisher, hired Evelyn as a chorus girl.[3]

The carriage left Broadway, turning onto Twenty-fourth Street, finally coming to a halt before a brownstone house set back from the sidewalk. Evelyn Nesbit looked up in surprise, disappointed that their rendezvous would occur in such a nondescript building. She had thought she might meet Stanford White at the Waldorf Hotel; but they had arrived instead at a large four-story house distinguished from its neighbors only by its shabby, unkempt appearance. The building seemed forbidding, even menacing, as it sat silently in the afternoon sunshine. There was no sign of life within the house, and Evelyn, as she glanced upward, scanning each floor, saw that heavy curtains covered all the windows. She felt a sudden chill — should she enter this gloomy place? — as she imagined the tomb-like silence inside.[4]

Edna Goodrich paid the driver his fare and was now ascending the steps to ring the bell. The door opened inward automatically at her touch, without that familiar click that would indicate the release of a lock, and she began climbing a flight of rickety wooden steps to the second floor.

Evelyn Nesbit stood in the doorway, looking up into the darkened stairwell.

"Where on earth are we going?" she asked anxiously.

"It's all right," Edna answered, pausing to reassure her friend. "Come right along. Go on up," she added cheerfully.

Evelyn began to follow her companion, and as she started up the steps, a door opened at the top of the stairwell. A light appeared, casting its rays on the topmost steps. A man's voice, deep and resonant, a welcoming voice, boomed out a sudden greeting — "Hello" — and as she reached the top of the stairs, Evelyn could see Edna Goodrich leaning into Stanford White, embracing him and kissing him on the cheek.[5]

White stepped backward as Evelyn entered the room. He gazed at her, admiring her figure, his eyes lingering over

Evelyn as she stepped shyly forward. She was just as beautiful as he had anticipated from her photographs in the newspapers; indeed, now that he had met her, Stanford White realized that she was one of the most beautiful girls he had ever seen. Her cream-colored leghorn hat, trimmed with artificial flowers above the brim, was tilted slightly to one side. A taffeta ribbon circled the crown of the hat and fell away behind her, down her back, entwining itself around the long curls of her copper-red hair. Her cream-white blouse and her frock, an ankle-length summer dress of white mull, gave Evelyn a trim, youthful look, making her appear even younger than her sixteen years, an effect exaggerated by the timorous expression that crossed her face as she entered the apartment. White studied her carefully, noticing her large hazel eyes and her full lips. He saw that her nose had a slight upward tilt; her chin was precise, chiseled to perfection; and her forehead was clear and radiant.[6]

He glanced momentarily at Edna Goodrich, giving her a look of appreciation that she had introduced him to this marvelous vision. A second man, Reginald Ronalds, approached, and both men listened attentively as Edna Goodrich introduced Evelyn, telling them that Evelyn had recently joined the chorus in the musical *Florodora* playing at the Casino Theatre. Evelyn was a newcomer to the city, having moved with her mother and younger brother to New York only eight months before, in December 1900.

Stanford White introduced his friend to Edna Goodrich and Evelyn Nesbit. Reginald Ronalds, thirty-five years old, had graduated from Yale University in 1886 and had fought with Teddy Roosevelt's Rough Riders in Cuba during the

Spanish-American War. Despite his claim that he worked on Wall Street, no one, not even his closest friends, had any precise idea how Ronalds made his living; but since he always appeared to have plenty of money, it hardly seemed to matter. In truth, Ronalds lived an indolent existence, dining at his clubs, appearing at the fashionable dances, mingling with the city's aristocracy, and generally enjoying the leisurely life of a man-about-town. Everybody liked him—he was one of the wittiest men in New York—and he was rarely absent from any of the more important events on the social calendar.[7]

The dining table had been set for four people. The two men fussed over Evelyn during the luncheon, teasing her for her girlish appearance, bantering with her, and peppering her with questions. Did she find New York as glamorous as she had imagined? How did she like her role in the *Florodora* chorus? Where did she dine? Whose invitations had she accepted? Did she prefer Delmonico's or Rector's for supper? Evelyn gave her attention more to Reginald Ronalds than to Stanford White— Ronalds was the younger, better-looking man, six feet tall with blue eyes and blond hair—and he joked and flirted with her, appearing all the while solicitous for her welfare, forbidding her to drink more than a single glass of champagne.

Evelyn relaxed; her shyness had left her; the champagne had washed away her inhibitions and she had forgotten her initial apprehension. She felt a slight disappointment that Reginald Ronalds had to leave early—he had to go to his office, he explained—but Stanford White invited his other guests to stay a little longer. And neither Edna Goodrich nor Evelyn Nesbit was in a hurry to depart; both women were in

Florodora, and the evening performance did not begin until seven o'clock.

Stanford White suggested a tour of the house. They ascended the stairs, bypassing the rooms on the third floor, climbing to the topmost level. A large studio with a high ceiling ran the entire length of the fourth floor. This room, like the dining room, was elaborately decorated: artificial light illuminated the red velvet curtains that shut out the sunlight; antique divans and couches, covered with velvet cushions, lined the four sides of the room; and a card table and four chairs stood near the windows at the front of the building.

A swing, attached to the high ceiling by two velvet cords, hung in the center of the room. A large circular paper screen, stretched taut in a thin wire frame, was attached to a pulley suspended from the ceiling. This screen, decorated with a Japanese motif, could be raised above eye level so that it hung directly over the swing.

Stanford White took Evelyn by the hand, helping her to sit on the padded velvet seat of the swing. Edna Goodrich stood a few feet in front of her, pulling slightly on the rope to raise the Japanese screen. Evelyn could feel White's hands on her back, pushing her higher and higher so that her outstretched feet came closer and closer to the screen. Edna, holding the rope in her hands, began to laugh as she watched Evelyn's futile attempts to touch the screen with her feet, and Evelyn also started to laugh at her own helplessness. No matter how hard she strained in her seat, no matter how she urged herself forward, her feet could not pierce the screen that hung invitingly a few inches in front of her.

Evelyn realized that White was controlling her movement with his hands, pushing her just so much, so that despite her efforts, she could not break the paper. But finally, with a single strong push of his hands on her back, Evelyn soared higher than before and her feet split the screen in two.

White replaced the torn screen and Edna Goodrich now took her turn, climbing onto the seat of the swing. Evelyn held the rope, lifting the screen into the air, laughing in her turn as Edna also eventually pierced the paper.[8]

It was all great fun and it had been so unexpected; and they continued to amuse themselves until almost four o'clock. Reluctantly the party disbanded. White announced that he had to go to his office on Fifth Avenue. Edna and Evelyn, meanwhile, had to go uptown to the Casino Theatre to prepare for that evening's performance.

Evelyn Nesbit's encounter with Stanford White seemed to epitomize the sudden good fortune that had accompanied the family's move to New York. Evelyn, along with her mother and brother, had scraped and struggled, often in desperate poverty, for years. Now, it seemed, everything had changed. Two years earlier Evelyn Nesbit was holding a menial job in a Philadelphia department store; now she was on the Broadway stage.

She had been born on Christmas Day in 1884 in Tarentum, a village outside Pittsburgh. Her father, Winfield Scott Nesbit, was a Pittsburgh lawyer, commuting each day to his office on Diamond Street. Many years later Evelyn would recall her early childhood with fondness. She remembered the affection that had existed between her father and her mother, Florence, an affection that included her and her brother, Howard.

But Winfield Scott Nesbit had died unexpectedly in 1893, and his death proved traumatic for his widow. Florence Nesbit was singularly ill-prepared for her loss: she had no formal education and little practical experience outside the home. She had lived in her husband's shadow, and his death left her suddenly bereft.

Nothing was now more painful to Florence Nesbit than the daily humiliation of her impoverishment. Her former acquaintances and friends soon dropped away, and eventually she sold the house in Tarentum, moving the family to Cedar Avenue in the East End, one of the least desirable neighborhoods in Pittsburgh. She rented out rooms to lodgers, took in laundry, and tried her hand at dressmaking, all the while struggling with melancholy and depression, but her efforts were never enough, and gradually the family slipped into poverty.[9]

Her decision in 1899 to move the family to Philadelphia, a larger, more cosmopolitan city, proved to be a turning point. Florence Nesbit secured a position as a saleswoman in Wanamaker's, the largest department store in the city.

She grew to dislike the work there—it required stamina and self-discipline to stand at the counter all day talking to customers—but Florence quickly found new friends among the other lodgers at the boardinghouse on Arch Street where she and her children lived. Everybody made a great fuss over her fourteen-year-old daughter. Evelyn Nesbit was such a pretty girl, so adorable and sweet, and everyone who saw her immediately remarked on her beauty.

An artist, John Storm, visiting his sister at the Arch Street boardinghouse, noticed Evelyn and asked Florence Nesbit if her daughter would pose for him. Soon other artists also were using Evelyn as their model. Violet Oakley designed stained-glass windows for several Philadelphia churches, and Evelyn was one of the models immortalized in glass as a celestial angel. Philadelphia, then the publishing capital of the United States, had many book and magazine illustrators working for such firms as Curtis Publishing and J. B. Lippincott, and Evelyn was soon in demand as an artist's model. She had worked briefly with her mother as a stock girl at Wanamaker's, a job she disliked, and she was thrilled that she could now earn money posing in costume for artists and illustrators.[10]

If Philadelphia had provided such opportunities for Evelyn, would New York City not prove even more profitable? Her daughter's triumph in Philadelphia as an artist's model encouraged Florence Nesbit to imagine that Evelyn might achieve even greater success; and so, in 1900, she moved with her two children to New York, taking rooms in a boardinghouse on West Twenty-second Street.

Florence, who had been initially reluctant to allow her daughter to pose as a model, had long since shed her inhibitions on the matter and now acted as Evelyn's agent in New York. One painter, Carroll Beckwith, hired Evelyn immediately, paying her five dollars to pose for two afternoons each week in his studio in the Sherwood Building on West Fifty-seventh Street.

Beckwith was an important figure in New York's artistic community, and soon other artists, hearing of Evelyn's beauty, contacted Florence Nesbit for permission to employ her daughter.[11]

That permission was rarely denied. Frederick Stuart Church, then fifty-nine years old, hired Evelyn to pose for him each week in his studio on Forty-fourth Street. The sculptor George Grey Barnard used her as the model for his marble figure *Innocence,* and Charles Dana Gibson, a well-known sketch artist, portrayed Evelyn in several of his classic illustrations of the American girl.[12]

Evelyn could command a fee of five dollars for each sitting—the customary amount for an artist's model in 1901—and the money she made supported the family during the first year in New York. But she could obtain more than twice that amount posing for the photographers who supplied the New York magazines with illustrations for the fashion pages. Very soon her picture was ubiquitous.[13]

It was inevitable that her image, widely reproduced in the pages of such newspapers as the *New York World* and the *New York Journal,* should attract the attention of theatrical agents looking for new talent to put on the stage. Ted Marks, one of the first agents to contact Florence Nesbit about her daughter, promised that he could get Evelyn a role in the musical *Florodora,* then playing at the Casino Theatre.

But the manager, John Fisher, had been reluctant to hire Evelyn Nesbit. She was young, too young to go on the stage, and he knew that he might invite an investigation by the authorities if he employed her. But one of his chorines was leaving *Florodora*

The Casino Theatre stood at Thirty-ninth Street and Broadway from 1882 until it was demolished in 1930. The Casino, designed in a style best described as Moorish Revival, included a tower that resembled a minaret. The musical comedy *Florodora* played at the Casino from November 1900 until it moved uptown in October 1901 to the New York Theatre. *(Library of Congress, LC-DIG-det-4a08580)*

the next week. Evelyn was very pretty and could dance passably well, and so, in June 1901, she joined the company as a chorus girl with a weekly salary of fifteen dollars.[14]

Florodora had had a two-year run on the London stage, at the Lyric Theatre on Shaftesbury Avenue, before moving to Broadway in November 1900. The first act, set on an island, Florodora, in the Philippines, tells how Cyrus Gilfain, the owner of a perfume factory, expects his daughter Angela to marry his manager, Frank Abercoed. But Frank has fallen in love with Dolores, a girl who works in the factory.

The second act of the play moves to Wales, where Gilfain has bought a castle. A ghost haunts the castle, eventually forcing Gilfain to confess that he stole the title to the perfume factory: Dolores is the rightful owner. Everything ends happily: Frank Abercoed marries Dolores; Angela Gilfain marries an army officer; and Cyrus Gilfain marries Lady Holyrood, an aristocratic widow.[15]

Florodora, despite its improbable plot, was popular beyond all expectations, playing to acclaim in both London and New York. Its catchy tunes, attractive girls, and extravagant costumes all conspired to make the play, a comic opera, an immediate success in New York, and it eventually ran for more than five hundred performances on Broadway.[16]

The *Florodora* sextet—some of the most beautiful women in New York—was the centerpiece of the show, the fulcrum on which *Florodora* pivoted. These dancers were the stars of the Broadway stage, celebrities whose talents and beauty had earned them fame. Evelyn Nesbit, never more than a mere chorus girl, a bit player on the stage, would watch from the wings, admiring their poise and grace, aspiring to become a member of the famous ensemble. All six women—Frances Belmont, Susan Drake, Daisy Green, Edna Goodrich, Kather-

The musical comedy *Florodora* played at the Casino Theatre from 1900 to 1901. The members of the *Florodora* sextet—reputedly six of the most beautiful women in New York—are shown here in a scene from the second act. This illustration originally appeared in a 1900 souvenir album. *(Billy Rose Theatre Division, New York Public Library for the Performing Arts)*

ine Sears, and Clarita Vidal—knew Stanford White well, and it was one of them, Goodrich, who would first introduce Evelyn Nesbit to the architect.[17]

Evelyn had given little thought to her first encounter with Stanford White. It had been amusing to spend the afternoon in his apartment, playing on the velvet swing; but it was just one novel experience among the many that she had had since her arrival in New York. Stanford White, moreover, had not impressed her; his friend Reginald Ronalds had been better-looking, younger certainly, and more amusing. White, then forty-seven, had seemed somehow remote, more distant, less a companion than a vaguely avuncular presence.

It came as a surprise, therefore, that she should receive a second invitation from White a few days later. White had also asked Elsie Ferguson, an actress then appearing in *The Strollers* at the Knickerbocker Theatre, along with her companion, Thomas Clarke, a dealer in porcelain and antique furniture. The second occasion was not dissimilar from the first: White and his three guests had luncheon in the dining room on the second floor, later ascending to the fourth-floor studio to play on the velvet swing.[18]

White, on this occasion, was less reserved, more carefree, more relaxed, and altogether better company. He was not handsome in a conventional sense, Evelyn thought; but there was a warmth in his manner that seemed to invite intimacy even with those acquaintances who had known him for only a short time. He was tall and imposing, six feet two inches, long-limbed, with gray-green eyes and a shock of spiky red hair. He seemed at first sight slightly awkward in his movements, almost as if he were self-conscious about his appearance. He had been good-looking as a young man, twenty years before, but he was now middle-aged, slightly overweight, and he was no longer as dashing as he believed himself to be.[19]

There was something almost childlike about his exuberant enthusiasm, a quality that could be simultaneously endearing and exasperating. He was generous, charitable toward those less fortunate than he, but too often he acted spontaneously,

always on some whim, rarely paying heed to the consequences, rarely thinking too far into the future.[20]

Evelyn gave as little thought to her second encounter with
White as she had given to her first. White had impressed her
as a man who seemed more considerate and thoughtful than
the majority of men she had met since her arrival in New York,
but there was little else in their encounters that captured her
interest. Evelyn had long been aware that she attracted attention on account of her beauty, but it had never occurred to her
that Stanford White had any intentions toward her.

It was so unexpected, therefore, that less than a week after
the second meeting, her mother should receive a letter from
Stanford White inviting her to visit him in his office on Fifth
Avenue. Who was this man, Florence asked her daughter,
who had asked to see her? Would it be proper, she wondered,
for her to accept an invitation from someone to whom she had
not yet been introduced? Evelyn had told her mother about
her two encounters with Stanford White; she had described
her adventures on the velvet swing; and she had portrayed
White as sympathetic and kind, slightly eccentric perhaps, but
surprisingly extroverted for someone so eminent. Evelyn had
spent two afternoons in his company, yet, she confessed to her
mother, she still knew almost nothing about him. He was an
architect, she knew—and he was involved in some way with
the theater—but otherwise she could provide her mother
with very little specific information.

Florence Nesbit accepted White's invitation to visit him at
his office, and she returned singing his praises. He was the
perfect gentleman, she told her daughter. His interest in

Evelyn was, according to White, simply a consequence of his benevolent regard for those girls struggling to gain a foothold on the Broadway stage. He had significant investments in several New York theaters; he knew many actors and actresses; and his connection with the stage provided him with an agreeable diversion from his sometimes stressful architectural practice. He regarded himself, he had told Florence, as a patron of the arts, and there was no better way for him to promote the cultural life of New York than by supporting the theater.

Life had treated Florence Nesbit cruelly in the eight years since the death of her husband, yet she had remained untouched by the cynicism that typically accompanies misfortune. She was an innocent abroad, an ingénue who could never perceive the hidden motives that often undergird the actions of others. She accepted Stanford White's kind words at face value, not suspecting that he might, in claiming the role of guardian over her daughter, be prompted by self-interest. She, Florence, had been tossed from one misfortune to the next, humiliated by her poverty, crushed by her failure to live as a respectable woman, and obliged to hire her daughter out as an artist's model; and suddenly the skies had cleared with the arrival into her life of this considerate, thoughtful, generous man. Who was she to turn away such a philanthropist as Stanford White? Who was she to deny him the opportunity to take her daughter under his watchful guardianship? And the more she learned about Stanford White, the more fortunate she considered herself that such a distinguished man should take an interest in her daughter.[21]

*   *   *

By 1901 White's career as an architect had traced a triumphal arc of accomplishment that extended over three decades. His father, Richard Grant White, had never succeeded in his attempts at a literary career—the family had lived always in genteel poverty—and he had never been able to afford to send his two sons to college. Stanford White, the elder of the two boys, had been fortunate, therefore, to begin an apprenticeship in 1872 at the age of nineteen as a protégé of Henry Hobson Richardson, the leading exponent of the Romanesque style in the United States and one of the principal partners in the New York firm Gambrill & Richardson.

Stanny, as he was known to his friends, soon realized his luck in gaining such a mentor as Richardson, who, for his part, came to appreciate that he could trust Stanford White to faithfully execute even the most complex tasks associated with the firm's many commissions. White drafted the perspective drawings for the tower of Trinity Church in Boston in 1874 and hired the artists to design the murals for the church's interior; he assumed responsibility for the decorative detail on Oakes Ames Memorial Hall in Easton, Massachusetts; he contributed to the interior decoration of the senate chamber of the New York State Capitol at Albany; and he worked closely with Richardson on several lucrative commissions for private houses in Newport, Rhode Island.[22]

In 1877 White, having served his apprenticeship and now employed as a draftsman at Gambrill & Richardson, joined with a few close friends in establishing the Tile Club, an informal group of artists and writers who met weekly for social

Stanford White served an apprenticeship with Henry Hobson Richardson before entering a partnership with Charles McKim and William Rutherford Mead in September 1879. White designed countless landmark structures in New York, most notably the Washington Square Arch, Madison Square Garden, the Herald Building, and the Judson Memorial Baptist Church. *(Library of Congress, LC-DIG-ds-10592)*

conversation in one another's homes. The Tile Club lasted only a decade, disappearing in 1887, yet it was an important institution, drawing together members of the city's cultural avant-garde. Augustus Saint-Gaudens, one of the most celebrated sculptors of his generation, was a member, as were Louis Comfort Tiffany, Winslow Homer, and William Merritt Chase. Stanford White faithfully attended the weekly meetings, designing the studio on Tenth Street that subsequently served as the club's meeting place after 1882.[23]

In August 1878 White journeyed through France on an architectural tour with Saint-Gaudens and a second acquaintance, Charles McKim. They traveled from Paris as far south as Marseille, making sketches of some of the buildings that they encountered on their way. McKim returned to the United States later that year, but White remained in Europe, staying with Saint-Gaudens in Paris, traveling through France, Belgium, and Italy, and returning to the United States in September 1879.

Charles McKim, following his return to New York, had joined with William Rutherford Mead, a draftsman working for the architect Russell Sturgis, in establishing a new firm. Stanford White had worked alongside McKim at Gambrill & Richardson in the early 1870s, and White also knew Mead; and so, on White's return to New York, the three men established the firm of McKim, Mead & White, hiring draftsmen and renting office space on lower Broadway.[24]

The creation of McKim, Mead & White in 1879 coincided with the start of a prolonged economic boom in the United States. An entrepreneurial class, capitalists who had made vast fortunes in railroads, iron and steel, shipbuilding, banking, and retail, had come into being in the decades after the Civil War, and members of this class were eager to display their wealth through the construction of extravagantly luxurious private residences. McKim, Mead & White was a direct beneficiary of their largesse, and soon the firm had received commissions from wealthy New Yorkers for country houses in Massachusetts, Rhode Island, New Jersey, and along the North

The firm of McKim, Mead & White opened in 1879 in offices at 57 Broadway and soon became one of the leading architectural firms in the United States. In 1894 the firm moved to offices at 120 Fifth Avenue. This photograph, taken around 1905, shows, from left to right, William Rutherford Mead, Charles McKim, and Stanford White. (*Avery Architectural and Fine Arts Library, Columbia University*)

Fork of Long Island. The work of McKim, Mead & White began to appear also in New York City: Charles Tiffany hired the firm to build an imposing mansion on Seventy-second Street at Madison Avenue; Henry Villard, the president of the Northern Pacific Railroad, commissioned McKim, Mead & White to build an opulent apartment complex between Fifti-eth and Fifty-first Streets for members of his immediate family; and other projects included the design of town houses for Lloyd Phoenix and Gibson Fahnestock.[25]

By 1887 the partnership of McKim, Mead & White had established itself as the most lucrative architectural practice in the United States. No firm recorded larger profits in the late 1880s. In the five-year period from 1887 to 1892, McKim, Mead & White received nearly two hundred commissions with an aggregate value of $13 million. The nouveaux riches—those New York families that had suddenly accumulated great fortunes—adopted the style and manners of the Renaissance princes to signify their rapid rise up the social ladder; and it was no coincidence that McKim, Mead & White abandoned its earlier preference for the American colonial and Queen Anne styles in favor of an architectural mimicry of the Italian Renaissance.[26]

It seemed appropriate, therefore, that in 1887 the managers of the National Horse Show Association should grant the commission for a new exhibition hall to McKim, Mead & White. New York had never possessed a suitable venue for the annual horse shows; the original Madison Square Garden, located on Madison Avenue at Twenty-sixth Street, had served this purpose for several years, but the building, a former railroad depot, was now dilapidated and shabby, an embarrassment to the city.

Stanford White's completion three years later of the new Madison Square Garden confirmed his reputation as one of the nation's leading architects. White had purposely designed the building to convey the illusion of buoyancy and lightness. There was nothing elegant in its basic shape—it was simply a straight-walled rectangular box that filled up its allotted area—but the decorative detail on the exterior transformed it into one of the most beautiful buildings in New York.

White had taken Filippo Brunelleschi's fifteenth-century

Stanford White designed the new Madison Square Garden in the Renaissance Revival style. The structure, on the northeast corner of Madison Square, included a large amphitheater, concert hall, restaurant, and theater. The flat roof, at the base of the tower, was used for musical comedy during the summer months. The New York Life Insurance Company took ownership in 1913, and the building was demolished in 1925. *(Avery Architectural and Fine Arts Library, Columbia University)*

24

masterpiece the Ospedale degli Innocenti as the inspiration for his design of Madison Square Garden. A colonnade—a series of slender columns spaced at regular intervals—ran along the front of the building, forming an arcade, an enclosed space that served to protect passengers alighting from their carriages in inclement weather. The decorative detail on the upper façade, above the colonnade, resembled the ornamentation on the church of the Certosa di Pavia, a Carthusian monastery in Lombardy. White had placed six semicircular arched windows on the façade, and above each of these windows he had inserted a bull's-eye window, a smaller circular opening that allowed additional light to enter the building. The exterior decoration— a combination of pale-yellow pressed brick and cream-white terra-cotta masonry—together with the large windows that looked out over Madison Avenue, created an impression that the building was lighter and more airy, somehow less substantial, than it actually was. Madison Square Garden was the largest and most capacious structure in the city—nothing in New York's history up to that point could rival it—yet even at night, when the gas lamps illuminated it only faintly, it had a cheerful, exhilarating appearance.[27]

An enormous amphitheater, with seating for seventeen thousand spectators, provided the interior space for horse shows, boxing matches, religious revivals, political meetings, and the like. Madison Square Garden also contained a restaurant on the first floor, a ballroom and concert hall above the restaurant, and an indoor theater lavishly decorated with silk draperies.

The building had a flat roof, a large outdoor space that

contained another stage and seating for almost two hundred spectators. New York possessed several outdoor theaters suitable for performances on summer nights, and the arrangement on the roof of Madison Square Garden was typically informal: the audience sat either on elevated benches running along the sides of the roof or at small tables positioned in front of the stage. There was space between the tables for waiters to move from table to table between acts, taking orders and serving drinks.[28]

The shareholders who had invested in the project—a group that included members of the Astor family and the bankers George Bowdoin, J. Pierpont Morgan, Adrian Iselin, and James Stillman—had not imagined that Madison Square Garden would include a tower. The new building had been originally intended as an amphitheater for horse shows, and there was no functional requirement to superimpose a tower above the main structure; it would be a wasteful and expensive addition. But Stanford White had always meant his creation to serve as an architectural landmark, a building that, on account of its beauty and style, would distinguish itself from its neighbors, and nothing, he argued, would serve that purpose better than the addition of a tower. The directors and principal shareholders eventually acquiesced in the plan, and White's tower, modeled after the campanile of the Cathedral of Santa Maria in Seville, reached three hundred feet, making Madison Square Garden one of the tallest buildings in the city.[29]

The inauguration of Madison Square Garden on June 16, 1890, marked the zenith of Stanford White's celebrity. The new edifice, one of the most attractive structures yet to appear in the city, was a signal of the emergent importance of New York City; and the opening ceremony was as much a tribute to the architect as a celebration of the building.

Levi Morton, the vice president of the United States, sent a telegram to say that he had been detained at the capital and was unable to attend. But William Tecumseh Sherman, the famed Civil War general, had accepted an invitation and was present with his wife and two daughters. The leadership of the Democratic Party — New York's political elite — was well represented among the audience, and Abram Hewitt, the former mayor, also put in an appearance. Theodore Roosevelt, a member of the Civil Service Commission, had traveled from Washington earlier that day to attend the inauguration of the new building.

Some of New York's most important capitalists had come to celebrate the opening of Madison Square Garden. Chauncey Depew, the president of the New York Central Railroad; August Belmont, the American representative of the Rothschild banking family; and Hermann Oelrichs, a director of the North German Lloyd Steamship Company, along with a host of lesser industrialists, financiers, and bankers, were all in attendance. The social elite of the city, the wealthiest and most prestigious families in New York, an indiscriminate mixture of old wealth and new, sat in private boxes elevated above the main floor of the amphitheater. Below them, a vast crowd of New Yorkers, more than twelve thousand, watched as the Vienna Orchestra played a series of waltzes and polkas. Alfred Thompson, the librettist, had written two ballet scores for the occasion, and the spectators loudly applauded each piece before finally departing the new Madison Square Garden.

"Never hitherto in New York was seen such a brilliant gathering," the *New York Press* proclaimed the next day. "Last night at the Madison Garden was, in a word, a night not to be soon forgotten.... The public spirited men who have furnished the capital for this venture showed their wisdom in intrusting the building of this great amusement hall to architects of the highest reputation, and the result is to be a structure of which they and the public at large may well be proud."[30]

Madison Square Garden, according to the *New York Times,* was not merely an architectural masterpiece, noteworthy for the beauty of its ornamentation, but also a worthy addition to the square, a part of the city already distinguished by its attractive appearance. "Much has been written about this great amphitheatre," the *Times* advised its readers, "but it must be seen to be appreciated. Everyone should go and take a look at it, because it is one of the sights of the city."[31]

It was the largest building in New York, yet its immense size had not compromised its splendor and majesty. "There is something tremendously imposing," the *New-York Tribune* proclaimed, "in its vast dimensions, and, what is more commendable, something exceedingly agreeable in the excellence of its proportions and the impression of combined strength and gracefulness in its constructive details.... The Madison Square Garden will be one of the most admirable places of its kind in the world."[32]

No single commission, either before or after, would confer as much celebrity and recognition on Stanford White as Madison Square Garden. McKim, Mead & White had received the

James Gordon Bennett Jr. hired Stanford White to design a new building for the *New York Herald* newspaper on Thirty-fourth Street. The building, modeled after the Loggia del Consiglio in Verona, included a statue of Minerva above the main entrance and bronze statues of owls on the eaves. After the *Herald* moved to Thirty-fourth Street in 1895, the building was found to be impractical and was demolished in 1921. *(Avery Architectural and Fine Arts Library, Columbia University)*

commission, but the other partners had played no role in the project, and the glory and success accrued exclusively to Stanford White. His subsequent career extended over three decades and encompassed many significant buildings. None, however, brought more distinction than the landmark on Twenty-sixth Street.

Stanford White's fame as the genius behind Madison Square Garden brought him a series of lucrative commissions in the 1890s. Everyone, it seemed, wanted to hire White to design some new project. James Gordon Bennett Jr., the owner of the *New York Herald,* one of the city's most successful newspapers, decided to move his building from Park Row, a short, squalid street close to City Hall, to an uptown location at the intersection of Broadway and Thirty-fourth Street. White's design, a single-story palace in the Italian Renaissance style, an imitation of the Loggia del Consiglio in Verona, was about as impractical a newspaper building as one could imagine, and rival newspapers gleefully predicted that the *Herald* would suffer as a consequence. "It is an odd, medieval-looking structure," the *New-York Tribune* sneered, "set down in the midst of the surrounding practical Yankee architecture."[33]

Few projects in the city in the 1890s promised as much as the construction of a new campus for New York University. The university, originally established in 1831 in a single building in Washington Square and subsequently hemmed in on all sides by a mélange of disreputable manufactories and slum tenements, had led an increasingly cramped existence. In 1892 the chancellor of the university, Henry McCracken, announced that New York University had hired Stanford White to design a new campus on land north of Manhattan, on an elevation adjacent to the Harlem River on the southern boundary of the Bronx.

White's blueprint, submitted later that year, included a library, an engineering building, sports facilities and a gymnasium, student dormitories, a museum of natural history, a chapel, and buildings for philosophy, languages, and literature. The campus quickly took shape under White's supervision, and undergraduate instruction moved to the Bronx location in October 1894.

New York University, according to White's design, occupied a picturesque site on the heights overlooking the Harlem River to the east with a view of the Hudson River and the Palisades to the west. The library building, decorated in buff-colored Roman brick with limestone trim and built around a sky-lit rotunda containing sixteen Connemara marble columns, was the centerpiece around which the other buildings were grouped. The university now possessed the most attractive campus imaginable, one that would enable it to compete successfully with such rival New York institutions as Columbia University and City College.

Other commissions followed rapidly, one after the other, each new project seeming to confirm the brilliance of the architect's vision. William K. Vanderbilt and J. Pierpont Morgan hired White in 1892 to construct a building for the Metropolitan Club, and White's design, an imposing palazzo in white marble on Fifth Avenue, opened in 1894. McKim, Mead & White was the firm in New York most closely associated with the city's aristocracy, and other wealthy coteries provided the firm with similar commissions during the same period. The Harvard Club, the Century Association, the University Club, the Players' Club, and the Lambs all hired McKim, Mead & White either to modify existing clubhouses or to build new ones.

White's earlier success in constructing a new campus for New York University also led to commissions from other American colleges and universities. McKim, Mead & White won the competition to design Radcliffe College in Cambridge, Massachusetts, and successfully bid on the contract to build a new campus for Columbia University.

Other commissions, less lofty, less aristocratic, but always profitable, flooded in during the 1890s and beyond from insurance companies, banks, hospitals, railroads, and retail stores around the United States. No architectural firm at the turn of the century won more contracts or earned greater profits; and no firm left a more enduring impact on the architecture of New York.

Florence Nesbit had scant knowledge of White's record of accomplishment; she knew only that he was someone important, a man who could use his influence in her daughter's favor. Indeed White had already demonstrated his generosity in ways that surprised even Florence. She no longer lived at the boardinghouse on Twenty-second Street; Florence and Evelyn had moved that summer, at White's expense, to a suite of rooms at the Audubon Hotel on Broadway. Her twelve-year-old son Howard, a sickly child who suffered from asthma, no longer needed to endure the dust and dirt of New York; Howard had enrolled, at White's expense, at the Chester Military Academy, a private school in the country a few miles west of Philadelphia.

And when Florence mentioned that she wished to visit friends in Pittsburgh, White was quick to offer his encouragement. It might be difficult, she had hinted to White, for her to pay the expense of the train ride; but she so desired to make the journey. No matter, White had replied; he would gladly pay for her ticket and would even provide some extra money—pocket money, he had joked—to cover any additional costs.[34]

But there was one more problem, she reminded him. Who would look after her sixteen-year-old daughter? Whom could she trust to make sure that no harm would befall Evelyn while she, Florence, was in Pittsburgh?

White, speaking now in a slightly less jocular manner, reassured Florence that he, White, would guarantee the child's safety. Evelyn would live quietly, without distractions, performing each evening at the theater, but spending no time with the young men who so persistently bothered her at the stage door. It was admirable, he told her, that a mother should have such concern for her child; but she need suffer no anxiety while the girl was in his care.[35]

Evelyn saw Stanford White every day following her mother's departure. He would arrive at the Audubon Hotel in the afternoon, spending an hour or so with her before escorting her to the Casino Theatre for the evening performance of *Florodora*. Sometimes, around nine thirty, she would take one of the cabs waiting outside the stage door, usually with some of the other chorus girls, to drive to the apartment that Stanny rented in the tower of Madison Square Garden. His friends— writers, artists, actors, and actresses—would come and go throughout the evening, catching up with the latest gossip, each guest vying with his or her neighbor to relate some sensation that had happened that day in New York.

One evening at one of these parties, toward midnight, as she was preparing to make her departure, Stanny mentioned to Evelyn that an old acquaintance, someone he had known for several years, was interested in having her pose in his studio. Rudolf Eickemeyer was one of the best photographers in New York, Stanny told her, known around town for his portraits of society ladies. His studio was close by, on Twenty-second Street, and Evelyn could visit for a few hours during the day before going on to *Florodora* in the evening.

Rudolf Eickemeyer photographed Evelyn Nesbit in his studio on Twenty-second Street in the fall of 1901. Eickemeyer titled this photograph *Ready for Mischief.* Stanford White, also present in the studio during the session, suggested that she wear a Japanese kimono. *(Library of Congress, LC-DIG-ds-10596)*

Evelyn readily agreed. Every actor in New York needed a set of portrait photographs to find work in the theater, and sooner or later *Florodora* would end its run. Evelyn would pose for Eickemeyer and receive a set of the prints as her reward.

She met Stanny the next day at the studio. As Eickemeyer and his assistant prepared the lighting, Stanny took Evelyn to the dressing room to show her some silk kimonos, imported from Hong Kong, that he had brought for her to wear. She posed for Eickemeyer in the kimonos, patiently following the instructions that Stanny called out to her. It was more fatiguing than she had previously imagined; but eventually both White and Eickemeyer were satisfied. Then, as she relaxed, relieved that the sitting had finally ended, White mentioned that he was hosting a dinner the next evening at his town house on Twenty-fourth Street. He had invited a few friends, and he would be delighted if Evelyn would accept his invitation to join the party. It did not matter, he told her, that she would arrive after the other guests; they would all know that *Florodora* did not end until around nine o'clock.[36]

She quickly agreed. Her mother was away in Pittsburgh, and Evelyn was always reluctant to spend her evenings alone. She had now known White for several weeks and she had never felt the slightest discomfort in his presence. And besides, White had promised her that other guests would attend; it would be foolish, she told herself, to imagine that anything untoward might happen. She had always enjoyed herself at Stanny's parties and she had no reason to think that the next day would be any different.

2

Rape

"What do you think?" Stanny asked, greeting Evelyn as she appeared in the doorway. "They have turned us down." He had been waiting about an hour, he explained, but none of his friends had appeared, and it was already almost ten o'clock.

"Oh, it's too bad," Evelyn replied, a look of disappointment on her face. "Then we won't have a party."

She had come directly from the theater, leaving at the end of the performance to take a hansom to Stanny's town house on Twenty-fourth Street.

"They have turned us down," Stanny repeated, "and probably gone off somewhere else and forgotten all about us. They probably won't come."

Evelyn was disconsolate at this unexpected news. She had already unbuttoned her coat, and now she removed the fur stole from around her neck; it hung dejectedly from her left hand. It seemed almost too much for her to endure that she should have to spend the remainder of her evening alone in her empty apartment at the Audubon Hotel.

She looked up, turning her face toward Stanny, silently

imploring him to salvage something from this unexpected disaster.

"Had I better go home?" she asked, letting the stole slip from her fingers as she placed it on the back of a chair.

"No, we'll have a party all to ourselves," White replied. He placed his hand on her shoulder, ushering her into the dining room and indicating the dinner table laid with plates and dishes. "We will sit down and have some food anyhow in spite of them."[1]

Evelyn suddenly realized that she had not eaten that night. She was famished. She chatted absent-mindedly during the dinner, telling Stanny the *Florodora* gossip and confiding her hope that the company would retain her when the play moved to the New York Theatre later that year.

Stanny listened to Evelyn, prompting her occasionally, saying little, letting her chatter on. Finally, when he realized that she could say no more that might interest him, he asked Evelyn if she would like a tour of the house. He knew that she had been to his studio on the fourth floor; but had she seen the other rooms? There was a great deal he could show her, he suggested, a great many works of art that he had collected.

White led Evelyn to the rear of the building, taking her up a narrow flight of stairs to the third floor. She stepped into a large room, and as White followed behind, he explained that he had obtained the paintings on his most recent trip to Europe.

How lucky he was, she replied, to travel so frequently; it had always been her ambition to go to London and Paris. There was a piano in the room, and Evelyn sat on the stool, playing a few bars that she had recently learned, while White sprawled lazily on a divan, his long legs stretched out in front of him.

Evelyn ran her fingers up and down the keyboard, picking out some tunes from *Florodora*. She swiveled around on her stool, turning to face Stanford White, seeming to ask his approval of her efforts. He took her hand, saying that there was one more room that she had not yet seen, and led her to the rear, drawing back some curtains to reveal a hidden door that opened into a smaller room.

A large four-poster bed stood in the center of the room. Evelyn advanced shyly, sitting tentatively on the edge of the bed, as Stanny poured some champagne into a glass that stood on a small table. He gave her the glass and Evelyn held it in her hand, watching the champagne effervesce, the bubbles rising rapidly to the surface. She took a sip while Stanny stood looking down at her, watching as she raised the glass to her lips. It tasted bitter, she complained, and she didn't care to finish it — but Stanny seemed strangely insistent.[2]

Evelyn drank some more champagne — reluctantly — and sat quietly, watching the bubbles in her wineglass. Stanford White said nothing, still watching her as if he were waiting for some reaction.

A minute went by, then two minutes, and Evelyn started to feel a slight throbbing in her ears. She felt suddenly very dizzy; her wineglass seemed about to slip from her fingers. She reached out to place it back on the table, and as Stanny took it from her, Evelyn fell back unconscious onto the bed.[3]

She awoke with a sudden start — how long had she been unconscious? — and Evelyn realized that she was lying naked on the bed. Stanford White was lying next to her and he also was naked. She began screaming, and White, alerted by her screams, leaned over to reassure her, telling her not to be concerned.

"Don't cry," he said, attempting to calm her. "Please don't. It's all over." He reached across the bed as if to stroke her, but his movement seemed only to heighten her distress.

"Keep quiet," he spoke softly. "It is all over. Now you belong to me. Nothing so terrible has happened," he consoled her in a gentle voice, attempting to hold her in his arms to comfort her. "You must not worry."[4]

Evelyn shrank from his touch, attempting to push him away. She saw, on the sheet between her legs, splotches of blood, bright red, and her screams became louder and more intense.

"You are so pretty; so young, so slim," White continued, seemingly oblivious to her screams, talking, as if to himself, about Evelyn's naked body. "I love you," he murmured, "because you are so young and slim."

She fumbled for her clothes, desperate now to hide her body from his gaze. White, still speaking, watched her as she struggled to put on her chemise.

"Don't tell anybody," he cautioned. "What would be the use? It would only make trouble for you and for me."

This must be their secret, he told her; she should confide it to no one; and she should never tell her mother about this night.

White had started now to put on his clothes also. "Forget it, little girl," he said as he fastened his boots. "Let us be happy."[5]

Evelyn Nesbit returned that night to the Audubon Hotel, to the apartment that she shared with her mother. But it was impossible for her to sleep. She stayed awake until dawn, sitting at the window that looked out over Thirty-ninth Street and Broadway, watching the passers-by go about their nocturnal tasks.

Stanford White called on her the next afternoon. He no longer possessed that boundless self-confidence that had always been his trademark. He seemed abashed, even ashamed; he approached her hesitantly, uncertain that she would listen to his words.

Evelyn received him in silence; she sat staring out of the window, looking across at the apartment buildings on the other side of Broadway.

"Why won't you look at me, child?" White began.

"Because I can't," Evelyn replied abruptly.

He spoke softly, telling her not to worry, saying that everyone did such things all the time. All his friends, all his acquaintances, he said, did such things. There was no need for her to imagine that the events of the previous night had been unusual.

She turned her head to look at him, and White could see in her glance that he had aroused her curiosity.

"Does everybody that you know do these things?" she inquired.

"Yes," he replied, speaking almost nonchalantly, "they all do."

Do the dancers in *Florodora* also behave in that way? Evelyn asked.

The question, posed so innocently, seemed to amuse Stanford White. He smiled broadly, in a manner that suggested he had lost his earlier trepidation, before answering that, most assuredly, all the dancers in the *Florodora* troupe behaved that way.[6]

His answer seemed to surprise Evelyn. She began to name some of their mutual acquaintances, people prominent on the Broadway stage, and, yes, White replied in turn, each one did such things. But it was important, he cautioned Evelyn, to remember that no one ever discussed this behavior; no one mentioned it or admitted to it. Some of the girls in *Florodora* were too foolish in this regard. They gossiped and, as a consequence, they destroyed their reputations.

Stanford White felt a sense of relief when he left Evelyn's apartment later that afternoon. She had accepted his explanation, it seemed, and she had assured him that she would not tell her mother. It was slightly surprising, he felt, that she should have believed him so completely. He had not imagined that even a sixteen-year-old could be so naïve as to accept such a story.

It had been an unpleasant experience for Evelyn, but she found it difficult to remain angry with Stanny for long. He had, she knew, taken advantage of her, but his assertions that everyone acted in such a way provided Evelyn with a measure of reassurance. It had not been so bad, she persuaded herself, and, remarkably, their friendship continued as before.

No one was more popular in New York society than Stanford White, and Evelyn could convince herself that Stanny had chosen her as the special object of his affection. She saw him frequently in the days and weeks that followed, spending time with him in the evenings after each performance of *Florodora*.

She left the theater each evening around nine o'clock, taking one of the cabs at the stage door to go to the tower apartment in Madison Square Garden. At Twenty-sixth Street, at the base of the tower that rose above the square, she alighted from the cab and pushed the bell to call the elevator. The operator, an elderly man with a sad, wizened face, gave her his customary greeting, and very quickly, almost before she could take another breath, the machinery propelled her to the topmost floor of the tower.

The elevator doors rattled open with a slight clatter, allowing her to step into a hallway. Evelyn knocked on the door that stood before her, waiting for Stanny's valet to allow her to enter.

She came into a magical space, the salon at Madison Square Garden where Stanny held court each evening with his friends and acquaintances. The tower with which Stanny had embellished the building held seven apartments, each apartment occupying the entire floor and commanding views of the city on all four sides. Stanford White had claimed the topmost apartment as his own, and it was this apartment that Evelyn entered.[7]

Evelyn could usually recognize a familiar face at Stanny's parties—other actresses from the Broadway shows were always present—and she could also count on meeting Stanny's many friends.

Ethel Barrymore, just twenty-two, was a frequent guest. Barrymore had achieved sudden fame that fall, in October 1901, in her role as Madame Trentoni in the comedy *Captain Jinks of the Horse Marines*. Ethel Barrymore's elder brother, Lionel, would also appear at the tower from time to time, gossiping wickedly with friends before mysteriously flitting away again, back to one of his Broadway haunts. The vaudeville star Lillian Russell, accompanied by her paramour, the financier James (Diamond Jim) Brady, would arrive late at night after her performance at the Broadway Musical Hall, and Fay Templeton, then appearing in *Hoity-Toity,* a burlesque show, would also make an appearance.[8]

Evelyn's friends from *Florodora* were often present. She was always pleased to see Fannie Donnelly, invariably accompanied by the magazine writer Frank Crowninshield. Other members of the *Florodora* troupe would show up occasionally. Susan Drake and Daisy Green, both favorites of Stanny, would appear arm in arm, laughing and giggling together, both slightly tipsy after drinks at Delmonico's.

George Lederer, the manager of the Casino Theatre, was also a visitor to the tower. Lederer, still a comparatively young man —just thirty-eight—had already achieved astonishing success as a Broadway impresario. His production of *The Belle of New York,* a musical comedy, had run for two years after its transfer to the London stage. Lederer had thus silenced those critics who had claimed that an American production would never find favor with British audiences, and in later years he staged successful productions on both sides of the Atlantic. His musical comedies and vaudeville shows, notorious for their risqué lyrics and their beautiful girls, were always in demand in New York, and *Florodora,* first staged by Lederer at the Casino Theatre in 1900, was no exception, playing to packed houses night after night.[9]

Stanford White belonged to several clubs in New York—the Salmagundi Club, the Players', the Lambs, the Harmonie, and the Metropolitan—and his friends from these clubs would also often attend the evening parties. The Tile Club had long ago disappeared, but several of its members, friends of White in the 1880s, would occasionally attend. The sculptor Augustus Saint-Gaudens, despite his ill health, appeared from time to time. The artists William Merritt Chase and John Henry Twachtman would visit the tower, albeit infrequently. The illustrator Charles Dana Gibson, a celebrity famous for his humorous sketches in *Harper's Weekly* and *Collier's,* was present, always on the lookout for attractive girls who might pose for his drawings. Rudolf Eickemeyer, the photographer for whom Evelyn had posed at the end of 1901, frequently attended. Eickemeyer had photographed Evelyn several times since their first encounter, always posing her in a slightly risqué manner, and they had since become friends.[10]

White's salon, close to the theaters and restaurants frequented by the *bon ton* and conveniently located in Madison Square, was a meeting place where the cultural avant-garde—writers, editors and publishers, musicians, artists, actors and actresses, sculptors and painters—could discreetly mingle and gossip, secure in the knowledge that few people outside their charmed circle would ever learn its secrets.

Stanny's guests would often stay late into the night, sometimes until one o'clock in the morning. Evelyn would remain behind, waiting impatiently for their departure, and then, after hearing the elevator descend to the street, she would turn to embrace Stanny. Evelyn would linger a few more minutes, enjoying her interlude with Stanny before she too would descend to the street to catch a cab home.

Stanford White modeled the tower of Madison Square Garden on the campanile of the Cathedral of Santa Maria in Seville. The copper statue of Diana, by the sculptor Augustus Saint-Gaudens, acted as a weather vane. *(Avery Architectural and Fine Arts Library, Columbia University)*

But often, on clear nights, they called the elevator back to the seventh floor and took it higher, as far as an open-air platform that then led by way of stairs to the summit. Stanford White had designed the topmost section of the tower with three separate levels, much as one would design a wedding cake, each level elaborately decorated with balustrades and tourelles, all done in the baroque style. A spiral staircase wound its way from the lower platform to the top of the tower, arriving finally at the level that stood directly beneath the copper statue of the goddess Diana at the pinnacle.

The elevator opened onto the first level, the open-air platform enclosed on all four sides by a stone balustrade. Evelyn would lead the way up the narrow iron stairway, stepping gingerly, holding onto the railing with her hand. Stanny followed behind, treading more confidently, waiting patiently for Evelyn to make her way up the steps. On the second level they paused briefly, stopping to catch their breath, resting for a few minutes before making the final ascent. Evelyn led the way again, finally stepping onto the topmost platform.

They stood, side by side, more than three hundred feet above street level. On a clear night, with a full moon, they could see far into the distance, as far north as Central Park. To the southwest they could make out the faint glimmer of the torch of the Statue of Liberty in the harbor.

Even in the middle of the night, they could see the ferries crisscrossing the East River, chugging from Manhattan to Long Island City and back again, their lights twinkling in the darkness. The ferry service from Manhattan to Brooklyn had declined recently, in the years since the opening of the new suspension bridge, but the bridge itself was a spectacular sight—the heavy granite caissons supporting the limestone towers, a network of steel cables holding the roadway along which Evelyn could see a steady procession of carts, carriages, and the occasional motorcar. Stanny had shown her, on her first visit to the summit, the construction of a second bridge to Brooklyn, one that would link Manhattan to Williamsburg, but this bridge, not yet complete, always seemed slightly forlorn. Its two towers, tied together by steel cables, stood on either side of the river, but its causeway was empty and abandoned, without any glimmer of traffic.

To the west, the Sixth Avenue train would come into view, rumbling along the elevated tracks, appearing in the far distance like a child's toy, electrical sparks flying away from the wheels, its passengers staring from the windows into the inky darkness. Farther west they could see the Jersey shore, an obscure and remote hinterland, dotted with small towns—Weehawken, Hoboken, Secaucus—with strange names.

Occasionally Evelyn and Stanny, each wearing a heavy coat against the wind, his arms around her shoulders, would stand on the platform waiting a little longer, until daybreak, and then they could watch the city below begin its daily round. Within a matter of minutes, it seemed, both Broadway and Fifth Avenue had become clogged with traffic, with endless lines of carts and carriages stretching north and south. They could see the rooftops below and the spires of the churches, and on the horizon, on the eastern edge, the sun would begin to shine its light over what seemed, at such moments, to be the greatest city in the world.[11]

*   *   *

Evelyn still lived with her mother in an apartment suite at the Audubon Hotel, but now she started spending more and more of her time with Stanny at his Madison Square Garden apartment. The Audubon Hotel was conveniently located at Thirty-ninth Street and Broadway, a few steps from the Casino Theatre, but it was inconveniently placed in the center of the Tenderloin district, that part of the city notorious for its brothels and gambling dens.

Madison Square, by contrast, had retained its distinction as one of the most desirable areas of New York. Fashionable hotels and expensive shops lined Fifth Avenue on the west side of the square; a row of elegant town houses ran along Twenty-sixth Street on the north side; and two impressive buildings, the New York Supreme Court, completed in 1900, and Madison Square Presbyterian Church, a Gothic pile built in 1853, occupied Madison Avenue on the east side of the square.

New York has typically, in its long history, been too large, too complex, and too diverse to have an acknowledged center. It has sprawled over too vast an area and has encompassed too many diverse roles—financial, political, and cultural—for any one district to command the obeisance of the others. Yet Madison Square, at least at the turn of the century, effectively served as the city's center. Its location, at the intersection of Broadway and Fifth Avenue, provided easy access to other parts of the city, and its hotels, restaurants, theaters, and shops all drew New Yorkers to spend their time and money in the square and the adjacent streets. It was one of the most exclusive residential neighborhoods in the city; and it was distinctive also as the meeting place of the city's political elite. The Fifth Avenue Hotel, an elegant white marble building facing the west side of the square, hosted meetings of the Republican Party establishment, while the Hoffman House, an adjacent hotel, was the gathering place for Democratic politicians. On election nights, each set of politicians awaited the results at its favored hotel while, in the square itself, large crowds cheered the returns as they were projected onto the façade of the St. Germain Hotel through a set of ingenious lantern slides.[12]

Stanford White never displayed much concern with politics; even the campaign to overthrow the corrupt Democratic machine failed to awaken his interest. But he was friendly with the politicians whose help he might need for the approval of various building projects, and he was always careful to provide them with tickets to the shows and exhibitions at Madison Square Garden.

Evelyn knew nothing of such arrangements. Stanny was always preoccupied with various architectural projects, soliciting commissions, arranging proposals, coordinating workmen, and meeting deadlines; but Evelyn knew little about such work. It irritated her, of course, that Stanny was so frequently away from New York, but there was good reason, he explained, for his absences. The firm often contracted for work in other parts of the country, and it was always necessary that one of the partners supervise the construction. He also traveled to Europe at least once a year, and these trips too were a necessary component of his work. His clients often demanded that he furnish their houses with the most expensive accoutrements, and he journeyed to France, Italy, and

Britain to seek out antique furniture, silverware, tapestries, and paintings that he could use to decorate the mansions of his wealthy patrons.

Evelyn consoled herself for Stanny's absences with the knowledge that her life with him was never dull. Her role in *Florodora,* always a very minor part, had, after eight months, become almost humdrum by its repetition; yet her privileged position within Stanny's circle of friends was sufficient compensation. It seemed of little account that he was married and that he occasionally spent the weekends with his wife, Bessie, and his son, Lawrence, at the family estate on Long Island. Stanny, after all, frequently disparaged his wife, telling Evelyn that Bessie had gained too much weight since their marriage. It was impossible for Evelyn to feel any jealousy toward a woman who had so obviously lost Stanny's affection.

But one day, idly glancing at some papers, Evelyn noticed a small black book, slightly tattered and torn, a book that she had never seen before. Stanny was away from the apartment, working at the office. She hesitated. Stanny was always insistent that she not touch his papers; but the temptation was too great, and with a slight sense of guilt, Evelyn began to leaf through the pages. She noticed a list of names written in Stanny's sprawling, spidery handwriting. Some of the *Florodora* girls had made it into the black book, and she saw that girls from other Broadway shows were included also. She recognized her own name on the list and saw that her birth date had been written in black ink next to her name. Evelyn remembered that Stanny had given her a diamond necklace from Tiffany's on her birthday, and she vividly recalled the impression it had made on her.

Why had Stanny written this list of names? Did it serve to remind him of each girl's birthday? Did he give a birthday present to each girl on the list? Evelyn realized with a sudden blush that Stanny's black book had provided her with evidence of his infidelity.[13]

It was mortifying for Evelyn to realize that she was not the special object of Stanny's affection. He had claimed that his frequent absences were on account of his architectural practice, but Evelyn, her suspicion aroused, no longer could believe that he was faithful to her. She could never confront him with her knowledge — she was afraid that he might then exclude her from his circle — but she nursed her anger at his betrayal and calculated her revenge.

Could she arouse his jealousy by showing affection to other suitors who had so persistently courted her? Evelyn knew some of the members of the Racquet Club, a group of wealthy young men who played tennis on the courts at their clubhouse on Forty-third Street. Bobby Collier, the heir to a publishing house, flirted with Evelyn, taking her to Sherry's, escorting her to the Metropolitan Opera, and introducing her to his friends. Condé Nast, the business manager at *Collier's Weekly,* also courted Evelyn for a while, writing affectionate *billets-doux* and sending her roses, while James (Monte) Waterbury, the dilettante son of a prominent businessman, had a brief fling with Evelyn in the spring of 1902. James Barney, a recent Yale graduate and a member of the Racquet Club set, also took a shine to Evelyn, buying her diamond brooches from Tiffany's, sending flowers to her apartment, and taking her to the theater.[14]

But such affairs were never likely to end happily for Evelyn.

The young men who flirted with her had no intention of marrying an impoverished actress with few prospects. She had little to recommend her beyond her looks, and they quickly tired of her company. James Barney abruptly ended his affair with Evelyn not long after it had begun, moving to Paris to study architecture at the École des Beaux-Arts. Later that year, in July 1902, Bobby Collier married Sara Van Alen, the daughter of a wealthy Wall Street stockbroker, and the following month Condé Nast married Clarisse Coudert, an heiress who, though still in her twenties, was independently wealthy.[15]

Florodora ended its New York run in January 1902. It had been a triumph, one of the most popular shows on Broadway. George Lederer, keen to repeat his success, rented the Knickerbocker Theatre that spring for a new comedy, *The Wild Rose,* that had recently had its premiere in Philadelphia. Lederer had taken a fancy to Evelyn Nesbit during the *Florodora* run, and he now hinted that he would give her a musical role in *The Wild Rose* when it moved to New York in May. But first, he stipulated, she had to take singing lessons. Evelyn did her best, going each day to Arthur Lawrason's studio on Sixty-ninth Street, practicing in the evenings in her apartment, but she had little discernible talent as a singer. Lederer, a sympathetic, generous man, was reluctant, nevertheless, to cast Evelyn adrift, and he eventually gave her the part of Vashti, a Gypsy girl.

The Wild Rose was not a success, ending its run less than four months later. Lederer's generosity toward Evelyn had also run its course, and he conspicuously failed to offer her a part in any of the other musicals that he produced that year.

Evelyn auditioned in October 1902 for *The Silver Slipper,* a musical scheduled to open the following year at the Grand Opera House, but she failed to get the part.

Evelyn's acting career came to an inglorious end the next month. Norma Munro, a society matron who had inherited her father's publishing business, had invested $80,000 in a new theater, Mrs. Osborn's Playhouse, on Forty-fourth Street. The first production, *Tommy Rot,* a musical comedy, provided Evelyn with one more opportunity to display her acting talent, but the show ran for only thirty-nine performances. Mrs. Osborn's Playhouse, in any case, was less a professional theater than a caprice of Norma Munro. It was too far uptown to attract an audience, and the stars of the Broadway stage refused a connection with such a doubtful venture. Mrs. Osborn's Playhouse went into bankruptcy the following month.[16]

Evelyn was still only seventeen, too young to dwell for long on this disappointing end to her theatrical career. Her disappointment was tempered, moreover, by a new friendship, a friendship with one of the most amusing and intriguing men whom Evelyn had yet to encounter in her time in the city.

John (Jack) Barrymore was twenty years old, tall and thin, with brown eyes, a chalky-white complexion, jet-black hair swept back from his forehead, and a prominent chin. He seemed a whir of motion, constantly firing off humorous remarks, perpetually suggesting some wheeze that would set the town talking, always gossiping, without the slightest hint of malice, about this friend or that acquaintance. He was original; he was charming; he flattered Evelyn with compliments; and there was an immediate, instantaneous attraction between them.

But Barrymore's energy could never find its focus. His sister, Ethel, was already a Broadway star, and his older brother, Lionel, was making his mark on the stage also; but Jack had already told Evelyn that he had no interest in following his siblings onto the stage. What was he to do? He had had no education; he was not fitted for a profession; he had no money, no talent, no social position, and, it seemed, no future. He had been expelled at sixteen from Georgetown Preparatory School for visiting a brothel with some classmates; he had attended drawing classes at the Art Students' League but had failed his exams; he lived hand to mouth as an illustrator; and he seemed, to everyone who met him, to be about as irresponsible as one could imagine a young man to be. Jack Barrymore had no plans for the future, no thought that he should prepare himself for adulthood.[17]

Stanford White had often invited Ethel Barrymore to his tower apartment, and he knew both brothers, Lionel and Jack, passably well. Stanny and Evelyn had drifted apart that year — she no longer came so frequently to his apartment — but he still had affectionate feelings for her and was solicitous for her welfare. He was dismayed that Evelyn seemed to have fallen in love with young Barrymore and horrified that she seemed ready to accept his proposal of marriage. Jack Barrymore was a reckless drifter, a wastrel, and no one, Stanny believed, could exert a more harmful influence over Evelyn.

Did she not realize, he asked her, that Jack Barrymore was

an alcoholic and a womanizer? Barrymore was only twenty, yet he was already notorious for his carousing. His father, Maurice, had contracted syphilis and had gone insane; and there was every indication that Jack Barrymore meant to follow along the same path. Did she seriously intend to marry such an indolent young man? How would they live, Stanny demanded, if she married Jack Barrymore?[18]

He had an especial reason to dislike Barrymore. White had designed the memorial arch in Madison Square to

Several generations of the Barrymore family have been prominent as actors. This photograph, taken around 1904, shows, from left to right, John Barrymore, his sister, Ethel, and his brother, Lionel. John (Jack) Barrymore began his stage career as a comic actor, but in 1922 his portrayal of Hamlet won him recognition as one of the greatest actors of his generation. Ethel and Lionel were equally famous during the first half of the twentieth century for their many roles onstage and in films. *(Library of Congress, LC-USZ62-56616)*

commemorate the defeat of the Spanish fleet at the Battle of Manila Bay. His design of the arch had included the allegorical figure *Victory*, a sword in her right hand, a shield in her left. It had infuriated him to learn that Barrymore, after spending an evening in a nearby saloon, had climbed the arch to steal the sword, marching with it in triumph down Broadway.[19]

But Jack Barrymore's inability to earn his keep was more troubling than his propensity for practical jokes. He led a chaotic life, borrowing money from friends, living in a slum apartment on Fourteenth Street, and only occasionally earning a few dollars when he sold his drawings to the newspapers. His sister, Ethel, had hoped that Jack would find his métier as an actor, but even this goal seemed beyond him. In October 1901 Ethel, then playing a return engagement of *Captain Jinks* in Philadelphia, had persuaded the stage manager to hire Jack as a replacement during the absence of the actor playing Charles Lamartine. The role was undemanding, but Jack had failed to learn his lines. He seemed not in the least embarrassed that he provoked ridicule and laughter from the audience, but even Ethel now realized that her younger brother would never be successful on the stage.[20]

None of it made any difference to Evelyn Nesbit. She was seventeen; Jack was twenty; she was madly in love with him, and what did it matter that he had no money? They were both young, both starting out on the great adventure of life, and something would surely turn up.

Stanford White held a hurried consultation with Evelyn's mother, Florence. The widow of an old friend, a fellow member of the Players' Club, had established a school for girls in

Pompton, a small town in western New Jersey, near the Ramapo Mountains. It was at a remote location, far from the temptations of New York, and White would be willing, he told Florence, to support Evelyn's studies at the school. It would effectively end the courtship between Evelyn and Jack Barrymore—the young pup would not even be able to afford the train fare to Pompton—and Evelyn would benefit in receiving a sound education.[21]

Florence Nesbit was delighted with the plan. She too was alarmed that Evelyn had fallen in love with Jack Barrymore, and she too was anxious to prevent their marriage. She had long pinned her hopes, her expectations, on her only daughter, and it was a severe disappointment to her that Evelyn's acting career had fizzled out. Evelyn's star had never shone very brightly on Broadway, and now it seemed to have dimmed completely. Her daughter had never had much of an education, and White's proposal would be Evelyn's opportunity to learn something more than the lessons provided by her *Florodora* experience.

White's offer to pay for Evelyn's schooling seemed entirely in character, and Florence once again expressed the gratitude she had always felt for his kind, disinterested support. He had continued to pay for her son, Howard, to attend the Chester Military Academy. White had already given her family so much and had asked nothing in return; very often Florence Nesbit wondered to herself that she and her children had been so fortunate as to have him as a patron.

Evelyn, to everyone's surprise, readily agreed to the proposal to study at the school. Her most recent experience on the stage, playing in *Tommy Rot* at Mrs. Osborn's Playhouse, had not been a happy one: all the actors were uncomfortably aware that they were in a failing production that had received caustic reviews in the press. Evelyn herself realized the inadequacy of her education. Stanford White's offer to pay her expenses was too good an opportunity to refuse, and if it meant her separation from Jack Barrymore—well, so what? She could always resume her relationship with Jack when she returned to New York.

Evelyn first arrived at the school in November 1902, shortly after the start of the fall semester. The school, established in February 1894 by Beatrice DeMille in honor of her late husband, Henry, occupied a large yellow-and-white three-story frame house a few miles from the village of Pompton. There could not have been a more bucolic spot: the main school building, framed by the mountains, stood at the edge of Pompton Lake, a pristine expanse of water edged with pine trees and boasting innumerable species of waterfowl.[22]

Evelyn had appeared on Broadway only a few months before, and her photograph had once been ubiquitous in the New York newspapers, but her new schoolmates knew nothing of her past life. She now reveled in her anonymity. She was a model pupil, studying French, music, art, and English literature, occasionally performing in school plays and participating in outdoor games. Evelyn, like most of the older girls, lived away from the main building, in a small cottage on the school grounds. On autumn weekends the teachers would take the girls on hikes in the surrounding hills, and in the winter, when snow and ice covered the ground, they would go skating on Pompton Lake.[23]

It was an idyllic existence, so pleasant and tranquil as to make her previous life on the stage appear almost impossibly remote. She had forgotten her romance with Jack Barrymore, and she rarely even thought about her benefactor, Stanford White, despite his generosity toward her.

Her mother came to Pompton to visit her for a few days at Christmas. Florence told her daughter her news from New York: she had recently moved from the Audubon Hotel to a suite of rooms at the Algonquin Hotel on Forty-fourth Street. Stanford White continued to pay her rent, but she now heard from him infrequently. It was slightly troubling, she told her daughter, that they were so dependent on the whim of one man. What would become of them, how would they support themselves, if something, some catastrophe, were to happen to Stanford White so that he could no longer make the payments?

But a far different crisis suddenly disrupted Evelyn's studies. One morning, toward the end of January 1903, as Evelyn was about to leave her cottage to go to class, she felt a severe abdominal pain. She collapsed onto a settee, wincing in agony, clutching her stomach with both hands. A classmate, seeing Evelyn doubled up on the settee, ran to the main building, returning to the cottage with one of the teachers.

A local physician, William Colfax, arrived at the school thirty minutes later. It was a case of acute appendicitis; it would be necessary to operate as quickly as possible; and it would not even be advisable, Colfax warned, to attempt to move Evelyn to the nearest hospital.[24]

Later that day, around noon, Florence Nesbit arrived in Pompton. Beatrice DeMille had telephoned her at the Algonquin with the news that Evelyn was desperately ill. One of Evelyn's admirers, a man named Harry Thaw, had been visiting Florence Nesbit that morning, and Thaw offered to drive her in his motorcar from New York to Pompton. The train service to western New Jersey was infrequent and irregular; it would be quicker, he advised Florence, to travel by car.

Florence Nesbit, before her departure, had telephoned Stanford White to tell him the news. White also responded quickly, arranging for his physician, Nathaniel Bowditch Potter, to travel to the school. Potter, professor of clinical surgery at the College of Physicians and Surgeons, agreed with Colfax's diagnosis that Evelyn had acute appendicitis, and the operation was performed later that day. He remained at Pompton for several days, watching over Evelyn, prescribing morphine to dull the pain, and providing advice to the local physicians. Evelyn had previously been healthy and she could expect to recover in a few weeks. But the facilities for medical care in the village were rudimentary, and Potter advised her to return to New York under his care until she was fit enough to resume her studies at Pompton.[25]

Evelyn recovered slowly, spending several weeks recuperating at Stanford White's expense in a private sanatorium in New York. Her friends, performers from *Florodora* and other Broadway shows, visited the hospital, sharing with her their gossip about the New York stage. Jack Barrymore was nowhere to be seen—he had quickly found a new girlfriend after Evelyn departed for Pompton—but other young men called regularly to offer their support for her recovery.

She had briefly met Harry Thaw at Rector's twelve months earlier—Elba Kenny, one of the *Florodora* girls, introduced them—and Thaw was now a frequent visitor, bringing flowers and offering his assistance. He had left New York shortly after their first meeting, he told her, and had spent that year, 1902, traveling in Europe, visiting archaeological sites in Greece and Italy and seeing friends in France and Britain, before returning to the United States in the autumn.[26]

Thaw, thirty-one, had a reputation among the smart set as a wealthy playboy who spent his money with abandon, hosting extravagantly expensive dinners, showering his lovers with diamonds, traveling each year in Europe with a retinue of friends and servants, and generally living in the most aristocratic manner possible.

His father, William Thaw, had made his first fortune from the freight business, carrying goods in Conestoga wagons from Philadelphia across the Allegheny Mountains to Pittsburgh. William Thaw had been an early investor in the Pennsylvania Railroad, and his rapidly accumulating wealth had enabled him to purchase thousands of acres of coalfields in western Pennsylvania. He had been an enthusiastic booster of his birthplace, Pittsburgh, donating millions of dollars to the city's cultural and educational institutions, yet his estate at his death in 1889 still amounted to more than $12 million.[27]

The bulk of the inheritance, held as a family trust, passed to his widow, Mary Copley Thaw. She had effective control of the estate, and the revenue from the railroad stock and the landholdings provided each of William Thaw's ten children — five from his first marriage, to Eliza Blair; five, including Harry, from his marriage to Mary Copley — with an annual income of $80,000.

Harry's brothers — Josiah and Edward — remained in Pittsburgh after their father's death. They joined the city's business elite, working independently to make their own fortunes, while assisting their mother in the administration of the family trust and settling into lives of comfortable prosperity.

But Harry Thaw, unlike his brothers, seemed determined to live a life of extravagant ease and dissipation. Thaw, eighteen at the time of his father's death, had already been expelled from the University of Wooster, a college in western Ohio, on account of his dismal grades. He had been a reluctant student, spending more time at the racetrack than at the library, and the faculty, perceiving Thaw as a disruptive presence, voted to dismiss him from the college. He returned to Pittsburgh to enroll at the Western University of Pennsylvania, a college in Allegheny City, but his time there was no more successful, and he left during the first semester. In November 1890 he entered Harvard University, but he did no better, spending most of his time drinking and playing cards, and in February 1892 the president of Harvard, Charles Eliot, expelled him from the university.[28]

Thaw returned a second time to Pittsburgh to stay with his mother and to ponder his future. He had no need to make a living: Mary Thaw, oblivious to her son's reckless behavior, assured Harry that he too, like his siblings, would receive

$80,000 each year from the estate. There was little point, Harry realized, in resuming his studies or attempting a profession; he could live quite comfortably on his share of the family fortune.

It was still the custom for wealthy Americans to spend time in Europe, residing for several months each year in a major city, London, Paris, or Rome, seeing the sights, mingling with the local aristocracy, and making the occasional excursion to some exotic destination in North Africa, Russia, or Palestine. Europe contained cultural resources — the theater, the opera house, museums, art galleries — that far surpassed in their splendor comparable institutions in the United States; and, equally significant, they were more exclusive, less democratic, less republican, even in France, than their equivalent in the United States. The American bourgeoisie at the turn of the century held aristocratic traditions and styles in high regard. The opportunity to interact with members of the British aristocracy was especially alluring, and nothing could confer more prestige on an American parvenu than the marriage of his daughter to a peer of the realm.

Harry Thaw soon adopted this lifestyle as his own, sailing to Europe for the first time in 1894. He traveled with a retinue of servants from his mother's household, spending several weeks in London before crossing the English Channel and journeying through France, Germany, and Austria-Hungary as far as Budapest. He continued to Constantinople, visiting the Greek islands, and eventually arriving at Cairo before crossing the Mediterranean to Naples and north to Rome. He returned to Europe every year, always staying in the best hotels, dining in the most expensive restaurants, gambling at the most exclusive casinos, and patronizing the most notorious brothels.[29]

Evelyn Nesbit had no knowledge of Thaw's checkered past. She knew only that he was wealthy and that he traveled frequently to Europe. He had seemed slightly eccentric at their first meeting in January 1902. On that occasion, she recalled, he had spoken too rapidly, in short, clipped sentences, in a manner that made him appear self-conscious, almost as though he were carefully guarding his remarks. He had sent roses to her apartment in the Audubon Hotel, but Evelyn, preoccupied with other matters, had given him little thought, and his departure for Europe that month had ended their acquaintance.

He had now reappeared, visiting her frequently in the hospital. He seemed almost excessively solicitous, sending flowers every day, ordering delicacies for her from the Waldorf Hotel, and pestering the doctors and nurses, demanding that they provide the best possible care. There was nothing, it seemed, that he would not do for her; his generosity appeared unlimited. They became friends, and Evelyn soon began to depend on Harry Thaw for small favors, acts of kindness that speeded her recovery.

There was little that was noteworthy about his appearance: he was a tall man, around six feet, clean-shaven, with thin lips, a broad nose, and a rounded chin. He was well dressed, neat and careful in his movements, and almost deferential in his attitude. Although he was thirty-one, his boyish appearance and ready smile made him appear younger. There was

Harry Kendall Thaw attended three colleges—the University of Wooster, Western University of Pennsylvania, and Harvard—but he was an indifferent student, and he left each college before graduating. His mother, Mary, provided him with an annual allowance of $80,000, on which he lived a life of leisure, spending several months each year traveling in Europe. *(Library of Congress, LC-DIG-ds-10586)*

something charming, Evelyn thought, about his readiness to please her, and it gave her great satisfaction to know that, once again, there was someone upon whom she could depend.[30]

And so when Harry suggested in February 1903 that Evelyn travel with him, at his expense, on his next European tour, she readily agreed. The doctors had advised her to avoid strenuous exercise, and it would certainly not be possible for her to attempt a return to the stage. She needed rest and relaxation, and an extended vacation abroad would enable her to return to full health. She could not travel alone with Harry, of course — they were not married — but he had already suggested that her mother, Florence, accompany them as a chaperone. All three of them, Harry promised, would journey in grand style, staying at the most luxurious hotels and dining at the most exclusive restaurants. What could be more enjoyable, more pleasant, than the opportunity to stay for a while in London and Paris, to visit the museums and art galleries, to go to the theater and admire the sights?[31]

But Evelyn's mother was less enthusiastic. Florence Nesbit, on her recent trip to Pittsburgh, had renewed an acquaintance with a friend of her late husband. Charles Holman, a stockbroker, had subsequently visited her in New York and had offered his hand in marriage. It would be inconvenient for her to spend several months traveling around Europe while her future husband waited for her to return. Harry Thaw had proposed an ambitious itinerary, one that would require her prolonged absence, and it seemed unreasonable that she, Florence, should spend so long away from home.

She mentioned Harry's plan to Stanford White, and their conversation only increased her reluctance to travel to Europe. Harry Thaw, White told her, was a wealthy man, the son of a Pittsburgh millionaire, who spent part of each year living in Paris and traveling around the continent. Thaw was generous with his friends, spending his money impulsively and never calculating the cost. But he also had a reputation as an obnoxious, often hostile, individual, someone who had been seen to lose his temper at the slightest provocation, flying into a rage over some trivial incident. There were rumors that he was a drug addict who indulged in heroin and cocaine, and, even worse, there were whispers among the smart set that Harry Thaw frequented prostitutes, tying them with restraints and whipping them.

None of the clubs in New York, White told Florence Nesbit, were willing to admit Harry Thaw as a member; there had always been a blackball whenever he applied. His wealth would normally have been sufficient—the Union Club or the Knickerbocker Club would have admitted him—but his reputation always denied him the privilege.

Nothing good could come from an association with such a man as Harry Thaw, White cautioned. It would be foolhardy, and perhaps even dangerous, for Florence and Evelyn to travel in Europe in Thaw's company. They would be beholden to Thaw, dependent on him for their expenses, staying in foreign lands, far from any support and assistance that they might otherwise receive from their friends. And she, Florence, would be putting Evelyn, still only eighteen years old, in harm's way. What would they do in an emergency? To whom would they turn for help? There was no telling what Thaw might do, and they would be foolish to take the risk.

But Evelyn reassured her mother that such fears were groundless. She, Evelyn, had heard the same rumors about Harry from some of her friends, the girls she had known in the *Florodora* chorus. She had already asked Harry if there was any truth in the gossip about him and he had laughed, telling her that he had heard such rumors many times. They were the work of blackmailers who were trying to extort money from him. It was common practice in New York for unscrupulous crooks to threaten to tell such tales; but he had never thought to pay them any attention. He had never indulged in any drug use, he told her, and he never frequented prostitutes.

Harry had quickly convinced her of his honesty, and Evelyn told her mother that there was no cause for alarm. Harry was perhaps a little hot-tempered, too quick to feel slighted, but he had always behaved toward her in a kind and considerate manner. It was ridiculous, Evelyn protested to her mother, to imagine that Harry would indulge in cocaine or associate with prostitutes.[32]

Florence Nesbit eventually acquiesced. Harry planned to stay in Pittsburgh during April for the wedding of his sister Alice, and he would then return to New York to prepare for the journey. He would travel ahead to Paris with his valet in May to make the arrangements while Florence and Evelyn, accompanied by a maid, would sail on a later ship. Evelyn had every expectation that she would have a wonderful time — nothing untoward, she thought, could happen. What could possibly go wrong?

3

MARRIAGE

HARRY THAW SAILED FROM NEW YORK IN THE FIRST WEEK OF May, arriving in Paris ten days later, while Evelyn and her mother traveled at the end of the month on the SS *New York*, a luxury passenger ship of the American Line. Stanford White, unhappy that they had accepted Thaw's offer to go to Europe, accompanied them to the harbor, warning Florence Nesbit to be on her guard against Thaw. He could not, in good conscience, allow them to travel without any money—they would otherwise be entirely at Thaw's mercy—and at the last moment, just as Florence was about to board the ship, White slipped an envelope, containing a letter of credit for $500, into her hand.[1]

Six days later, after an uneventful voyage, the SS *New York* docked at Southampton. Evelyn and her mother, accompanied only by a maid, traveled along the coast as far as Folkestone, taking a boat across the Channel to Boulogne and then continuing onward by train to Paris.

Harry had rented an enormous apartment in the Eighth Arrondissement, on the Avenue Matignon, close to the shops and restaurants on the Champs-Élysées. Every morning, after breakfast, Evelyn and Harry would go sightseeing, or to a museum or an art gallery, and in the afternoons he would take her shopping. They visited the Louvre many times, often accompanied by a guide, listening to his précis as they walked through the rooms. Nothing gave Evelyn more pleasure than the sculpture galleries: the Winged Victory of Samothrace, portraying the goddess Nike descending from the skies, surpassed anything she had seen back in New York in the Metropolitan Museum of Art, and the Venus de Milo, a marble statue of the goddess of love, seemed impossibly delicate, full of grace and beauty.[2]

But Leonardo da Vinci's famous painting the *Mona Lisa*, the jewel of the Louvre's collection, was a disappointment. Evelyn recognized the enigmatic expression of the subject, the faint smile of the woman in the portrait, but there was otherwise nothing noteworthy about the work. It was a mystery, she decided, that this painting had attained its status as a masterpiece.

There was more enjoyment to be found in an adjacent gallery, in an exhibition of paintings of the Barbizon school. The Louvre had owned Jean-François Millet's controversial painting *The Gleaners* since 1890, and in 1902 the financier Georges Thomy-Thiéry had donated several other important works, notably Théodore Rousseau's *Edge of the Forest*, to the museum's collection. *The Gleaners*, showing three peasant women picking ears of corn, had been controversial during the Second Empire for its sympathetic portrayal of the lower classes, but by 1903, when Evelyn Nesbit saw it, the painting had won a reputation as the epitome of the realist movement.[3]

There was nothing in New York, not even the Metropolitan Museum, that could compare to the Louvre, and the opportunity to view its collections brought Evelyn and Harry back to the museum day after day. There was too much to see in the few weeks that they had planned to spend in Paris; but no matter, Harry told Evelyn — they would certainly come again another year.

Their afternoons were spent shopping in the fashionable districts of the capital. Evelyn's favorite destination was the Rue de la Paix, the street that connected the Place Vendôme to the Place de l'Opéra. The jewelers at Cartier knew Harry Thaw well — he was one of their best customers — and Evelyn loved to spend an hour or so browsing the showcases, picking out a diamond brooch, a lavaliere with a ruby pendant, or some pearls. It was a great convenience for her that the most fashionable couture houses — Jacques Doucet, Georges Doeuillet, Maison Paquin, Paul Poiret, and the House of Worth — were all located nearby, either on the Rue de la Paix or near the Place Vendôme, and Evelyn would often spend her afternoons choosing designs for a gown or an evening dress, selecting the fabric, and arranging for delivery. Her favorite salon was Doucet, a fashion house that had earned an extraordinary reputation for the elegance of its style, but she also frequented the House of Worth, an establishment known for its precision and detail.[4]

Florence Nesbit had accompanied Harry and Evelyn to

Paris as her daughter's chaperone, and occasionally all three would dine together in the apartment. But Harry preferred to spend his evenings alone with Evelyn, out of sight of her mother. His favorite restaurant, Lapérouse, located on the Quai des Grands-Augustins, was reputedly the best seafood establishment in the capital, and in fine weather they would drive to the restaurant along the banks of the Seine, crossing the river on the Pont Neuf.

On the weekends, Harry would take Evelyn on a carriage ride farther afield, outside the city limits. They toured the royal château and gardens at Saint-Germain-en-Laye and visited the palace at Fontainebleau, the traditional residence of the French monarchs. They also spent time at the Palace of Versailles, walking through the great halls and strolling through the gardens. But Versailles had suffered decades of neglect during the Second Empire and there were, even in 1903, few visitors. Renovations had begun ten years earlier, but Versailles still seemed strangely abandoned and forgotten.[5]

There was more enjoyment to be had at Longchamp, a racetrack within the Bois de Boulogne, a large park on the western edge of the city. In fine weather they would drive out to the Bois in an open carriage to watch the horses compete over the flat, to place bets with the bookmakers, and to mingle with the Parisian aristocracy. Harry was a familiar figure at Longchamp and at the Maisons-Laffitte racetrack, north of the city, and at both places he introduced Evelyn to his acquaintances.

It was a heady experience for the eighteen-year-old chorus girl. Evelyn Nesbit had been, six months previously, a pupil at the DeMille school in Pompton, studying her lessons with her classmates, and now she was in Paris, mingling with the elite of French society. Both Emma Calve, an opera singer who had recently starred in the role of Carmen at the Opéra-Comique, and Lina Cavalieri, an actress who frequently performed at the Théâtre de l'Odéon, knew Harry Thaw well. Evelyn also met the ballet dancer Cléo de Mérode, a mistress, so it was said, of the Belgian king, Leopold II. There were innumerable Russian princes, British lords, Italian dukes, and Spanish noblemen, all watching the races and placing bets on the horses, and on one memorable occasion Evelyn encountered Sultan Muhammed Shah, the third Aga Khan, on one of his visits to the Maisons-Laffitte track.[6]

Elisabeth Marbury, a theatrical agent, and her companion, the actress Elsie de Wolfe, had moved from New York to Paris in the 1890s. Marbury was well known in theatrical circles on both sides of the Atlantic for her success in bringing the plays of French and British authors to the attention of American audiences. Her influence on Broadway was commensurate with her reputation in Paris and London: she worked to ensure that her authors received their royalty payments while simultaneously providing the theater companies in New York with entertaining plays.[7]

Her residence, Villa Trianon, an eighteenth-century estate near Versailles, had originally served Louis XV as a retreat from the distractions of the French court. Villa Trianon had evolved into an essential destination for wealthy Americans in Paris who wished to spend time with their counterparts from Britain, France, and other European countries. Both Marbury and Elsie de Wolfe promoted Villa Trianon as an exclusive meeting place for an international aristocracy, hosting salons and concerts, staging theatrical productions, and generally welcoming anyone who could claim either wealth or fame.

Harry Thaw had been to Villa Trianon on his previous visits to Paris, and he first introduced Evelyn to his hosts in June 1903, on the occasion of her first sojourn in the capital. Her beauty, her youth—she was still only eighteen—and her Broadway experiences all combined to make her, for a short while at least, the center of attention. Elisabeth Marbury had known Stanford White in New York, and she was intrigued to learn, through gossip and conjecture, that this young American girl, apparently so innocent and impressionable, had spent time with White two years before. What was she now doing with Harry Thaw in Europe? Did she intend to go back on the stage when she returned to New York, or did she wish to settle down, perhaps with Thaw?[8]

Evelyn's experiences in Paris exceeded her expectations in every way. Stanford White had spoken often of his travels in France, but his stories, invariably amusing and entertaining, had given her little sense of the delights that she now enjoyed. Harry Thaw also had exceeded her expectations. Harry had proven himself the perfect host, showing her the sights, taking her hither and thither, sparing no expense, and generally taking care to satisfy her every whim. Evelyn had heard the rumors about Harry from her friends, but she had seen no evidence either that he took drugs or that he frequented prostitutes. He had treated her well, with respect and consideration, and it seemed only natural that their time exploring the city together would bring them closer, in a feeling of mutual affection.

She was taken aback, nevertheless, when Harry suddenly asked her to marry him. She had had no warning, no premonition; the request came as a surprise. Evelyn hesitated, unsure how to deal with a situation that she had not foreseen. She was still only eighteen, she replied, too young to think of marriage, and she was not yet ready to settle down. They had known each other only a short time, and besides, she had begun to think about a return to the stage. What would be the response of his family if they knew that he was engaged to be married to an actress?

Her words seemed to have no effect, and for the first time, Evelyn realized that Harry was unaccustomed to hearing any refusal. He loved her, he replied, and he wished to marry her. His mother might not be happy that he had married an actress, but she would eventually come around—she always accepted his decisions—and he did not give a fig what society might think. He cared greatly for her, and he was sure that they would be happy together.

"Don't you care for me?" Harry asked. "Don't you care anything about me?"

"Yes," she replied hesitantly. She appreciated everything that he had done for her. His solicitude for her recovery after her illness; his kindness and his consideration while she was in the hospital; and now his generosity toward her in France—it had all been wonderful . . .

Harry leaned forward, scanning her face for some clue that might provide an explanation for her hesitation. She had always seemed content to be with him, and they had enjoyed their time together. Was there some other cause, some reason, apart from their relationship, that explained her reluctance?

"Tell me," he said, "why won't you marry me?"

He had heard the gossip about Evelyn and Stanford White but he had paid little attention, until now, to such rumors. It had seemed scarcely credible that she would give her affection to such a man as White. Why, the disparity in their ages, at least thirty years, would have made any relationship between them improbable. But Harry had always been uncertain; and he had never previously asked her about her friendship with White.

He leaned forward again, gently taking hold of her hands, as he asked her about the architect.

"Is it because of Stanford White?" he said.

Tears welled in her eyes and she moved her head slightly, tilting it to one side as if to avoid his gaze. She nodded her reply — "Yes" — freeing her hand from his grasp to wipe away a tear that threatened to roll down her cheek.[9]

It was as if Harry's questions had released a flood of memories. They stayed awake until dawn, Evelyn telling him everything that had happened two years before between her and White, describing their initial encounter, her adventure on the velvet swing, and her mother's visit to White's offices. Stanford White had given her mother some money to go to Pittsburgh, and she, Evelyn, had seen him almost every day during her mother's absence.

Harry, his interest aroused, pressed her for details, demanding to know more, following the thread of her story to discover where it might lead. Evelyn continued to talk, telling him that she had posed for the photographer Rudolf Eickemeyer, and then, the next day, she had taken a cab from the Casino Theatre to Stanford White's town house on Twenty-fourth Street.

White had taken her upstairs, to a small bedroom on the third floor, where she had fallen unconscious after drinking some champagne. She had awoken to discover herself naked in bed with White, telltale spots of blood on the sheets.[10]

Evelyn felt a great sense of relief: at last, after two years, she had told someone about the rape. It was as if a burden had lifted itself from her shoulders, and at that moment, she experienced a sudden, unexpected sensation of well-being.

But her story seemed to provoke a profound revulsion in Harry Thaw. He had listened intently to her narrative, all the while nervously biting his fingernails, his whole body tense with anxiety, his face twisted in an expression of disgust. Evelyn knew that she had told a shocking story, a violent tale of deceit and deception; but she was taken aback, nevertheless, by the severity of Thaw's reaction.

He had started to sob; he had buried his face in his hands; and now he was no longer sitting in his chair but had begun pacing nervously about the room, his shoulders hunched together, his left hand tightly clutching his right forearm.

"The beast! The filthy beast!" Thaw's voice, now rising almost to a shout, startled her with its rage. "A sixteen-year-old girl! Damn him!"[11]

Evelyn had started to speak, attempting to hush his words, but he had already returned to his chair, anxiously interrogating her further about the rape.

What role, he demanded, had her mother played in this awful event? Why had Florence Nesbit entrusted her daughter to the care of such a man as White? Had it been negligence on her part, or had she deliberately put Evelyn in harm's way on account of the gifts that she had anticipated receiving from White? Stanford White had won their trust by his apparent generosity; but they should never have accepted his gifts.[12]

In any case, Harry told Evelyn, her story had not diminished his love for her. She had said that the rape had somehow tainted her, that White's act had disgraced her, and that she was not worthy to be his wife. But that was not true—the rape had not diminished her in his eyes. He still desired that they should be married.

Evelyn hesitated again. She was not ready to give him an answer; and Harry was too upset, too distraught at that moment to push his suit any further.

Florence Nesbit knew nothing of the secret that Evelyn had confided to Harry that night. But Florence, isolated and lonely in Paris, was herself desperately unhappy that she had agreed to accompany Evelyn to France. She had come to Paris as a chaperone for her daughter, but Harry and Evelyn explored the city without her, leaving her alone in the apartment. She knew no one in Paris; she could not speak French; and she had little interest in walking about the city by herself. It was a miserable situation, and her obvious discontent heightened the antipathy that Harry Thaw and Florence Nesbit had always felt for each other.

They finally left Paris in August, traveling to London. Florence insisted that she and Evelyn live apart from Harry, and he moved into a suite at the Carlton Hotel, on the Haymarket, while Florence and Evelyn took up rooms at Claridge's, a hotel in Mayfair. It would be only a short visit to the British capital, Harry announced: he intended to stay only two weeks in London before returning to Paris in preparation for their extended tour of the continent.[13]

But Florence Nesbit had had enough. She positively refused to spend more time with Harry Thaw, and she intended to return to the United States as soon as possible. She would no longer act as a chaperone to her daughter.

Her return to New York should have spelled the end of Harry's plans to tour Europe with Evelyn. It would be too scandalous for a man to travel alone with an unmarried woman. But Harry assured Evelyn that there was no cause for alarm; he would hire someone in Paris as a replacement for her mother.[14]

Harry and Evelyn spent that autumn traveling through Europe. They sailed from England to France, stopping at Paris for a few days to hire a chaperone, the widow of a British army officer, before going north to Holland. They boarded a steamboat on the Rhine, traveling south into Germany, eventually making their way to Munich.

There was no destination so romantic, so picturesque, as the Austrian Tyrol, and Harry had arranged that they should spend three weeks in a small castle in the Trientine Alps. They left Munich at the end of August, crossing into Austria-Hungary and traveling south to Innsbruck, continuing by carriage to Meran, a spa town close to the border with Italy.

Meran, located at the intersection of the Passer and Etsch Rivers, was known for its mineral waters, its gardens, and its temperate climate. The empress consort Elisabeth of Austria, the wife of Franz Joseph I, had visited the town frequently, but Meran had remained unspoiled, largely ignored by the tourists who flocked to the Tyrol each summer and fall.

Harry had reserved rooms for three weeks in September in a castle nestled among the mountains, more than three miles from the nearest house. The castle watchtower, a stone structure attached to the main building, provided magnificent views across the mountain range, and in the far distance, trapped between the mountain peaks, a small lake could be seen, its sky-blue waters shimmering in the sunlight.[15]

They left Meran at the end of September, traveling through the mountain passes into Switzerland, stopping at Lucerne, Bern, and Zurich before returning to Paris in October. Harry and Evelyn resumed the daily schedule they had pursued on their first stay in the capital, visiting the museums and art galleries, shopping on the Rue de la Paix, attending the ballet and the opera, and dining at the most exclusive restaurants.

But Evelyn was dismayed to learn in Paris that her secret — her confession that Stanford White had raped her — had become known to Harry's friends. She had entrusted Harry with the most intimate details of her past life, and she had told no one else; but he had betrayed her trust. It was distressing to learn that Elisabeth Marbury, someone with many acquaintances in New York, a woman who was friendly with Stanford White, now knew everything. Harry's betrayal would ensure that everyone, on both sides of the Atlantic, would learn about the rape.[16]

Even her mother had now heard the report that Stanford White had raped Evelyn. Florence Nesbit had returned from London to the United States earlier that summer, leaving Evelyn alone with Harry Thaw. But an acquaintance, Ida Simonton, had learned about the rape during a visit to Villa Trianon before traveling back to the United States. Simonton had booked a cabin on the same passenger liner on which Florence Nesbit sailed to New York, and as the boat chugged its way across the Atlantic, she revealed the entire episode to her companion, naming Stanford White as the perpetrator of the rape.

Nothing could have been more shocking to Florence Nesbit than the knowledge that Stanford White, her benefactor, the man in whose care she had placed Evelyn, had taken advantage of her absence to rape her daughter. It was too painful to believe, too distressing to accept, and to her relief, when she confronted White in New York with the accusation that he had raped Evelyn, he denied everything.

It was a false story, White replied, an invention of Harry Thaw, intentionally designed to blacken his reputation. Thaw had always been hostile toward him, believing that he, White, had blackballed him from the Union Club. There was no truth in the rumor, White repeated, that he had raped Evelyn. It was a wicked lie that Thaw had told in the hope of sending him to the penitentiary.[17]

⋆　　⋆　　⋆

Evelyn returned to the United States later that year, on October 24, 1903. She was now alone in New York: her mother had gone on to Pittsburgh to visit her fiancé and Harry had remained in Paris for a few weeks to settle some business matters. She still felt some fatigue and lassitude, symptoms of the illness that had afflicted her earlier in the year, but her time abroad had been an exhilarating experience. It was unfortunate, of course, that Harry had revealed her secret, but now even that no longer seemed so worrisome as it had first appeared. And Evelyn was preoccupied with her return to the stage. The producer Sam Shubert had offered her a part in a new show, *The Girl from Dixie*, a musical comedy that was scheduled to open in Hoyt's Theatre in December.[18]

She had not expected to see Stanford White — his presence in her life had already begun to seem a distant memory — but a chance encounter on Fifth Avenue, an exchange of greetings as their carriages passed each other, reawakened their friendship. They saw each other frequently that November; White called at her apartment at the Savoy Hotel, and she occasionally visited the tower apartment at Madison Square Garden. He had last seen her in May, as she had been about to embark on the SS *New York*, and he was curious to hear about her travels in Europe. Evelyn reported that it had been a wonderful experience to spend time in Paris, seeing the sights and meeting the most interesting people; and it had been equally enjoyable to travel through Switzerland, Germany, and Austria-Hungary.

White was familiar with many of the places that Evelyn

had visited during her time in the French capital. He also had spent many hours viewing the paintings and sculptures in the Louvre, and he had dined at several of the restaurants that she mentioned. He knew both Elisabeth Marbury and Elsie de Wolfe and had visited Villa Trianon on many occasions. But he did not fail to remind Evelyn again that she must be careful in her relations with Harry Thaw. White cautioned her that Thaw was a morphine addict, a man with a violent, unpredictable temper who was capable of doing her a great deal of harm.

Evelyn protested that she had seen no signs of drug use during her time in Europe with Harry. How could she believe such stories? But it was true, White replied, and if she would not believe him, why, there were other people in New York who knew about Harry Thaw. He could introduce her to several acquaintances who would corroborate his warnings.

Charles Dillingham, a friend of Stanford White, also spoke with Evelyn that month, advising her to be cautious. Dillingham, an urbane, smartly dressed man in his mid-thirties, had previously been the theater critic for the *New York Evening Post* before establishing his career as a producer of Broadway shows. He already had an enviable reputation on account of the success of *The Little Princess,* a play set in a girls' boarding school, and in November 1903, when he met with Evelyn Nesbit, he was the producer of two shows, *The Office Boy,* a musical then playing at the Victoria Theatre, and *Babette,* a comic opera at the Broadway Theatre.

He had heard many stories from his actors about Harry Thaw, he told Evelyn, and none of them had been favorable.

The accounts came from different sources, but they were all remarkably similar. Thaw frequently placed advertisements in the theatrical press, asking to interview actresses for a stage production. He would meet his victim, typically a young girl, at rooms he rented in a boardinghouse on Fifty-seventh Street. He would ask her about her background, her connections in the city, attempting to ascertain if she had relatives living nearby. If she lived alone, if she was vulnerable, if she had no protector or guardian, he would attack straightaway, tying his victim with cords and assaulting her with a dog whip. Such assaults were invariably brutal, leaving the victim with welts across her body, but Thaw had always avoided prosecution by paying large sums of money, thousands of dollars, to his victims.[19]

It became difficult for Evelyn to dismiss such accounts as entirely fictitious. Why would a man such as Charles Dillingham invent such stories? He was a well-known figure on Broadway who had produced several successful shows, with another, *Her Own Way,* soon to debut, and he had no reason to lie to her about Harry Thaw. Stanford White also was respected and reputable, and his warnings about Thaw seemed well intentioned, designed to safeguard her against danger.

White suggested that she should visit his lawyer, Abraham Hummel, for advice. Hummel was one of the best attorneys in New York, and he would give her the assistance that she needed. He was an ugly little man, White confided, with a grotesquely twisted body and a large head, but she need not be alarmed by his appearance; he was a brilliant lawyer with vast experience in the New York courts.

Evelyn trusted White and believed that he was acting selflessly to protect her interests. There was no disadvantage in speaking to a lawyer, and Evelyn made the journey downtown, to the Clock Tower Building at 346 Broadway, where Hummel had his office.

He was exactly as White had described him: no taller than five feet, with a head that seemed far too large for such a small body. His face had a chalky-white pallor, and Evelyn could see some tiny cherry-red warts on his cheeks and brow. His thin lips, sharp nose, pinprick eyes, and broad forehead gave Hummel a rat-like appearance; but there was nothing evasive or furtive about his manner. He was, on the contrary, excessively courteous, almost obsequious, in his greeting.[20]

Hummel was a divorce lawyer who specialized also in suits for breach of contract; he had succeeded in dozens of actions brought by actresses against wealthy men. He had settled a case against Harry Thaw several years before: a woman named Ethel Thomas had sued Thaw for assault, but Thaw paid her off before the case came to court. That was always the way, Hummel remarked; no one wanted the publicity that would come with a lawsuit.

Evelyn spent the afternoon talking about her friendship with Harry Thaw, describing their initial encounter at Rector's and the solicitude he had shown her during her illness. He had invited her to travel with him in Europe, and she had sailed with her mother at the end of May, meeting Thaw in

Paris and staying in France for about five weeks. Her mother had returned to the United States in June and she, Evelyn, had spent the remainder of her time traveling with Thaw through Holland, Germany, and Austria-Hungary.

Her description of the castle near Meran seemed to catch Hummel's attention more than any other detail of her journey. The location, high in the mountains, far from any town, had been stunningly beautiful, Evelyn remembered, but the castle itself, a large rectangular structure with crenellated walls, was a forbidding place. She had seen only a few servants, two or three maids and a butler, but otherwise she and Harry had spent their time alone.

Abraham Hummel listened attentively to Evelyn's descriptions, carefully noting the details that she provided, occasionally asking questions designed to complete her account. It would be best, he advised, to have a written record of her experience, something on which she could rely if there were a lawsuit. He would prepare a document that they could use against Thaw in such an event.

The suggestion puzzled Evelyn. Was it necessary to have a written summary of her remarks? What purpose would that serve? But her inexperience and her youth were no match for Hummel's shrewd calculation. He called his stenographer into the office and Evelyn listened as he dictated a summary of her account.[21]

Nothing could have been more surprising to Harry Thaw, on his return to New York in the middle of December, than to realize that Evelyn Nesbit had no desire to continue their friendship. He had expected to see her again on his arrival, but he received no response to the notes that he sent to her apartment. He called on the telephone, but her maid invariably replied that her mistress had left and there was no telling when she might return.

It was a mystery, a puzzle that confounded Harry. They had parted amicably, even, one might say, affectionately, when Evelyn had taken the boat back to New York. They had had no contact since her departure, and nothing, therefore, could have passed between them to end their friendship.

It took a chance encounter, a coincidental meeting at the Café des Beaux-Arts on Fortieth Street, to solve the mystery. Neither one had expected to see the other that afternoon, and Evelyn was hesitant even to acknowledge Harry's presence in the restaurant. But their tables were almost adjacent, and once they began to talk, Harry quickly realized why Evelyn had shunned his company.

She had heard horrible stories about him, reports that he lured young girls to his apartment, beating and whipping them and abusing them in the most dreadful ways. There was one account that he had scalded a young girl with boiling water. She had heard also that he was a morphine addict, that he frequently took cocaine and other drugs. It had been all too terrible to hear such stories, and she had no desire to see him again.[22]

Harry listened impassively, saying nothing as Evelyn explained her reluctance to continue their friendship. He merely shook his head from time to time, waiting for her to finish speaking. Finally she paused, expectantly, surprised that Harry had shown so little reaction to her words.

"I see," he began, speaking with an air of resignation, "that they have been making a fool of you." There was no anger in his voice, no indignation at the accusations that his enemies had leveled against his reputation. Stanford White, he explained, had always hated him and had done everything possible to destroy him. The reports that he had abused young girls were common currency among the blackmailers who had attempted to get his money. White had merely repeated the rumors that he, Harry, had heard so many times before, but there was nothing new in such gossip, he told Evelyn, and no truth in such tales.

Did Evelyn have any evidence, apart from the gossip that she had heard, to persuade her that White's stories might be true? She had just spent several months traveling with Thaw. "If I had taken morphine," he asked, "wouldn't it have shown itself some time or other?" Stanford White knew a great deal about such things, more than he, Harry Thaw, had ever learned; and if anyone were guilty of such behavior, it was White.[23]

It was preposterous that White, of all people, should make such accusations. He was one of a group of wealthy roués, all members of the Union Club, who organized frequent orgies in secret locations scattered about the city. Other members of the group included Henry Poor, a financier; James Lawrence Breese, a wealthy man-about-town with an avocational interest in photography; Charles MacDonald, a stockbroker and principal shareholder in the Southern Pacific Railroad; and Thomas Clarke, a dealer in antiques.[24]

There had been a notorious episode in 1895 when James Breese had held a dinner for some friends at his apartment. Stanford White had been present that evening with his partners Charles McKim and William Rutherford Mead. The sculptor Augustus Saint-Gaudens, several artists—Carroll Beckwith, Alden Weir, and Charles Dana Gibson—along with the architect Whitney Warren, had also attended. Some financiers and bankers, men well known on Wall Street, had accepted Breese's invitation, and several literati—journalists, writers, and magazine editors, all presumed to be trustworthy—had come to the dinner. The caterer, Louis Sherry, had arranged a magnificent dinner with a limitless quantity of champagne, but the highlight of the evening came at midnight. Six waiters carried an enormous spherical pie into the room; the headwaiter cut the crust; and a young girl, almost nude, magically appeared. The girl, Susie Johnson, had been paid well for her performance, but there had been a tragic denouement. Later that year, she had disappeared without a trace, and her distraught parents had been unable to discover her fate.

An account of the dinner subsequently appeared in the *New York World*. The newspaper condemned the men, all prominent New Yorkers, for their selfish corruption of young girls. Susie Johnson, according to the *World,* had come from a decent family but she had been tempted into prostitution. Stanford White's accomplices in the affair had used their social standing to escape prosecution. No one had been willing to indict them for their misdeeds, and the authorities, by their passive acquiescence, had thereby enabled them to continue with their crimes.[25]

It came as no surprise to Harry that Stanford White should accuse him of morphine addiction—it was an attempt by White to distract attention from his own misdeeds—but how had Abraham Hummel become involved in the affair? There were few lawyers, Harry told Evelyn, so crooked as Hummel. He had a reputation in the city as a blackmailer who frequently used the threat of a lawsuit for breach of contract to extort money from wealthy men. No one wanted to have his name linked to some disreputable woman, and most men were willing to pay any reasonable sum to settle the matter out of court. The accusations might be entirely false, without a shred of evidence to support them, but it was always preferable to avoid the publicity that would inevitably attach itself to a lawsuit.

Evelyn admitted to Thaw that she had talked with Hummel one afternoon in his office, telling him about her travels in Europe, describing the incidents in Paris that had led to her mother's return to the United States, and detailing the itinerary that she and Harry had followed on the continent. Hummel had been especially interested in their stay in Meran in the Tyrol, asking her many questions about the castle in which they had spent almost three weeks during September.

Harry was intrigued to learn that Hummel had dictated a document, an account of her travels, to one of his stenographers. What was in that document? Where was it now? Had she signed anything, any papers, during the interview in Hummel's office? Evelyn could give only vague replies to Harry's questions, saying that she had not read the document very carefully—there had been little opportunity—and yes, she might have signed some papers that afternoon; but she was not sure...

There was a scheme afoot, Harry told her, a conspiracy. But what trick did Hummel intend to play? Stanford White had learned that his rape of Evelyn was no longer a secret. Perhaps, Harry speculated, White and Hummel were preparing some ruse that would protect White from prosecution. But Hummel was a shrewd, cunning lawyer who would never reveal anything if it did not work to his advantage, and it would not be possible to learn the nature of the conspiracy unless he chose to disclose it. They could only wait and see what might transpire.

It was a dizzying turn of events for Evelyn Nesbit. She was caught between two forceful, strong-willed men, each of whom accused the other of the most terrible behavior. Evelyn, still just eighteen years old, was naïve and impressionable, too quick to believe anything she heard, and it was impossible for her to determine which man might be telling the truth. Could it be that their mutual dislike had increased to such a degree that each was ready to repeat the most scandalous gossip that he had heard about the other? Perhaps there was no truth in either account; perhaps each man had allowed his antipathy for the other to exceed all reasonable bounds.

Evelyn traveled a second time to Europe with Harry, sailing from New York the following year on the SS *Kaiser Wilhelm der Grosse* at the end of March 1904. It was again necessary that a chaperone travel with them, and Harry persuaded a friend, Ben Donnelly, to accompany them on the journey. They went first to Paris, staying at the Hôtel Palais d'Orsay, before taking the train south to Monte Carlo. They stayed at the resort for two weeks, playing *trente et quarante* at the casino during the day and attending the opera at the Salle Garnier at night. Then it was on to Italy, going first to Verona and then to Lake Como, pausing briefly at Bellagio.

They followed a zigzag, almost haphazard itinerary, returning to Paris for a few weeks before crossing into Switzerland by motorcar. Harry traveled impulsively, deciding their route on a whim, yet his wealth invariably opened all doors, securing them the best rooms in the most exclusive hotels. They reached London in October, staying only to visit Harry's sister Alice before boarding a ship back across the Atlantic to New York.[26]

Evelyn had imagined that their wanderings would distract Harry from thoughts of Stanford White—but nothing, it seemed, could dissuade him from his pursuit of the architect. Earlier that year, in February 1904, shortly before his departure from New York, Thaw had enlisted Anthony Comstock, secretary of the Society for the Suppression of Vice, in his crusade to bring Stanford White to justice. Comstock, then fifty-nine years old, had campaigned for many decades against obscenity, successfully persuading the United States Congress in 1873 to ban the delivery by the postal service of lewd and obscene publications. Comstock's remit, as secretary of the Society for the Suppression of Vice, encompassed anything that he considered

immoral, including literature on birth control and the preven-
tion of venereal disease. Thaw's complaints that Stanford White
and other men were luring young girls to secret locations in
New York and raping them seemed legitimate, and Comstock
promised that he would assign detectives to investigate Thaw's
accusations.[27]

Nine months later, after Thaw had returned from Europe,
the two men spoke again about White. Thaw reported that
workmen had heard the cries of young girls coming from the
building that contained the photographic studio of Rudolf
Eickemeyer, the same studio in which Evelyn Nesbit had posed
for Eickemeyer in a kimono. Comstock again promised to
investigate, saying that he would assign detectives to watch
Stanford White and to stand guard over the places that White
was known to frequent. Comstock also informed Thaw that
he had attempted to rent one of the tower apartments in Madison Square Garden in order to spy on White; but none of the
apartments had become vacant that year.[28]

Harry Thaw had complained publicly about Stanford White,
accusing him of various crimes, but already the gossip columns in the New York newspapers were remarking un-
favorably on Thaw's own behavior. He had traveled to Europe
twice with Evelyn Nesbit, an unmarried woman, and social
convention dictated that a chaperone accompany Evelyn while
she was with Thaw. Yet Florence Nesbit, on the first trip,
had chaperoned her daughter only during her stay in Paris
and London; and no one had yet been able to determine who, if

anyone, had accompanied Evelyn for the remainder of the journey.

Thaw claimed that his friend Ben Donnelly had been the chaperone for Evelyn on the second visit to Europe in 1904, but no one could have seemed less suited for the role. Donnelly, a former football player at Princeton, subsequently played for professional teams in Pittsburgh and Chicago, earning a reputation as a brutal thug who would do anything, no matter how unsportsmanlike, to win games. His later career as a football coach had been lackluster and his teams had achieved little success. He had drifted aimlessly since the end of his coaching career, finding intermittent employment here and there, and he had readily accepted Thaw's offer of employment as a chaperone to Evelyn Nesbit.[29]

The newspaper reports that Harry might have traveled alone with Evelyn Nesbit in Europe were a source of acute distress to his family. His mother, Mary Thaw, a proud woman who had always jealously guarded her social position, was indignant that her eldest son was so recklessly endangering the family name. Evelyn Nesbit, an obscure actress who had played in risqué musical comedies on Broadway, was, in the opinion of Mary Thaw, little better than a courtesan, and it would be too scandalous to public morals to imagine that Harry had lived with such a woman.

Her other children had married well, choosing husbands and wives whose social position was secure; but there seemed no solution to the problem that Harry posed. One daughter, Alice, had wed George Francis Alexander Seymour, a member of the British aristocracy, the eldest son of the sixth Marquess of Hertford, and a second daughter, Margaret, had married George Lauder Carnegie, a nephew of the steel magnate Andrew Carnegie. Her two other sons, Josiah and Edward, had also chosen wisely, each marrying the daughter of a prominent Pittsburgh businessman.[30]

Mary Thaw had threatened to withhold Harry's share of the inheritance if he continued in his determination to marry Evelyn Nesbit. But Harry was too strong-willed to pay much attention to his mother's demands, and she knew, even as she made the threat, that it would be futile. If Harry was determined to marry Evelyn, then it was at least preferable that he marry her as soon as possible and thus avoid the continuing scandal that had attached itself to the relationship. Mary Thaw would consent to the marriage and accept Evelyn Nesbit as her daughter-in-law, but only, she informed Harry, if she could be allowed to forget that Evelyn had ever been on the stage. There were to be no reminders of her disreputable past as an actress.[31]

Harry renewed his proposal of marriage and Evelyn eventually accepted. She had always been uncomfortably aware that Harry's relatives — his mother, his brothers and sisters — might not willingly accept her into the family. The marriage would also compel her to abandon her stage career, to relinquish any chance of success on Broadway, and might even, as Harry had suggested, require her to leave New York to move with him to Pittsburgh.

There was so much to consider and so many possible pitfalls. But marriage would mean financial security. Evelyn had always lived from day to day, never knowing what the future might hold. It no longer seemed possible for her to make a living as an actress, and now she could not count on the generosity of Stanford White. Her education had been only intermittent, and she was ill-equipped for any profession. Her future seemed to depend almost exclusively on marriage to someone wealthy, a man who would support her.

The wedding, on April 4, 1905, was almost pitiful in its brevity, an expression of the disdain that Mary Thaw felt for her new daughter-in-law. There had been bright sunshine earlier in the day, but that afternoon, when Evelyn Nesbit arrived for the ceremony, it had already started to rain. Her mother, Florence, and her stepfather, Charles Holman, accompanied Evelyn to the residence of William McEwan, pastor of the Third Presbyterian Church in Pittsburgh. Harry Thaw greeted them, welcoming his bride with a bouquet of red roses. His mother and his younger brother Josiah were also present as witnesses, and after McEwan had conducted everyone to his study, a large room lined with bookshelves, the pastor began the service.[32]

No one else was present to see Harry Thaw take Evelyn Nesbit as his wife. Harry's sisters, Alice and Margaret, unwilling to accept Evelyn as a sister-in-law, had declined their invitations, and Edward, his youngest brother, had also refused to acknowledge the marriage. The bride had hoped to invite one or two of her *Florodora* friends, and Harry had suggested that a couple of his friends might also attend; but Mary Thaw had insisted on a private ceremony, one that would receive as little notice as possible.

It was an almost perfunctory occasion, designed solely to satisfy the legal requirements, and soon, in less than an hour, it was over. Three carriages waited outside to take everyone to Lyndhurst, the Thaw family home, for a celebratory dinner, and later that evening Harry and Evelyn caught the train for New York in preparation for their honeymoon.

The next day the newlyweds traveled west, taking a train from New York to Chicago. They stayed there only two days before heading north, to Milwaukee, to visit one of Evelyn's former classmates at the DeMille school. They spent several days with a guide in the Grand Canyon before continuing on to Yosemite, eventually reaching San Francisco before returning home to Pittsburgh.[33]

Neither Evelyn nor Harry had given much thought to the future; Harry had vaguely anticipated that they would settle in Pittsburgh after the honeymoon. Lyndhurst, the family residence on Beechwood Boulevard, was an enormous mansion, one of the grandest residences in the city, and Harry and Evelyn moved into the house at the end of May 1905.

But Evelyn quickly became disillusioned. Mary Thaw, on account of her philanthropy, exerted great influence within the Presbyterian Church in Pittsburgh; she had given generously to religious charities in the city and throughout western Pennsylvania. But her reputation was less potent in other circles, and it soon became apparent that the social elite of the city was reluctant to accept Evelyn into its ranks. She occupied her time in self-improvement, studying French and taking piano lessons, but there was little opportunity for her to meet companions of her own age, and she soon began to think of herself as a prisoner, trapped in a large, rather gloomy mansion.[34]

Harry also felt restless. There was little for him to do in Pittsburgh, and he had few friends in the city. He was frequently absent, claiming that his business affairs in New York often compelled him to go east, and Evelyn, resentful that her husband occasionally abandoned her, felt a growing sense of isolation and loneliness. Had she made the wrong decision in marrying Harry Thaw? She had been married only a few months, yet already she had begun to contemplate filing for divorce.[35]

The sense of crisis that imperiled the marriage found reinforcement in the sudden appearance of the photographs of Evelyn that Rudolf Eickemeyer had taken in 1901. The copyright had somehow passed to a printing company in Elizabeth, New Jersey, that had started to distribute images of Evelyn commercially. In December 1905 Haudenshield & Co., a butcher in Diamond Square in Pittsburgh, issued its calendar for 1906, including among the illustrations a photograph of Evelyn Nesbit, dressed in a kimono and reclining on a bearskin rug.

Lawyers for the Thaw family pounced immediately, threatening Haudenshield & Co. with legal action if the butcher continued to distribute the calendar to his customers. The butcher was initially defiant, claiming to have been unaware of the identity of the girl in the photograph, but a financial settlement was reached and the attorneys were able to confiscate the remaining calendars.[36]

A second photograph of Evelyn appeared in January 1906 in

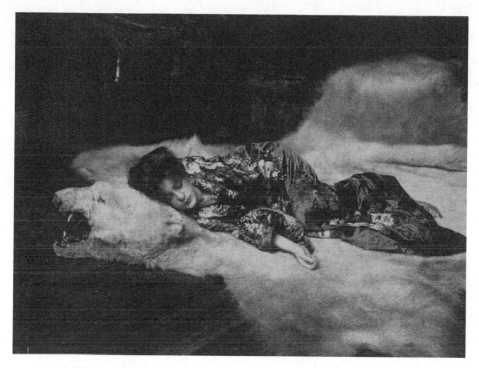

Rudolf Eickemeyer originally titled this 1901 photograph of Evelyn Nesbit *The Little Butterfly*. The photograph subsequently appeared in an exhibition at the Carnegie Art Gallery in January 1906 under the title *In My Studio*. *(Library of Congress, LC-DIG-ds-10597)*

an exhibition at the Carnegie Art Gallery. The portrait, identified only as a photograph by Rudolf Eickemeyer, showed a young girl asleep. There was nothing in the exhibition to identify the model as Evelyn Nesbit—Eickemeyer had named his work only *In My Studio*—but no one had any doubt about the matter.[37]

It was a lamentable situation and nobody felt a greater sense of humiliation than Mary Thaw. She had given her consent to the marriage on the condition that there be no reminder of Evelyn's disreputable past as an actress; it was not to be mentioned in her presence. Yet just a few months later, suggestive photographs of Evelyn as a young girl started to pop up in the most unexpected places. Mary Thaw had always cherished her position as a grande dame, giving generously to various cultural institutions in the city, guarding her reputation for moral probity, and actively supporting the local clergy; but her son's marriage to Evelyn Nesbit cast a shadow over all her endeavors.

Harry Thaw was disconsolate. His wife was lonely and unhappy, regretful that she had agreed to live in Pittsburgh; his mother was angry and indignant that the photographs of Evelyn had undermined her social position and made her family the target of malicious gossip. Perhaps, he suggested to Evelyn, it would help their marriage if they traveled again for a while in Europe. They could spend some time in New York, visiting friends and renewing acquaintances, before taking a boat across the Atlantic.

Evelyn readily agreed. Nothing would please her so much as the chance to leave Lyndhurst. She had enjoyed her previous journeys to Europe, and she looked forward to seeing Paris and London again. They would leave Pittsburgh at the end of June, Harry said, spending several days in New York before sailing on the SS *Amerika* to Hamburg. It would be splendid to visit New York again, to chat with old friends, to catch up on the latest gossip, and to see some of the Broadway shows. A musical comedy, *Mamzelle Champagne*, was opening at Madison Square Garden on June 25. Everybody would be there on opening night, Harry predicted, and it promised to be a very special occasion.

4

Murder

June 25, 1906–July 15, 1906

"Hello, Larry," White exclaimed, seeing the stage manager Lionel Lawrence appear in front of the curtain. "How are all the girls?"[1]

Stanford White sat in his usual seat, at a small table near the front, waiting for the play to begin. The rooftop theater at Madison Square Garden was empty; but the audience would soon arrive, ascending in the elevator, occupying the seats at small tables in front of the stage and filling up the two benches that ran along each side.

The show that evening, *Mamzelle Champagne,* was a typical Broadway production, a musical comedy in two acts, with attractive girls and tuneful songs. It had already played in Atlantic City, and it was opening that night in New York to coincide with the start of the summer season. The reviews had all been tentative: the leading man, Harry Short, was an unknown with little Broadway experience, and the story was skeletal—a champagne bottle, transported from Paris, reveals its secrets—but it was opening night, and there was always a good audience at the first performance.[2]

Lionel Lawrence paused momentarily, stopping to exchange greetings. Lawrence had first met White several years before, when he had directed *The Giddy Throng,* a comic opera, at the New York Theatre. He liked White's easy familiarity, his lack of pretension, and his jovial good humor, but he had little time now, thirty minutes before the start of the show, to stop and chat.

"Say, Larry," White called out, indicating a young woman seated by the stage on the far side of the theater, "who is the little peach over there? I want to meet her."

Lawrence recognized one of his actresses, Maude Fulton, a twenty-five-year-old making her Broadway debut.

"Some other time," Lawrence answered. "I'll make you acquainted, old man, some other time. . . . I can't introduce you tonight," he pleaded. "This is a first night and I have not a minute."

"All right, Larry," White replied cheerfully, "but bear in mind that I mean it, and I'll keep you to your promise. . . . I like the looks of that girl and want to meet her."[3]

White seemed carefree, apparently intent on enjoying the play. But his demeanor masked an anxiety over his financial troubles. His debts had accumulated gradually, silently multiplying over the years until they had reached almost a million dollars. Two acquaintances, Alfred Vanderbilt and J. Pierpont Morgan, had lent him large sums of money, but there was little chance that he would be able to repay his creditors. His partners, Charles McKim and William Rutherford Mead, had tolerated his extravagance for many years, but now their generosity had run its course. They had voted to end the terms of his association with the firm, removing him as a partner and insisting that he work as a salaried employee.[4]

It was a bitter irony that his connection to Madison Square Garden had proved financially ruinous. White had invested heavily in the project, and he was now a director and principal stockholder in the company that owned the building. But the mortgage had always been onerous; it had been a constant struggle to obtain bookings, and Madison Square Garden had rarely turned a profit. The main arena attracted shows of every description—bicycle races, horse shows, military parades, prizefights, political rallies, religious revivals—but the maintenance and operating costs always outran the receipts. Neither the restaurant on the first floor nor the concert hall above attracted sufficient customers, and only the interior theater had ever been profitable. And Madison Square was no longer a residential neighborhood—commercial office buildings had replaced the brownstones that previously lined its streets—and the theater district had moved uptown to Times Square. The land on which Madison Square Garden stood—an entire block between Madison Avenue and Fourth Avenue—had become increasingly valuable as the area changed, and the property taxes on the building had increased accordingly.[5]

One year before, White had reluctantly reconciled himself to selling part of his art collection to settle his debts. He had stored some of his most valuable artworks—sixteenth-century Italian tapestries, antique furniture, several seventeenth-century Flemish paintings, some statuary and decorative ironwork—in a warehouse on Thirtieth Street in preparation for the sale of the collection at auction. But disaster had struck: on February 13, 1905, fire broke out in a nearby printing shop; a northwesterly wind fanned the flames, and the blaze spread to the storage rooms, destroying White's collection. There had been a heavy snowfall the previous night; the streets were not yet clear, and the fire trucks were unable to make their way in time. Stanford White had been too distraught to speak to the newspapers about the catastrophe—he had not insured the collection—but a close friend, Thomas Clarke, had claimed that the loss would be severe.[6]

White's financial distress had gone hand in hand with a general decline in his health. He was now fifty-two; his hair had almost turned white, and he had recently gained a great deal of weight. Even the slightest exertion, merely walking up a flight of stairs, was sufficient to leave him short of breath. He had a recurrent pain on his right side, just above the rib cage, and all his joints seemed to ache in the most alarming manner.[7]

And finally, there was the wretched business with Harry Thaw. This irritating young man, the husband of Evelyn Nesbit, had long had an intense dislike of him and had recently hired private detectives to follow him around New York, all in the belief that he, White, was engaged in some nefarious activity. It was unsettling, even alarming, to know that Thaw's detectives were shadowing him; but what could he do about it? His friends had advised him to be on his guard—Thaw was mentally unstable—but Stanford White disregarded their warnings. Harry Thaw had a reputation for assaulting young girls who had few means of defending themselves; but Thaw was otherwise a coward who would not dare attack one of New York's most prominent citizens. He, Stanford White, had the resources and the determination to press charges if Thaw was so foolish as to assault him.[8]

Evelyn Nesbit watched absent-mindedly as the waiters moved about Café Martin taking orders. She had little appetite that evening and she played with the food on her plate, taking an occasional bite, listening as Harry and his two companions continued to talk among themselves. Truxtun Beale was telling them about his recent adventure in San Francisco. She glanced at her husband, directly opposite, as Harry interrupted to ask Beale about the shooting. Thomas McCaleb sat on her left, saying nothing, watching Beale impassively, his face expressionless, as Beale described how he had shot his victim.[9]

It had begun when a newspaper editor, Frederick Marriott, insulted Beale's wife in one of his columns. Beale had called on Marriott at his home, demanding an apology. Both men had drawn their guns: Beale had emerged unscathed, but Marriott was badly hurt. The jury at Beale's trial acquitted him of assault, accepting his defense that he had acted to safeguard the honor of his wife.[10]

Harry signaled to the maître d'hôtel that he was ready to pay the bill, remarking only that Beale had been very fortunate. It might have ended badly, he added, if the jury had taken a different view of the matter.

Evelyn Nesbit and Harry Thaw dined with friends at Café Martin on June 25, 1906, before walking across Madison Square to a performance of *Mamzelle Champagne* at Madison Square Garden. Café Martin, one of the most fashionable restaurants in Manhattan, opened in this location in 1901 after the previous tenant, Delmonico's, moved uptown in 1899. *(Library of Congress, LC-D401-70801)*

He had bought tickets for *Mamzelle Champagne,* a musical comedy opening that night, and the four of them left the restaurant by the exit on Fifth Avenue, crossing to the park opposite. Madison Square Garden stood before them, on the northeast corner of Madison Square, its vast bulk dominating the square, its tower, illuminated by arc lights, stretching skyward. It had been an unusually mild day—there had been no hint of the sticky humidity that typically gripped New York during the summer months—and the sun had already started to sink below the horizon. The golden rays of the sunset flooded the park, falling directly onto the front of Madison Square Garden. The pale-yellow brickwork and white terra-cotta reflected the sunlight with an intense gleam, and in the center of the main façade, high above the street below, the purple-pink decoration surrounding the Palladian window had become incandescent. Everyone could agree that Madison Square Garden was the most beautiful building in New York, an anomaly in a city so thoroughly devoted to business and commerce.

They made their way across the park, passing a statue of Admiral David Farragut on their left, leaving the park at the northeast corner, at the intersection of Madison Avenue and Twenty-sixth Street. An elevator took them from the side entrance of Madison Square Garden to the rooftop. The play was already in progress and the theater was almost full—only a few places were still unoccupied—and they threaded their way through the maze of small tables, eventually reaching their seats.

Every producer of a musical hoped to repeat the success that *Florodora* had experienced a few years before. Harry Pincus, the producer of *Mamzelle Champagne,* had employed the same ingredients—catchy tunes, beautiful girls, dramatic scenes—but the magic that had worked so well for *Florodora* was missing from *Mamzelle Champagne*. The audience was already slightly restless, fretful that the play seemed so unexpectedly dreary. Harry Thaw quickly became impatient, irritated that he had brought his friends to see such a dull play. He found it impossible to sit still and he excused himself, whispering a few words to his companions before making his way to the south side of the roof, adjacent to Twenty-sixth Street.

An acquaintance, J. Clinch Smith, was sitting alone by the balustrade, and Thaw, seeing an empty chair, sat down next to his friend. Smith had studied law at Columbia University, but his inheritance allowed him to live as a man of leisure, sailing his yacht on Long Island Sound and riding his thoroughbreds on his country estate.

"How do you like the play?" Thaw began.

It was terribly slow, Smith replied; it surprised him that the theater had chosen *Mamzelle Champagne* to open its summer season.

Thaw nodded his agreement, saying only that it might be a success nevertheless; it was always difficult to predict the fate of a musical revue.

"What are you doing in Wall Street nowadays?" he asked. There was not much more, he felt, that either of them could say about the play.

"I haven't bought any stocks in some time," Smith replied. "Do you know anything?" he added.

The best investment anyone could make, Thaw replied, would be Amalgamated Copper. The company controlled many of the most important mines in Montana and was able to keep the price of copper artificially high. There was tremendous demand for the metal on account of the mania for electrification; electricity was the future, and copper was necessary for its success. Steel would also be a good investment: the United States Steel Company was one of the most profitable businesses in the country. "In fact," Thaw advised, "if I had any money to invest I would put it all in steels and coppers, especially the copper."[11]

Neither man was now paying much attention to the actors on the stage. They continued to chat, their voices hushed, talking quietly so as to avoid giving annoyance to their neighbors. Thaw was intrigued to discover that Smith planned to sail to Europe later that week, and the two men compared notes on passenger liners.

It was astonishing, Thaw remarked, how quickly a ship could cross the Atlantic these days. He was leaving with his wife on the SS *Amerika* on Wednesday, and it would take them less than a week to reach Germany. It was a new ship, built the previous year for the Hamburg America Line, and he was looking forward to the journey.

"Do you know the *Amerika*?" he asked.

"Yes," Smith replied. "I only came out on her a few months ago." It was a beautiful ship, lavishly decorated in the first-class section, but the suites were very expensive.

"It is a ridiculous thing," Thaw agreed. "They charge for them $900."

"What do you want so much room for? There is nobody but yourself and your wife."

"Yes," Thaw answered. "I know that, but when I go to Europe I want to have my meals served in my own private apartment, and that necessitates more room."

He glanced out across the theater, scanning the audience, and he noticed Evelyn trying to catch his eye, beckoning him to return to his seat.

"Excuse me," he said, turning to Smith, "I am going down this way."[12]

Clinch Smith watched as Thaw made his way across the roof, walking along the side aisle and then threading a path through the maze of small tables. Evelyn Nesbit whispered some words to her husband, motioning to the empty seat by her side, and Harry Thaw sat down to watch the remainder of the play.

But Evelyn Nesbit also was impatient that *Mamzelle Champagne* was so dreary. She could not bear to sit still, to remain any longer in the theater. The play had not yet ended, but they started to leave, Evelyn and Thomas McCaleb in front, Harry Thaw and Truxtun Beale following.

Evelyn glanced behind her as they approached the elevator, looking to say some words to her husband, but he had disappeared. What had happened to Harry? How could he suddenly vanish? She looked around the roof, searching for him, thinking that perhaps he had returned to his seat to retrieve something. Where was he?

She was surprised to see, in the distance, directly in front of the stage, Stanford White sitting to one side, close to the balustrade, watching the play. He slouched in his seat, his right arm by his side, his left arm on the back of a neighboring chair. Suddenly she saw Harry, standing at the front of the theater, his right arm extended forward, his gun pointed directly at White.

At that moment Stanford White also noticed Thaw standing before him. White stiffened in his chair and started to rise to his feet; but it was too late. The first bullet entered White's shoulder, tearing at his flesh and splintering the bone. White slumped backward, sending his wineglass crashing to the floor, and a second bullet hit him in the face, directly beneath his left eye. Thaw fired again and the third bullet hit White in the mouth, smashing his front teeth.[13]

Stanford White died instantly, his body falling to the ground face forward, a thin rivulet of blood trickling outward from his head and spreading slowly across the floor. Harry Thaw stood motionless, staring impassively at his victim, his gun still in his hand.[14]

Two of the actors on the stage had engaged in a duel only moments before, and nearby spectators, those seated close to the stage, believed that the shooting of Stanford White was part of the play. But Lionel Lawrence, watching from the wings, had witnessed the murder and already realized that it might precipitate a general panic among the audience. The chorus girls onstage had seen the shooting also, and they stopped singing, their voices trailing away in their bewilderment.

"Sing, girls, sing!" Lawrence called to the chorus girls, "for God's sake, sing! Don't stop!"

The orchestra had stopped playing, the musicians still staring at the spot where White's body lay motionless, the entire ensemble paralyzed by confusion and fear. "Keep the music going!" Lawrence cried, urging the orchestra to continue, hoping to reassure the audience and prevent a panic.[15]

Harry Thaw, seemingly oblivious to the commotion, raised his right arm above his head, holding the gun by the barrel as if to indicate to the audience that he intended no further harm.

He now started to walk slowly down the center aisle, toward the rear of the theater, and as he advanced, the spectators started to rise to their feet, craning their necks to get a better view and to discover the cause of the disturbance.

Lionel Lawrence stepped from the wings, striding to the front of the stage, holding his arms in front of him with a gesture meant to reassure the audience that there was no cause for alarm. "A most unfortunate accident has happened!" Lawrence called out from the stage. "The management regrets to ask that the audience leave at once, in an orderly manner. There is no danger—only an accident that will prevent a continuance of the performance."[16]

Paul Brudi, the duty fireman, was the first person to reach Thaw, approaching him from behind and taking the gun, a blue-steel .22-caliber pistol, from his hand. Warner Paxton, a member of the audience, also came up behind Thaw, and both men, Brudi on the left, Paxton on the right, held Thaw, escorting him slowly down the center aisle toward the elevator at the rear of the theater.

There was no resistance, no attempt to escape on the part of Thaw. He had willingly given up his gun, and as he walked with his captors toward the exit, he started to speak, telling them why he had shot Stanford White.

"I did it," Thaw explained, turning to address Brudi, "because he ruined my wife."[17]

Neither Brudi nor Paxton gave him any response. Thaw continued to talk, speaking first to one man and then to the other, but they ignored him, tightly gripping his wrists as they slowly advanced along the center aisle toward the elevator.

Already they had arrived at the rear of the theater. Evelyn Nesbit, standing by the elevator doors, an anguished expression on her face, reached out for her husband, as if to embrace him.

"My God, Harry," she cried. "What have you done? What have you done? My God, Harry, you've killed him."

Thomas McCaleb had remained at Evelyn's side. He stepped forward as she spoke, resting his hand on her arm as if to comfort her.

"God, Harry," he exclaimed, "you must have been crazy."

But Thaw, a slight smile on his face, seemed indifferent to their anguish. He glanced first at McCaleb, then at Evelyn, as his captors paused before the elevator doors, waiting to descend to the street. "He ruined your life, dear," he said, speaking to his wife in a matter-of-fact way. "That's why I did it."[18]

Patrick Debs, the policeman on duty at Madison Square Garden, took Thaw into custody, walking with him toward the station house on Thirtieth Street. The prisoner seemed surprisingly acquiescent in his arrest, and the two men walked side by side along Madison Avenue. Debs was curious that Thaw should be so calm. He asked his prisoner if it was true that he had just killed Stanford White.

"He deserved it," Thaw replied, speaking without rancor. "He deserved everything he could get. He ruined a girl and then deserted her."

Why, Thaw asked, were they walking along Madison Avenue? Where were they going?

The police station was located a few blocks uptown, Debs replied, on Thirtieth Street, and he was taking Thaw to be booked. He, Thaw, would spend the night at the station house, and in the morning the magistrate would remand him into custody.[19]

It was not easy for Thaw to reconcile himself to his changed circumstances—his prison cell was cold and dark; his cot was uncomfortable; the clamor of the other prisoners kept him awake—and he passed a restless night. The next morning the police inspector, Max Schmittberger, took charge of the prisoner, ordering his transfer to headquarters on Mott Street. He would not grant Thaw any special privileges, Schmittberger declared, nothing to set him apart from the other prisoners. The police would escort Thaw to headquarters in the usual manner, chained and manacled, under armed guard, in a patrol wagon.[20]

A small group of journalists and spectators had already gathered at police headquarters to await Thaw's arrival. The guard escorted Thaw past the expectant crowd into the Mott Street building to be photographed. It was customary to identify prisoners by the Bertillon system of measurement, and Thaw cheerfully cooperated, allowing his captors to measure his head and fingers, to determine his height and weight, and to record the color of his eyes.

There was a pleasing novelty about the experience that Thaw had not anticipated. The police headquarters building was located halfway down Mott Street, in the center of the Italian immigrant neighborhood, and even at ten o'clock in the morning the market stalls were busy, each proprietor competing with his neighbor for the attention of passers-by. Peddlers and pushcarts moved up and down the street, challenging

The magistrate for the Third Judicial District remanded Harry Thaw into custody during a hearing at the Jefferson Market Courthouse. The courthouse was located in this Victorian Gothic building at Tenth Street and Sixth Avenue. *(New York City Municipal Archives, bps_17829)*

knots of pedestrians for the right-of-way, while hordes of ragamuffin boys and girls, intent on mischief, ran in and out of the doors of the tenement houses. Inside police headquarters, a motley collection of pickpockets, cardsharps, prostitutes, swindlers, and gangsters waited, together with Harry Thaw, to be photographed and measured. It was a world apart, as different from Madison Square and Fifth Avenue as one could possibly imagine, and Thaw experienced its novelty as both exhilarating and exciting.

Thaw and his police entourage traveled next to Tenth Street, to the Jefferson Market Courthouse, a distinctive redbrick building in the Victorian Gothic style. The magistrate, Peter Barlow, remanded Thaw into the custody of the coroner until the completion of the inquest into Stanford White's death.[21]

The Criminal Courts Building, a massive granite structure facing Centre Street, was the penultimate destination on Harry Thaw's itinerary that day. Thaw's attorneys, Daniel O'Reilly and Frederick Delafield, had already arrived at the courthouse, and Robert Turnbull, an assistant district attorney, was also present. Patrick Debs, the policeman who had taken Thaw into custody, presented an affidavit with the details of the arrest, and the coroner, Peter Dooley, committed Harry Thaw to the city prison.

Evelyn Nesbit called on her husband the next day. The prison, designed, incongruously, in the style of a French château, was an attractive building that provided no external sign of the cramped conditions within. Its location, between Centre and Lafayette Streets, had been the site of the original prison, nicknamed the Tombs on account of its resemblance

Harry Thaw was held in the city prison, nicknamed the Tombs, from June 1906 to February 1908. The Tombs, built in 1902, faced Centre Street, immediately next to the Criminal Courts Building. The bridge over Franklin Street, on the right of the photograph, allowed the guards to escort prisoners securely to the adjacent courthouse. *(New York City Municipal Archives, mac_1926)*

to a mausoleum. In 1902 the city had condemned the Tombs as inadequate and unsanitary and had built a second prison, also called the Tombs, on the same site. The new prison, an eight-story behemoth in gray-white limestone, with a steeply pitched roof and two conical towers, stood directly south of the Criminal Courts Building. Franklin Street separated the prison from the courthouse, but an enclosed passageway, four stories above street level, connected the two buildings. The Tombs typically held only those prisoners awaiting trial, and each morning around eight o'clock, the guards began escorting individual prisoners across the bridge that led to the courthouse for the disposition of their cases.[22]

Evelyn Nesbit, accompanied by Harry's younger brother Josiah Thaw, arrived at the prison at midday. The warden, Billy Flynn, escorted his visitors to the second tier, to the cells that housed those prisoners accused of homicide. Harry appeared remarkably cheerful, greeting his wife with a kiss, chatting amicably with his brother, and inquiring after his mother and sisters. It was inconvenient, he told Evelyn, that he must spend some time in the Tombs, but his imprisonment would not last long. Earlier that morning he had again met with his attorney Frederick Delafield, and he had learned that Black, Olcott, Gruber & Bonynge, a prominent New York criminal law firm, had agreed to join the defense. It was unfortunate, of course, that they could not now travel to Europe that summer; but it was necessary only to be patient to be assured of the right result.[23]

Evelyn Nesbit returned to Centre Street the following day, to the Criminal Courts Building, in response to a subpoena to appear before the grand jury. She had reluctantly agreed to appear in the jury room, but she would not answer questions, even if she risked being held in contempt of court. "I must respectfully decline," she began, speaking directly to the members of the grand jury, "to answer the questions you intend to ask me.... I might say something that would harm my husband, and I think a wife should do all she can to help her husband and nothing to hurt him. Therefore I beg of you all, not to insist upon putting these questions to me, because if you do, I will have to decline to answer."[24]

It was a brave response that won the approval of the jury. The foreman, Henry Smith, whispered some words to his colleagues and then informed the witness that there would be no further questions. Other witnesses did testify to the shooting, and, later that afternoon, the grand jury returned an indictment for murder in the first degree against Harry Thaw.[25]

He entered his plea the next day. The clerk of the court addressed Thaw in the customary manner, asking for his plea in response to the indictment, and Thaw, without pausing to consult his lawyers, replied that he was not guilty.[26]

That week, while Harry Thaw prepared for his upcoming trial, Bessie White organized the funeral of her husband. The body of Stanford White had lain, since the murder, in the drawing room of the family's Manhattan residence, a four-story town house near Gramercy Park. On Thursday, June 28, the undertaker brought the body to the Thirty-fourth Street ferry for the journey across the East River to Long Island City, where a special train waited to carry the casket to St. James, the village adjacent to the family estate on Long Island. Several dozen mourners, friends of Stanford White, accompanied the casket on the journey, each mourner caught in a shared sense of dismay that White had died such a violent death, so suddenly and unexpectedly.[27]

The service was brief, devoid of the panegyrics that might normally have accompanied the burial of so remarkable an individual as Stanford White. William Holden, the pastor of St. James Episcopal Church, recited a psalm and the choir sang a hymn. Leighton Parks, the rector of St. Bartholomew's, an Episcopal church on Madison Avenue, next pronounced a benediction. Bessie White and her son, Lawrence, then led the procession from the church to the nearby cemetery, and after the pastor had spoken some brief remarks, the gravediggers began to cover the casket with earth. Charles McKim and William Rutherford Mead both lingered to console the widow, promising Bessie White that they would settle any business matters that remained.[28]

It had been a modest ceremony, without any pomp or ostentation, in a Long Island village, far from the hustle and bustle of Manhattan. The funeral had originally been intended for St. Bartholomew's, but already too much controversy had accumulated around the memory of Stanford White for the congregation to consent to the service.[29]

Stanford White had been dead only three days, but the newspapers had already passed judgment, condemning him as a libertine who used his power and influence to lure unsuspecting girls to his apartment to rape them. The cause of the murder was, according to the newspaper accounts, the rape of Evelyn Nesbit as a young girl several years earlier. Several women, actresses on the Broadway stage, had reportedly corroborated this narrative, volunteering to the defense lawyers that White had raped them also.[30]

Anthony Comstock claimed that his organization, the Society for the Suppression of Vice, had uncovered evidence that coteries of wealthy men frequently sponsored orgies in which young girls, recruited from the tenements, were the victims. James Lawrence Breese, the society photographer, was the leader of one group of men, nicknamed the Carbonites, who met for riotous dinners in Breese's studio on Sixteenth Street. A second clique, according to Comstock, lured actresses and chorus girls, some as young as fifteen, to an apartment owned by Charles Dana Gibson on Thirty-fifth Street. "I will drive every moral pervert out of New York," Comstock declared. "The investigation must go on now to the bitter end, without fear or favor, no matter how rich or how prominent or how brilliant the perverts may be.... Many a man who has been generally held in the highest esteem must be tumbled into the mire, where he belongs."[31]

The prosecution of wealthy pedophiles was long overdue, Comstock proclaimed. It was the evident reluctance of the district attorney to investigate Stanford White that had led to his murder. "Thaw's act in slaying White," Comstock stated, "was the indirect result of the refusal by the proper authorities to bring White to book."[32]

Comstock's accusations found a ready echo in denunciations from the pulpit. Stanford White had engaged in the most wicked crimes, using his association with the theater to rob young girls of their innocence, and White's life, according to Madison Peters, a minister at the Church of the Epiphany, was a predictable consequence of the concentration of wealth, the corruption of morality, and the failure of the authorities to safeguard civic virtue. "These crimes, worse than murder," Peters declared, "must be avenged. That there are men of large wealth in this city who have made it a business to degrade womanhood—backing plays and players and using art studios to procure poor young girls...is a new revelation to the public: a new story that wealth has turned its rotting force to the corruption of innocent girlhood, whose misfortune is their poverty."[33]

Reuben Torrey, an evangelical preacher, was sanguine that the revelations about White would effect a reawakening. "Exposures of moral leprosy," Torrey commented, "always do good....The outraged public sense of purity and decency revolts and turns on these criminals and brings about moral regeneration....No jury will be found to convict Thaw, in my opinion." Thomas B. Gregory, a minister of the Universalist Church, agreed that, in a technical sense, Harry Thaw had indeed broken the law; but he had also fulfilled a higher law that transcended the formal statute. "When the libertine falls," Gregory proclaimed, "every healthy instinct of humanity feels, and cannot help feeling, that it is only the natural finale."[34]

Several of White's closest friends had already vanished, leaving little trace of their whereabouts. Reporters from the city's newspapers fanned out across New York, hunting for White's accomplices, hoping to provide the accused men with an opportunity to rebut the charges. James Breese could not be found either at his Manhattan residence or at his favorite haunt, the Metropolitan Club. The antiques dealer Thomas Clarke did not return to the city after attending White's funeral, and there was a suspicion that he had already left the

United States for an extended stay in Europe. Robert Lewis Reid, an artist, had not been seen at his studio, and the care-taker could provide no further information.[35]

His many friends, some of whom had known White for decades, stayed silent, refusing any association with a man who had become a moral leper. Even Charles McKim, who had worked closely with White since the 1870s, refused to condemn the murder of his friend. "There is no statement to make," McKim answered in response to a query from a reporter for the *New York World*. "There will be no information coming from us."[36]

A few brave souls did resist the tide of public opinion, remarking on the contribution that White had made to architecture in the United States. The sculptor Augustus Lukeman noted the surprising reluctance of the architectural profession to pay tribute to the dead man. "No voice appears to be raised," Lukeman said, "calling attention to the stupendous loss that has befallen the country in the death of Stanford White.... Mr. White was not only an artist, a great architect, if not the greatest of his age, but he had a generous spirit, which stimulated... the taste of the public to a higher standard of beauty." John M. Carrère, one of the partners of Carrère & Hastings, the firm responsible for the New York Public Library on Fifth Avenue, had worked as an apprentice for McKim, Mead & White, and he also mourned the death of White. "I have always looked up to him both as an architect and as a teacher. He was the foremost man of his profession," Carrère told a reporter from the *New York Times*. "Speaking generally of his position among American architects I consider that he had no superior."[37]

*   *   *

The emerging consensus that the authorities had been negligent in failing to apprehend such men as Stanford White both provoked the police to take more forceful action and emboldened such reform organizations as the Society for the Suppression of Vice in their campaign for moral purity. The arrest of Henry Alfred Short on July 1 for molesting young girls was one sign that the authorities looked to end the sexual exploitation of children. Short, a wealthy realtor and a member of the University Club, had lured Charlotte Fitzsimmons to his apartment with gifts of candy. He had repeatedly raped the fourteen-year-old, telling her that he would kill her if she told her parents; but the girl had eventually informed her father, and the police had raided Short's apartment, finding a trove of pornographic photographs.[38]

Anthony Comstock applauded such initiatives but continued to urge his acolytes to take independent action to combat such social evils as prostitution and pornography. Nothing in this regard was more infuriating to the Society for the Suppression of Vice than the complicity of newspaper proprietors in promoting prostitution, and no one was more culpable than James Gordon Bennett Jr., the owner and publisher of the *New York Herald*. Hundreds of paid notices, offering various services, appeared in the *Herald* every day; these advertisements never explicitly mentioned sex, but their meaning was nevertheless obvious. Such notices promoted prostitution, Comstock asserted, yet Bennett had always denied any responsibility, claiming that it was impossible for the *Herald* to distinguish between advertisements that offered companionship and those that offered sex.[39]

But the campaign for moral purity would not be denied, and on July 7, Charles Wahle, a magistrate in the Seventh District Police Court, issued a summons against the *New York Herald* for printing obscene and lewd matter. Charles Grubb, a pastor of the Methodist Episcopal Church, had initiated the complaint, but it was equally a triumph for Comstock and the Society for the Suppression of Vice.[40]

The campaign for moral rectitude simultaneously denigrated Stanford White and exalted Harry Thaw. White had reportedly continued to pester Evelyn Nesbit after the rape, even attempting to resume their relationship after she had married Harry Thaw. Who would not, under such circumstances, act as Thaw had acted, to avenge the honor of his wife? The authorities had taken no action and had done nothing to stop White. Surely, many commentators argued, Thaw had been justified in shooting Stanford White.

William Olcott, an attorney in criminal law, a partner at Black, Olcott, Gruber & Bonynge, had first encountered Harry Thaw on June 27, and already, less than a week later, he was starting to regret his firm's connection with the case. He had cautioned Thaw that he could avoid the electric chair only if he pleaded insanity; but the prisoner rejected his advice outright, saying that White's assault on his wife had given him every justification for killing the architect. "No jury will convict me of any crime," Thaw had explained, "when they hear the truth. I killed White because he ruined my wife. I am not crazy."[41]

Olcott had suggested to Thaw that his attorneys petition the Court of General Sessions to appoint a lunacy commission—a panel of three experts—to determine Thaw's mental condition. This commission could then recommend that the court commit the prisoner to an asylum. Thaw would remain in the asylum for a certain period, a few years, say, and could subsequently apply for his release on the supposition that he had regained his sanity. There would then be no necessity to endure the uncertainty of a trial, no need for an elaborate and expensive defense, and no danger that a jury would find Thaw guilty of murder.

But nothing could dislodge Thaw's belief that he had acted rationally and justifiably in killing Stanford White. There was no reason, Thaw stated, why he should spend any time in an asylum; he refused to apply for a lunacy commission, as Olcott had suggested, or to file a plea of insanity at trial. There was, he declared, no need for him to meet with the psychiatrists whom Olcott had hired, and he would not tolerate any examination that might question his sanity. "I am the boss," Thaw told Olcott, "and I won't plead insanity. I'm no more crazy than you are."[42]

It was in vain that Olcott argued for an insanity plea. Stanford White may have led a dissolute life, Olcott said, but there was no independent evidence, apart from Evelyn Nesbit's testimony, that the rape had occurred, and there would necessarily be no possibility of presenting any corroborating testimony that would support her account. The alleged rape had taken place in 1901, shortly after Evelyn moved to New York, several months before she first met Harry, and four years before their marriage in 1905. Was it meaningful to claim, therefore, that the murder of White had occurred in defense of Evelyn Nesbit when the supposed rape had been committed several years before? Would it seem reasonable to a jury that Thaw found his justification in an act that had happened so long ago? Why would Harry Thaw have waited such a length of time before killing his rival?

Thaw was adamant, nevertheless, that his defense—the "unwritten law" that a husband could legitimately kill a man who had dishonored his wife— would persuade the jury to free him. He had done the world a great favor, he believed, by killing White. He would assuredly win his case. Such a defense, Olcott replied, might find favor in the southern states, in Georgia, say, or Alabama or Kentucky; but it would not work with a Manhattan jury. Jurors in New York were too sophisticated, too knowledgeable, to believe that a man could kill another man solely on account of some supposed wrong.

But such arguments counted for little when set against the tsunami of public opinion that congratulated Harry Thaw for his act of killing White. Every day, sackfuls of mail, from every part of the United States, arrived at the Tombs, each letter praising Thaw for his courage. Opinion polls in the New York newspapers were equally celebratory, an overwhelming majority of New Yorkers supporting the murder and predicting that the jury would acquit Thaw at his upcoming trial.[43]

It infuriated Thaw to learn that, despite his instructions, William Olcott continued to act as if he would present an insanity defense at the upcoming trial. Various newspaper accounts reported that Olcott, suspecting the existence of hereditary insanity in the Thaw family, had surreptitiously traveled to Philadelphia to interview staff at the Friends'

Asylum for the Insane. Harriet Thaw, a cousin, had resided at the asylum for several years, and it was reasonable to assume that Olcott hoped to present evidence of insanity among Harry Thaw's relatives in order to win an acquittal.[44]

It was the final straw, an act of insubordination that Thaw would not tolerate, and on July 14 he informed Olcott that his firm's services would no longer be required. He had hired Hartridge & Peabody to represent him, and he asked Olcott to send the papers on his case to Clifford Hartridge at his offices on Broadway.[45]

But that day, at the very moment when Thaw was dismissing his attorneys, his mother arrived back in New York on the SS *Kaiserin Auguste Victoria*. Mary Thaw had left the city three weeks before, sailing from New York on the SS *Minneapolis*. Only on her arrival in England did she learn that Harry had killed Stanford White, and almost immediately she booked her return passage to the United States, arriving back in the city on July 14.[46]

She called on Harry the next day. It would be folly, she told her son, to imagine that a jury would acquit him of murder solely because Stanford White had assaulted Evelyn Nesbit five years before. There would be too great a risk that the jury would vote to convict; it would be far better either to petition for a lunacy commission or to plead insanity at trial. But Harry remained maddeningly obstinate, refusing to hear his mother's pleas, determined to state his case in court. "I am a sane man," he patiently maintained, "and I will never consent to have these alienists construe my actions, my conversation and my physical being as those of an insane person. The unwritten law must be my defense. I killed White because I had to. Instead of being guilty of murder I should be looked upon as a benefactor to mankind."[47]

Mary Thaw eventually acceded to her son's wishes. There could be no insanity defense if Harry refused to allow the psychiatrists to examine him, and there appeared no possibility that his resolve would ever weaken. But Harry's strategy would depend on a single witness—Evelyn Nesbit—whose testimony must persuade the jury that Stanford White had in fact drugged and raped her. No other person had witnessed the alleged rape, and no one could testify in support of Evelyn's statements on the witness stand. There was no physical evidence to corroborate her story, and everything, therefore, would necessarily depend on the coherence of her account.[48]

But how would it be possible for a young woman, twenty-one years old, with no courtroom experience and no knowledge of the law, to withstand the pressure that the district attorney would inevitably bring to bear? She would be alone on the witness stand, testifying to events that had occurred several years previously, trying to recall details that might now be only vaguely remembered, and all the time, at every moment, the prosecution would be seeking to expose contradictions in her account, to catch her in a lie, and to reveal her testimony as false. William Travers Jerome, the district attorney, a shrewd, calculating prosecutor, a man with extensive experience in the city's criminal justice system, would mercilessly interrogate her on cross-examination. It would be an unequal contest—Evelyn Nesbit would falter in her testimony—and everyone predicted that Harry would go to the electric chair.

5

FIRST TRIAL

January 23, 1907–April 12, 1907

"THE DEFENDANT IS ACCUSED OF THE CRIME OF MURDER IN THE first degree." The assistant district attorney, Francis Garvan, addressed the jury in a ponderous manner, each sentence followed by a slight pause. "It is claimed by the people of the State that on June 25, in this county, he shot and killed with deliberation and premeditation and intent to kill, one Stanford White."

There was nothing ostentatious about Garvan's opening address, nothing superfluous about his words, as he described how Harry Thaw had murdered Stanford White during a performance of the musical comedy *Mamzelle Champagne*. Thaw had acted deliberately, firing three bullets, then holding his gun above his head as if to indicate that he intended no further harm, calmly speaking to his wife before leaving Madison Square Garden. "He was placed under arrest, and was brought to the police station. He has been indicted by the

Grand Jury and is now here before you to be tried upon the charge."[1]

The hush of the courtroom was broken by a slight cough, and Garvan glanced toward the far side of the room. Harry Thaw, seated in the front row, his attorneys on either side, coughed a second time, muffling the sound with a handkerchief. The six defense lawyers sat stone-faced, paying no attention to Thaw, waiting impassively for Garvan to conclude his address. Daniel O'Reilly occupied the aisle seat, adjacent to the jury box; Henry McPike and A. Russell Peabody sat on his left; and three more lawyers—Delphin Delmas, John Gleason, and Clifford Hartridge—filled the remaining seats in the front.

Garvan had spoken for fifteen minutes and already he was approaching the end of his address. No one disputed the facts, Garvan continued, and the state need only show that the defendant had acted intentionally in order to prove his guilt. "The people claim that it was a cruel, deliberate, malicious, premeditated taking of a human life. After proving that fact to you," he said, addressing the jurors, "we will ask you to find the defendant guilty of the crime of murder in the first degree."[2]

The district attorney, Travers Jerome, nodded his approval, whispering some congratulatory remarks to his assistant as Garvan returned to his seat. The judge, James Fitzgerald, spoke next, saying that those people who expected to testify should leave the courtroom, and the clerk of the court, William Penney, stepped forward to escort Evelyn Nesbit to a side door. Delphin Delmas, the lead attorney for the defense, had warned Mary Thaw that he might call her to testify on her son's behalf, and she too gathered her belongings, walking alongside her daughter-in-law to wait in an anteroom outside the courtroom. Harry's siblings—his brothers, Josiah and Edward, his sister Margaret, and her husband, George Lauder Carnegie—all remained, seated behind the attorneys.[3]

Lawrence White, the son of the slain architect, was the first witness, telling the court that he had met his father for dinner on the evening of the murder. He had taken a cab uptown with a friend after dinner to see a musical at the New York Theatre, leaving his father to walk alone to Madison Square Garden for the opening of *Mamzelle Champagne*. He had returned to the family's town house on Gramercy Park, retiring around eleven o'clock, but reporters had awoken him shortly before midnight to tell him that someone had shot his father.[4]

A second witness, the coroner's physician, Timothy Lehane, also testified, saying that he had performed the autopsy on the day after the murder. He had found three bullets in White's body: two bullets had entered the skull, resulting in cerebral hemorrhage, the cause of death; a third bullet had hit White's arm.[5]

Other witnesses, members of the audience at Madison Square Garden, described the shooting, telling the court that Thaw had walked toward the stage to stand directly in front of Stanford White. He stood motionless for a few seconds before raising his gun and firing three shots. White collapsed, bleeding profusely, and Thaw, holding the gun above his head, retreated toward the rear of the theater, giving up his gun to the duty fireman.

There was little distinction between one account and another; they all agreed in the essential particulars. Even Delphin Delmas seemed content to let the testimony go unchallenged. Occasionally Delmas would cross-examine a witness, asking about some detail—what was the expression on Thaw's face? how was White sitting when Thaw shot him?—but his questioning seemed otherwise perfunctory; and very quickly, almost as soon as it had begun, the state had presented its case.[6]

Evelyn Nesbit lifted her veil as the clerk of the court, William Penney, waited to administer the oath. She removed her gloves, holding them in her left hand, her right hand raised as she repeated the words that Penney spoke to her. The crowd looked on expectantly, watching as she made her way across the front of the courtroom to the witness stand, waiting as she ascended the steps to sit in a high-backed chair on a raised platform.

She had placed her gloves on a small table by her side and she now sat erect, her back straight, her hands resting in her lap. She seemed so slim, so slight, almost impossibly young, closer in age to sixteen than twenty-two. There was nothing elaborate about her appearance: her dark-blue velvet jacket, white linen shirtwaist, and plain blue skirt provided no hint that she was married to one of the wealthiest men in the country. She wore a diamond solitaire ring and a gold wedding band on her left hand and a silver bracelet watch on her wrist. A black velvet ribbon fastened her hair away from her shoulders, at the nape of her neck, and a lawn tie, done in a bow, softened the severity of her white shirtwaist blouse.[7]

Delphin Delmas rose slowly from his chair, stepping toward his witness.

"You are Evelyn Nesbit Thaw?" he began.

"Yes."

"You are the wife of the defendant, Harry K. Thaw?"

"I am."

"On the evening of the twenty-fifth of June of last year were you in company with your husband at dinner at the Café Martin, in this city?"

"Yes."

"Kindly state who, if any one besides you two, composed the party?"

"Mr. Truxton Beale and Mr. Thomas McCaleb."

They had dined together that evening at Café Martin, a restaurant at Twenty-sixth Street and Fifth Avenue, leaving shortly after eight o'clock to walk across Madison Square for the opening night performance of *Mamzelle Champagne,* a musical comedy playing at Madison Square Garden. They had arrived in the middle of the first act, finding four seats at the rear of the theater. There had been nothing unusual, nothing untoward, about the evening; she had noticed nothing in her husband's behavior that might have caused comment; and she remembered only that he had left his seat for about ten minutes to talk to an acquaintance sitting by the balustrade on the south side of the rooftop theater. Harry returned to her side;

but she was not enjoying the performance, and they decided to leave shortly afterward.

"Will you kindly describe to the jury," Delmas asked, "how the party left?"

"We all went out together. . . . We were almost to the elevator and I was talking to Mr. McCaleb and turned around to say something to Mr. Thaw and he was not there."

She had looked around, searching the theater for her husband, when she suddenly noticed Stanford White seated at a table near the stage. Harry was motionless, standing directly before White.

"What was he doing?" Delmas asked.

"He had his arm out," Evelyn replied, raising her right arm, holding it straight before her, pointing it in the direction of the attorney, "like that."

"Did he then move forward?"

"No, he stood still a little longer."

"Did you hear any shots fired?"

"I did. . . . Immediately I saw Mr. Thaw I heard the shots. . . ."

"How many shots did you hear?"

"Three."[8]

Her voice was quiet, almost soft, yet she spoke in a matter-of-fact manner, each word so clear and distinct that even those spectators at the back of the courtroom could hear her answers. Occasionally she leaned forward as though to add emphasis to her testimony; at other times she placed her elbow on the arm of the chair, resting her chin on her hand. Sometimes Delmas would walk a few paces back and forth in front of her, twirling his eyeglasses in his hand, and she would follow his movements, always responding to each question in the same quiet, unhurried tone of voice.

Delphin Delmas, sixty-two years old, was a short, stubby man, about five feet six inches tall, slightly overweight, with a pompous manner. As a young man he had won a reputation as a clever, resourceful attorney, and he still treasured that reputation, now dulled with age, much as one might value an

Mary Thaw hired Delphin Delmas to represent Harry Thaw during his first trial for the murder of Stanford White. Delmas had studied at Santa Clara College in California before entering Yale University to study law. He served as a delegate to the 1904 Democratic National Convention in St. Louis and nominated William Randolph Hearst as the Democratic candidate for president. *(Library of Congress, LC-DIG-ds-10595)*

expensive overcoat that had become shabby through overuse. He had studied first at Santa Clara College in California, traveling east in 1863 to learn law at Yale University, eventually establishing a practice in San Francisco. His mannerisms in court seemed old-fashioned, reminiscent of the previous century; his sentences were too elaborate, excessively long-winded, and his gestures were overly dramatic, more for show than for effect. But he had learned his trade well, and he had not forgotten the tricks of a legal practice that had already lasted several decades. His knowledge of the law was compensation for his manner, and he almost invariably triumphed in the courtroom. He had a dour, disdainful expression and was often abrupt in his manner, but he was a clever lawyer who prepared each case meticulously, checking every detail that might win him an advantage.[9]

There was little chance, he had told Evelyn before the trial, that a jury would send Harry to the electric chair after hearing an account of the rape that Stanford White had inflicted on her. They had rehearsed her testimony beforehand, talking together for hours over the details that he needed her to describe in court. She should hold nothing back, Delmas had said; every detail, no matter how graphic, would serve both to damn Stanford White and to save her husband. But it was important, above all else, that she present her testimony about the rape in the form of a conversation that she had had with her husband. She had first told Harry about the rape in 1903, in their apartment in Paris, and it was that conversation, Delmas believed, that had tipped Harry over the edge into insanity.

The district attorney, Travers Jerome, would attempt to prove her account false, to trip her on some detail, to catch her in a contradiction, even perhaps to claim that the rape had never happened. But Jerome could cross-examine her only on the facts that had been entered into evidence on direct examination, which she had already presented to the court. He could not challenge the veracity of a private conversation that she had had with her husband, so their triumph over the district attorney would be assured, Delmas had said—but only as long as she avoided giving any direct testimony about the rape.

"When," Delmas asked, "had Mr. Thaw proposed for the first time to marry you?"

"In June, 1903, in Paris," Evelyn replied.

"At the time Mr. Thaw proposed to you, at that time did you accept his offer or did you refuse it?"

"I refused it."

"Did you state to him the reasons why you refused it?"

"I did."

"In stating the reasons to Mr. Thaw why you refused his offer, did you state a reason to him which you then stated was based upon an event in your life with which Stanford White was connected?"

"Yes."

"Will you kindly give us the whole of that conversation from beginning to end?"

Harry had proposed to her one evening during their stay in Paris, telling her that he loved her and that he wished to marry her. She had hesitated, and he had questioned her, wanting to know the cause of her reluctance, eventually surmising that it had something to do with Stanford White.

She told Harry that Edna Goodrich, a dancer in *Florodora,* had first introduced her to the architect, taking her to meet White at a town house on Twenty-fourth Street. They had had lunch with White and one of his friends, and later that afternoon they had played together on the velvet swing. White subsequently invited her mother to visit him at his offices and immediately, it seemed, he won their confidence. He had been generous, almost excessively so, providing the money for their suite of rooms at the Audubon Hotel and paying for her brother to study at the military academy outside Philadelphia. White always seemed willing to pay any expense, and when her mother, Florence, mentioned that she might travel to Pittsburgh to visit some friends, White offered to pay for the journey.

She, Evelyn, had seen White frequently during her mother's absence. One day he suggested that she pose for a photographer, Rudolf Eickemeyer, at a studio on Twenty-second Street.

"Did you describe or relate to Mr. Thaw what took place in that photograph studio?"

"I said they showed me a dressing room and I put on a very gorgeous kimono....I put on this Japanese kimono and Mr. White said it came from Hong Kong and I posed for a long time."

"Did you describe to Mr. Thaw the general appearance of those garments?"

"I did.... Then the next night after that I received a note from Mr. White at the theatre asking me to come to a party and he would send a carriage for me; the carriage would be waiting."

She had taken the cab downtown, to Twenty-fourth Street, expecting to see other guests, but Stanford White had been at the town house alone. They had dinner together, and White took her upstairs to the fourth floor, where he offered her a glass of champagne.

"He insisted that I drink this glass of champagne, which I did and I don't know whether it was a minute after or two minutes after, but a pounding began in my ears. . . . The whole room seemed to go around: everything got very black."

Evelyn had previously given her testimony without hesitation—there had not been the slightest trace of emotion in her words—but suddenly, without warning, she stopped speaking. She turned away slightly, toward the window, shifting in her chair as if to hide her face from view. There was a sudden hush in the courtroom, a painful silence that seemed to last forever, ticking away minute by minute, as the spectators watched her struggle to control her emotions. There was a slight twitching in her left cheek, and tears started to well up in her eyes. Her hands were clasped tightly together on her lap, the fingers of one hand gripping the fingers of the other hand. Suddenly a loud cry broke the silence and Evelyn buried her face in her hands, her muffled sobs echoing through the courtroom.

"Mrs. Thaw, I do not desire," Delmas spoke quietly, his voice full of sympathy, "to distress you any more than is necessary in this matter, but it is absolutely essential that you should go on with your testimony."

Eventually she recovered her composure, taking up again the thread of her story; but her voice was no longer calm as she recounted the dreadful details of that night. She had awoken to find herself lying naked on the bed next to Stanford

White. Telltale bloodstains on the sheets told her that he had raped her while she lay unconscious.

"When I woke up all my clothes were pulled off me and I was in bed. . . . I screamed and screamed and screamed, and he came over and asked me to please keep quiet, that I must not make so much noise."

"Did you tell Mr. Thaw what took place between yourself and White?"

"Yes. . . ."

"You told all of this," Delmas asked again, "to Harry Thaw that night in Paris after he had asked you to marry him?"

"Yes."

"What was the effect of this statement of yours upon Mr. Thaw?"

"It was very terrible. . . . He was very excited. . . . He bit his nails, he tore his hair. His face got very white. . . . He would get up and walk up and down the room. . . . He sat there and he cried. . . . Every now and then he would come and ask me particular things about it."

"Asked about the details of this occurrence?"

"Yes, sir."[10]

She had not anticipated that her story would cause Harry such anguish, and she had not realized the extent of his hatred for Stanford White. Later that year, at the end of October, she had returned alone to New York while Harry remained in Paris.

They met again, on Harry's return to New York at the end of December, at the Café des Beaux-Arts, and she told him how Stanford White had contacted her shortly after her arrival back in New York. She had been unwilling to see White again; but he had insisted on seeing her, and eventually she relented.

"You told Mr. Thaw," Delmas interrupted, "that Mr. White . . . had repeatedly called at your apartments at the hotel?"

"Yes."

"Proceed," Delmas instructed his witness. "Tell us all that you said to Mr. Thaw upon the subject."

White had attempted to kiss her on their first meeting, but she resisted his advances. He said that he had been concerned for her safety while she was in Europe. Harry Thaw was a drug addict who assaulted young girls, and he, White, had been fearful that Thaw might hurt her also. He introduced her to some of his friends, and they too told her the stories that had circulated on Broadway about Harry Thaw. White suggested that she speak to his lawyer, Abraham Hummel, and she took a carriage downtown to Hummel's office. She told the lawyer about her travels with Thaw in Europe, and he, Hummel, dictated a statement, an affidavit, to a stenographer in her presence.

"He said that I must be guided by his advice absolutely, that he had practiced law a great many years and knew just what to do. . . . Then he put in a lot of stuff that I had been carried off by Harry Thaw against my will, and I started to interrupt and he put up his hand for me to stop. . . . Mr. Hummel went on at great length about I had been taken away against my will and against my consent . . . and a lot of stuff that wasn't true, and that I had been ill treated by Thaw."

"Tell us all the details," Delmas prompted. "Tell us what you told Mr. Thaw."

"He asked me," Evelyn continued, relating her conversation with Hummel, "why I didn't sue Harry Thaw for breach of promise, and I answered that that would be absurd, that any breach of promise suit might be the other way because Thaw had asked me to marry him. . . . He said there would be lots of money in it. . . . Lots of rich men were sued for breach of promise of marriage by actresses, and he said I ought to sue Mr. Thaw, and he could easily win the case for me."

"Was that the substance of that interview, as stated by you to Mr. Thaw?"

"Yes," Evelyn replied. "Then Mr. Thaw asked if I had ever signed anything at Hummel's office. I told him I had not. . . . I said that I had signed absolutely nothing in Mr. Hummel's office."[11]

Who would now defend Stanford White? His behavior seemed the more contemptible because it had been so carefully calculated. His assault on Evelyn Nesbit's virtue — the rape in 1901 — had not been an act of passion, the result of a momentary loss of control, but had been long in preparation, each step of the scheme leading inexorably to the next. Two years after the rape, in November 1903, White had attempted to renew their acquaintance, hoping to have sex with her. She rebuffed him, but he attempted nevertheless to win her back, seeking to poison her relationship with Harry Thaw, telling her that Thaw was a drug addict who habitually whipped young girls. White had then conspired with Hummel to deceive her into drawing up a document, an affidavit, that he could use to blackmail Thaw.

*   *   *

Most observers realized that Delphin Delmas had so cleverly arranged matters that not even the district attorney could attempt to contradict the testimony of the witness. Evelyn Nesbit had testified only about her conversations with Thaw—the first in Paris in June 1903, the second in New York in December later that same year—and Jerome could cross-examine her, therefore, only on the content of those conversations. But how could Jerome challenge anything that she had said in a private conversation? It would not be possible. And it soon became apparent that Delmas would use his advantage to destroy whatever little remained of White's reputation.

"After you had told Mr. Thaw," Delmas prompted, "what had happened between you and Stanford White in 1901, did Mr. Thaw have any conversation with you in which he discussed the fate of other young girls who had met with similar treatment—?"

"If Your Honor please," the district attorney interrupted angrily, rising from his chair. "Stanford White is dead." Would there be no end to the destruction of White's character? Would the witness now tell the court every piece of gossip about the dead man? "Are there no limits," Jerome protested, "upon the condemnation which may be thrown upon the dead? I object to this question. It does not bear up on the case and we have gone far enough on this path."

"The learned District Attorney," Delmas replied sarcastically, "will bear in mind that I have no more desire to asperse the memory of the dead than of the living." But Stanford White had assaulted other young girls in his apartments. The

144

defendant had heard about those episodes also, and the cumulative effect of these tales had accelerated his mental deterioration. The defense attorneys had a responsibility to their client to provide the evidence that would account for his mental collapse. "We would be derelict in our duty," Delmas concluded, "if we omitted to supply every atom of proof which we conceive will aid these gentlemen," he pointed to the jury, "in arriving at a correct conclusion of his mental attitude."

But the judge sustained Jerome's objection. He would not allow the attorneys to introduce in this manner the gossip about Stanford White. The state had no means of contradicting such evidence, and, more significantly, Delmas had not yet provided any testimony to the court that Harry Thaw had been insane at the time of the murder. It was not sufficient, Fitzgerald ruled, merely to assert that Thaw had been insane; it was also necessary for the defense to provide the expert medical testimony that would support the contention.[12]

Evelyn Nesbit had begun her testimony on Thursday, February 7, and she remained on the witness stand for two days. She was an excellent witness, faithfully following Delmas's instructions, speaking always with a degree of self-assurance that seemed to confirm her testimony as truthful. But outside the courtroom, in every part of the United States, there had arisen a storm of protest that a young woman should speak so candidly of such terrible events and, worse, that the newspapers should reprint her shocking description of the rape. The publication of such explicit testimony, told in such detail, had no precedent and seemed to many observers to symbolize moral decay and degeneracy.

The National League of Catholic Women, then holding its annual convention in Chicago, took time away from more humdrum matters to pass a resolution calling on the city's newspapers to stop printing verbatim accounts of the trial. The Women's Christian Temperance Union, an influential reform organization with more than 200,000 members, condemned the publication of Evelyn Nesbit's testimony and called on Christian parents to protect their children by preventing them from reading the newspapers. In Chattanooga, the mayor, William Frierson, spoke at a mass meeting of citizens at the First Baptist Church against the publication of the sordid details, saying that such revelations would lead young men and women astray.[13]

Few observers attached any blame to Evelyn Nesbit for her testimony. Most commentators regarded her as the unfortunate victim of the affair and praised her for her resolute defense of her husband. It was the newspaper editors who were behaving irresponsibly, without any regard for morality. They had hoped to boost their sales by printing the scandalous details, and they were deservedly the target of public censure. A grand jury in Lebanon, Kentucky, indicted three newspapers in the state—the *Louisville Herald,* the *Louisville Times,* and the *Louisville Evening Post*—for printing offensive and indecent matter, and prosecutors in Ohio brought similar charges against the editor of the *Cincinnati Enquirer.* More significantly, Charles Wharton, a member of the United States House of Representatives from Illinois, introduced a resolution calling for legislation to empower the president of the

United States to prevent the distribution of the newspapers across state lines.[14]

Federal officials, including prominent members of Theodore Roosevelt's administration, debated the practicality of banning the circulation of the newspapers. Henry Stimson, the United States district attorney for the area that encompassed Manhattan, warned the New York newspapers that they had violated federal legislation that outlawed the distribution of obscene matter. It was irrelevant, Stimson announced, to claim as a defense that the newspapers had published the official transcript of a court proceeding: "The mere fact that such matter purports to be an account of a judicial proceeding furnishes no excuse for a violation of the statute."[15]

The federal authorities in Canada had already acted—the postmaster general, Rodolphe Lemieux, had issued a warning from Ottawa that he would enforce the law against any newspaper that printed obscene matter—and members of the Roosevelt administration in the United States were keen to follow suit. George Cortelyou, the postmaster general of the United States, discussed the situation with the president that weekend, and on Monday, February 11, Roosevelt issued a statement through his press secretary, William Loeb, to say that he hoped to do everything possible to prevent further publication.[16]

But other government officials were not sanguine that the federal authorities could successfully prosecute the newspapers. Would any jury vote to convict such newspapers as the *New-York Tribune* and the *New York Times* as obscene publications? It would, moreover, create a dangerous precedent; if the administration could succeed in this instance, it might be tempted to censor the newspapers whenever their editorials opposed government policy. Charles Bonaparte, the attorney general of the United States, acknowledged Roosevelt's desire to prevent publication but refused to declare an opinion on the question. "Somebody must clean out sinks and cesspools," Bonaparte proclaimed, "but I at least feel no inclination to take part in it as a matter of choice."[17]

But in any case, attempts at censorship were obviously now too late. The newspapers had already distributed Evelyn Nesbit's testimony far and wide, to every corner of the United States—even the president confessed that he had read her statements—and any attempt now to prevent publication would seem futile, even ridiculous. Her testimony on direct examination had ended, and other witnesses—the psychiatrists—had already started to give their evidence to the court.

Harry Thaw had rejected the suggestion that he might be insane, and he had previously refused any request that he be examined by psychiatrists. He had always regarded his trial as an opportunity to reveal to the world the extent of Stanford White's crimes, and an insanity plea would undercut his purpose. But Delphin Delmas had been persuasive, explaining that he would use psychiatric evidence only to supplement Evelyn's testimony. Evelyn would tell the world about the rape, and the psychiatrists would testify that her story had driven him insane.

It was a clever scheme, and Harry gave his consent. Britton

Evans, the medical superintendent at the New Jersey State Hospital for the Insane, was the first psychiatrist to visit the Tombs, examining Thaw on August 4, five weeks after the murder. Evans, accompanied by a second psychiatrist, Charles Wagner, returned to the Tombs on August 21, visiting the prison eight times over the next two months.

Evans recalled that Thaw had been nervous and agitated on his first visit, fidgeting constantly, talking without pause about the perceived slights that he had endured during his imprisonment. Thaw had been preoccupied with the belief that prominent New Yorkers, friends of Stanford White, were using their influence to send him to an insane asylum, thus preventing him from exposing their crimes in court. DeLancey Nicoll, a former district attorney, was a central figure in this conspiracy. Nicoll had been White's attorney and was still receiving a retainer from White's widow, Bessie, to hush up the scandal.

"What did you observe," Delmas asked Evans, "of Mr. Thaw's condition—mental condition—at the time of these various visits?"

"I observed that Harry K. Thaw exhibited a peculiar facial expression," Evans stated, "a glaring of the eyes, a restlessness of the eyes. . . . I observed a nervous agitation and restlessness, such as comes from a severe brain storm."[18]

Thaw told him that he intended to uncover evidence that would send White to the penitentiary. Thaw described how he had hired men from the Pinkerton Detective Agency to follow White; he had also asked Anthony Comstock to investigate the architect; and he had even contacted the district attorney, Travers Jerome; but nothing had come of his efforts. White, however, according to Thaw, had learned about this campaign against him and hired gangsters to assault Thaw; and Thaw had purchased a gun as a precaution against an attack. He had not intended to murder White, Thaw insisted. It had been an act of Providence that he used the gun to shoot White at Madison Square Garden—nothing more, nothing less.[19]

Thaw had allowed the psychiatrists to conduct a physical examination on their fourth visit, on September 22. His pulse, reflexes, muscular coordination, memory, eyesight, and sense of smell were all in excellent condition; there were no obvious signs of drug use and no symptoms of excessive drinking. But his mental condition was unstable and he was assuredly irrational. "He exhibited delusions of an exaggerated ego," Evans testified. "He felt himself of exaggerated importance and was subjected to persecution by numerous persons."[20]

Both psychiatrists, Britton Evans and Charles Wagner, on hearing a description of the defendant's behavior at the time of the shooting, agreed that Thaw had been insane when he killed Stanford White. Thaw had remained irrational for some time afterward, until September 1906, almost ten weeks after the murder, but his condition subsequently improved, and there was reason to believe that his mental instability had been only temporary. Thaw was less nervous, less agitated, and his behavior in subsequent interviews more closely approached the behavior of a normal person. "He was in a general way more composed," Evans stated, "more deliberate in manner, his greeting more cordial....He did not exhibit the same amount of nervousness. There was none of that peculiar suspicious glancing around the room."[21]

Travers Jerome could not recall a time when he had been so reluctant to cross-examine a witness. Evelyn Nesbit had shown extraordinary self-assurance a few days before, during the direct examination; but her composure would evaporate, Jerome realized, as soon as she understood how much he had uncovered about her past. Seven months had elapsed since the murder of Stanford White, and Jerome had used the time well, ferreting out the intimate details of Evelyn Nesbit's life. She was, he believed, a foolish, gullible woman with no thought for the consequences of her actions; she had allowed Thaw's attorneys to manipulate her; and she seemed unaware that she had put herself in a perilous position.

It was an outrage, Jerome felt, that she was sacrificing everything—her reputation, her honor—for such a scoundrel as Harry Thaw. It would have been easy for Thaw's attorneys to plead their client not guilty by reason of insanity. Thaw, no doubt, would have spent a few years in the asylum, but there would then have been no need for his wife to humiliate herself for his sake. Thaw had repeatedly said that he refused to go to the asylum because he wanted to expose Stanford White's crimes; but it was Evelyn Nesbit, not Thaw, who was performing that task. It was Evelyn Nesbit who was telling the world about the rape, while Thaw was merely observing, passively watching as his wife revealed the most intimate details of her life.

Jerome would be willing to spare Evelyn Nesbit his cross-examination, but only if Thaw's attorneys would agree that

Thaw should submit a plea of insanity. He had little confidence that they would accept his offer, but he would at least make the attempt.

"Your Honor," he began, "if in my opinion an honest case of insanity is made out here," he paused, looking at the attorneys on the other side of the room, "I am not going to take up the time of this learned Court in pressing this charge."

If both sides agreed to a hearing on the defendant's sanity, and if the lunacy commission decided that Thaw was currently insane, there would be no need for Evelyn Nesbit to subject herself to his interrogation. "I do not want," Jerome added, "to take this unfortunate young woman through the course I shall have to take her through if I can help it."

It was a generous offer, made in good faith, but Thaw's attorneys refused. They were confident that their client would win an acquittal and that Harry Thaw had no reason to accept Jerome's proposal.

"I thought to save the feelings of this girl," Jerome said, speaking in a subdued voice, with an air of resignation, "but if I must proceed I will."[22]

Travers Jerome, forty-seven, had first attracted public notice thirteen years before as an attorney for the Lexow Committee, an investigation by the state legislature into police corruption in New York City. The scandalous revelations by the committee resulted in the political eclipse of the Democratic Party and the election of the reform candidate, William Strong, in the mayoral election in 1894. Travers Jerome was a beneficiary of Strong's victory, receiving an appointment in 1895 as a judge on the Court of Special Sessions. Jerome used his position on the

This campaign poster shows William Travers Jerome as the Fusion candidate in the 1901 election for district attorney of New York County (Manhattan). Jerome earned a reputation as a forceful district attorney who fought to end gambling in New York. *(Library of Congress, LC-DIG-ppmsca-44773)*

court to great effect, campaigning vigorously against gambling and prostitution, and in 1901 he won election as district attorney on the reform ticket.[23]

Few politicians in the new administration were as influential as Travers Jerome. The new mayor, Seth Low, a lackluster, mediocre politician, had been unable to hold together the disparate factions that made up the reform movement, and it had quickly fallen apart. But Jerome had distinguished himself as the new district attorney; and his patrician upbringing and personal integrity set him apart from previous incumbents. A series of spectacular trials, each more scandalous and sensational than the last, had provided Jerome with enormous publicity, and he used his celebrity to campaign ceaselessly against crime and corruption in the city.

Jerome was a familiar figure in the hallways of the Criminal Courts Building. He was instantly recognizable: his sandy-brown hair, strong jaw, trim mustache, and pince-nez eyeglasses gave him an idiosyncratic presence. The sense of probity that had induced Jerome to support the reform movement in the 1890s had not deserted him; but he was now more pragmatic, less scrupulous in his choice of allies, often relying on members of the criminal underworld for information. He was a merciless prosecutor who always expected to win his cases, and he was never reluctant to use any available means to achieve his goal. He could be cruelly indifferent toward his adversaries, badgering the witnesses relentlessly, doing everything possible to belittle their testimony, seeming almost to take a sadistic pleasure in exposing their answers as fraudulent.[24]

Evelyn Nesbit had been an excellent witness for the defense. There had been nothing vague or uncertain about her replies to Delmas's questions, and she had provided an extraordinary amount of detail—detail that seemed to argue for her veracity. But she had inadvertently made one error, an error that would allow Jerome to challenge her testimony.

Stanford White had raped her, according to her previous statements, on the day after she first posed for Rudolf Eickemeyer in his studio on Twenty-second Street. But Eickemeyer had allowed the district attorney to examine his appointment books for 1901, and Jerome had discovered that Evelyn Nesbit first visited Eickemeyer's studio on Monday, November 4, 1901. The rape must have occurred, therefore, on the evening of the following day, Tuesday, November 5. But the municipal elections had taken place that day, and Stanford White, with his wife, Bessie, had hosted a dinner party for some friends at his town house on Gramercy Park. Jerome could therefore establish an alibi for White—an alibi that would destroy Evelyn's testimony—but only if he could prove to the jury that she had visited Eickemeyer's studio on November 4.[25]

Jerome held in his hand a large piece of cardboard, measuring eighteen by twelve inches, and he handed it to the witness, asking her to identify the photograph that was mounted on the front of the card. Evelyn recognized the photograph showing her dressed in a kimono, lying on a polar bear rug.

"Who was present when that photograph was taken?" Jerome asked.

"Mr. Eickemeyer and Mr. White...."

"How many poses do you recall—were there a good many?"

"I don't remember."

"You were never exposed to any indignity?"

"No."[26]

Jerome handed her a second photograph, again asking her to identify the picture. It showed her dressed in the skirt she had worn to the studio, a skirt that her mother had bought her earlier that year.

"I show you exhibit 31 for identification and ask you when that was taken?"

"In 1901."

"Were you acting at that time?"

"I think so."

"What company were you acting with?"

"The *Florodora* company."[27]

Jerome took a third photograph from the table by his side, showing it to the witness, but Delphin Delmas now interrupted. "This is a cross-examination," Delmas objected, "not upon what she told Mr. Thaw, but a cross-examination upon the events, facts, entirely independent from what she may or may not have told him." Such questions lay outside the rules of evidence. Evelyn Nesbit had not testified on direct examination about the photographs. The defense had not introduced them in evidence. How, then, could the district attorney cross-examine her about the photographs in this way?

But the judge, James Fitzgerald, now gave the state an important victory. Jerome had previously said that he intended to test the credibility of the witness. His interrogation, when directed toward that end, was therefore legitimate. "The question of the credibility of this witness," Fitzgerald stated, "is a material issue in this case. The objection will be overruled."[28]

Jerome continued to show her the photographs, pressing her for information about her visit to Eickemeyer's studio, trying to determine the day of the appointment; but Evelyn had realized the significance of his questions and she refused to be drawn. It was too long ago, she said, more than five years since she had first posed for Eickemeyer, and she could not provide Jerome with the information that he demanded.

Could she recall anything about the following day, Jerome asked, the day, according to her testimony, when White had drugged and raped her? That event, an intensely traumatic episode as she had described it, must have stamped itself on her memory. She had claimed to have lost her virginity in White's bedroom. What could she remember? How about the weather? Had there been snow on the ground? Had it rained?

"Do you recall the character of the weather that day?"

"No, sir."

But she could surely remember the date of that dreadful event? She had told Thaw that White had drugged and raped her and that she had lost her virginity. No one could possibly forget to mark such a traumatic episode

"Do you recall what day of the week it was? . . . Was it on a Sunday?"

"No," Evelyn replied, "it was not on a Sunday, because I came from the theatre." But she could not otherwise say what the day was.

"Do you recall what day of the month it was?"

"No, sir."

"Do you recall what month of the year it was? . . . Could it not have been in late October or early November?"

"No, I don't think so; it couldn't have been as late as that; I don't think it could have been November. I don't remember."[29]

Jerome had previously been reluctant to cross-examine Evelyn Nesbit, hoping to save her from the humiliation that would be the consequence of his interrogation. But her obstinacy, her refusal to answer his questions, annoyed and irritated him. He did not know the nature of her relationship with White; but he was certain that the rape never occurred as she had described it. He realized that it would be futile to continue his questions along the same path — she was obviously intent on giving him as little information as possible — but he expected to call Rudolf Eickemeyer as a witness at some point, and Eickemeyer would willingly testify to the date when he had first taken photographs of Evelyn Nesbit in his studio.

Jerome picked up some slips of paper from the table beside him, standing before Evelyn Nesbit, holding several canceled checks in his hand. Henry Deming, the president of the Mercantile Trust Company, was an acquaintance — both men were members of the University Club — and Deming had allowed Jerome to examine Stanford White's bank accounts. Jerome had discovered that the Mercantile Trust Company had sent checks, drawn on White's account, to Evelyn Nesbit throughout 1902.

"I hand you exhibits 65 to 73," Jerome said, showing the checks to the witness, "and ask you to pick out the ones bearing your signature."

She held the checks in her hand, glancing at each one before returning them to the district attorney. "They all have my signature," she replied.[30]

"You got these checks and indorsed them, didn't you?"

"I did," Evelyn replied.

The district attorney had taken her by surprise. How had Jerome come into possession of the checks? What else did he know about her relationship with Stanford White?

The checks were drawn for varying amounts, some for twenty-five dollars, others for fifty dollars. The payments had started in December 1901, several weeks after White had raped her, and continued at least until October 1902. Jerome started to leaf through the checks, reading the amount and date of each one, occasionally pausing to allow the stenographer to record the details.

"Who was furnishing that money?" he asked.

"Stanford White."[31]

"How long after you were drugged, as you say you were, did you begin to receive checks from Stanford White?"

"I don't recall," Evelyn answered. "It was some time after that."

"Did you not receive money…" Jerome paused, correcting himself. "Did you not have a letter of credit from Stanford White when you went to Europe?"

"Yes," Evelyn replied.

"Who got that money?"

"My mother."

"All of it?"

"Yes."[32]

Stanford White had provided a letter of credit for $500 for the journey to Europe in June 1903. But, Evelyn added, he had given it to her mother as the boat was about to sail from the harbor. She had not known about it until her mother mentioned it to her during the voyage to England.[33]

The district attorney had surprised her a second time; but Evelyn could now guess that her mother, Florence, had told Jerome about the letter of credit. Florence Nesbit had always refused to believe that Stanford White had raped her daughter. White had been a kind, generous man who had helped her and her children at a time when she was most in need. He had never refused any request, paying for the education of her children, securing an apartment for her in the Audubon Hotel, and occasionally giving her small presents of money. Stanford White had been her guardian during her time in New York, and his death had deeply upset her. It was impossible for her to believe that White had raped Evelyn; nothing could have been more hurtful than her daughter's accusations against her benefactor.

Florence Nesbit could not forget also that members of the Thaw family had uniformly treated her with contempt. The matriarch, Mary Thaw, held herself aloof, obstinately refusing any contact, still seeming regretful that her son had chosen Evelyn as his wife. Nor could Florence Nesbit forget that Harry Thaw, an obnoxious, self-centered young man, had ignored her during their time in Paris. It infuriated her to know that Evelyn was now besmirching the memory of Stanford White — all for the sake of that scoundrel Harry Thaw! — and Florence Nesbit had disowned her daughter. She had never liked her son-in-law, and it humiliated her to know that Evelyn was bringing dishonor on her family solely in order to save Thaw from punishment. Travers Jerome had asked her for her assistance, saying that he only wished to know the truth, and she had willingly cooperated with the district attorney, providing him with the information that he requested.[34]

Stanford White, according to Florence Nesbit, had frequently called at the Audubon Hotel, and Evelyn had often visited White at Madison Square Garden after performances of *Florodora*, occasionally staying out until the early hours of the morning. Jerome soon realized that the friendship between White and Evelyn Nesbit had continued for many months, long after the time when White had supposedly raped Evelyn.

"How often," Jerome demanded, "were you alone in the company of Mr. White?"

"I don't remember," Evelyn answered. She now spoke less assuredly, less confidently, uncertain how much Jerome already knew.

But she confessed that she had continued to see White alone, even after the rape. White would send a note to the theater, asking her to come see him, and she would take a cab downtown either to the tower apartment in Madison Square Garden or to the town house on Twenty-fourth Street.

"Did you," Jerome asked, "go out with him to lunch or to suppers in the tower very frequently?"

"Yes, sir."

"That was practically every week for a considerable period, was it not?"

"Yes."

"Sometimes two or three times a week?"

"Oh, yes, oftener than that sometimes."

"Sometimes every day?"

"Yes....He was constantly coaxing me to go with him

alone.... He was constantly nagging me. Sometimes he would coax me and sometimes scold me, and he would get very unpleasant about it.... He told me that he wanted me; he told me over and over again. He always wanted me to come back.... He tried to get me to come back."[35]

Travers Jerome was careful not to make any accusations against the witness—it scarcely seemed necessary—but her testimony had cast her relationship with White in a new light. She had been many times with Stanford White after that evening when he had first raped her. She had gone alone to see him, taking a cab downtown after each performance of *Florodora*. There had been no compulsion for her to be alone with White and, apart from his nagging, no coercion placed on her to see him. Had there been a consensual relationship? Had she been his mistress? Why had White continued to give her money for more than a year after they first met?

Her previous testimony, on direct examination, had cast her as an innocent victim who had suffered a brutal assault. But more and more, as Jerome continued to question her, it seemed almost as if Evelyn had encouraged the jealousy between her two suitors, continuing her relationship with Stanford White while traveling in Europe with Harry Thaw, holding White's letter of credit while living at Thaw's expense in Paris.

Florence Nesbit had accompanied her daughter to France in the summer of 1903, and after spending several weeks in Paris, they had left the capital for London. Harry Thaw had gone alone to England, traveling ahead to make the arrangements for their stay; and Florence had taken a train to Boulogne with her daughter to catch a boat across the Channel. There had been a delay at Boulogne, and Evelyn passed the time writing letters to her friends in New York, including a letter to Stanford White.

"Will you tell me," Jerome asked, again catching Evelyn by surprise, "why you wrote to Stanford White from Boulogne? Why did you write a letter from Boulogne to the man who had so grievously wronged you?"

"Because my mother begged me to write to him," Evelyn replied, dismayed that her mother had told Jerome even this detail. "Because my mother made me—she insisted on my writing to him. It was hateful to me to do so."

"What did your mother say to you?"

"She said that I was an ungrateful girl not to have written to Stanford White more than I had....She said I was very ungrateful to him not to have written to him."

Had she never confided to her mother that White had drugged and raped her? "Why didn't you turn to your mother and tell her those things when she urged you to write to White from Boulogne? She was your mother—why didn't you tell her?"

"Because I couldn't....I would rather have died than tell her. I could not tell her."[36]

It had been a welcome surprise for Jerome that Florence Nesbit had betrayed her daughter, providing him with information that he used to such effect to undermine Evelyn Nesbit's testimony. But even Jerome could not have imagined that another informant, one of his most bitter enemies, the attorney Abraham Hummel, would also offer him evidence against the witness, evidence that would contradict Evelyn's claim that Stanford White had raped her.

Two years before, in January 1905, Jerome had successfully prosecuted Hummel on a charge of conspiracy, accusing Hummel of bribing a witness to offer a false affidavit in a divorce case. The judge had sentenced Hummel to imprisonment for one year in the penitentiary; but Hummel had fought his conviction in the appellate courts and now, in February 1907, he awaited a final decision by the Court of Appeals.[37]

Jerome had indicted Hummel on a second charge, still pending, of subornation of perjury; and that felony indictment, more consequential than the conviction for conspiracy, would doubtless result in a second prison term for the attorney.

But Hummel now approached Jerome with a proposition. He had interviewed Evelyn Nesbit in his office in October 1903, shortly after she returned from Europe. She had signed an affidavit against Harry Thaw, Hummel told the district attorney, saying that Thaw had assaulted her with a dog whip. Thaw had told Evelyn, during their time in Europe, that he wanted to send White to the penitentiary and he had demanded that Evelyn accuse White of raping her. She refused, telling Thaw that the accusation was untrue, and he attacked her in her bedroom in the castle at Meran, seizing her by the throat, tearing away her clothes, and whipping her.

Every detail of Thaw's assault on Evelyn, Hummel said, was contained in the affidavit, and he would gladly give Jerome his copy... but only if the district attorney would abandon the indictment for perjury, still pending, that Jerome had presented against him.

The affidavit, Hummel told Jerome, would prove to the world that Evelyn's courtroom testimony, her claim that White had raped her, was a fabrication, a lie that had its origin in Harry Thaw's obsessive desire to send White to the penitentiary. Evelyn Nesbit had refused Thaw's original demand when he first presented it in 1903; but now, after White's death, she had agreed to testify falsely, telling the court an elaborate fiction that she hoped would save her husband from the electric chair.

But how could Jerome accept such an offer? How could he present as evidence an affidavit from Hummel when two years before he, Jerome, had prosecuted Hummel for offering a false affidavit? Everyone, including Jerome, knew Hummel's reputation as a deceitful, dishonest attorney, a shyster lawyer who had no regard for the law except as it served his self-interest. But the affidavit held out the possibility that Jerome could finally destroy Evelyn's testimony. It did not seem to matter that Hummel no longer possessed the original document and that he could provide Jerome only with a carbon copy. Nor did Jerome worry that Hummel might have fabricated the affidavit. The deal was struck: Jerome would withdraw the indictment against Hummel, and Hummel would provide the affidavit to Jerome.

"Evelyn Nesbit Thaw to the stand!"

The clerk of the court called out his command and the witness again stepped across the front of the courtroom, taking her place on the raised chair adjacent to the bench. She had borne the weight of her cross-examination for four days, never wavering in her testimony, never yet failing her husband, but now, on the fifth day, there was a hint of fatigue about her appearance. She no longer seemed so self-assured; her gaze, as she looked out across the courtroom, no longer seemed so fearless; the color had faded from her cheeks, and she seemed slightly diminished, almost as if she had lost weight.[38]

Travers Jerome, by contrast, appeared ebullient, almost cheerful, as he rose from his chair. He held in his hand the carbon copy of the affidavit that, according to Hummel, Evelyn Nesbit had sworn against Harry Thaw in 1903, the affidavit that claimed Thaw had whipped her.

"When you met Hummel at his office, in the fall of 1903," Jerome asked, speaking almost nonchalantly, "I understand you as saying that Hummel dictated a paper, dictated something to a stenographer in your presence."

"Yes," Evelyn replied. Her voice was abrupt, almost harsh, as if she had prepared herself for the onslaught of questions that Jerome was about to set loose.

"Before Hummel dictated to the stenographer, you talked with him?...Did you not tell him, Hummel, about your trip abroad, in all its details?"

"I told him about the trip abroad. I don't exactly know what you mean about all its details."

"Did you tell him what happened between you and Thaw there?...Did you not tell him that after travelling for five or six weeks the defendant had rented a castle in the Austrian Tyrol?"

"I told him that. I am not sure I told him after travelling five or six weeks; I don't remember that."[39]

"Did you tell him that the first night...you were very tired and went to bed right after dinner?"

"I don't remember whether I told him that or not. It is very possible."

"Did you tell him that in the morning you were awakened by Mr. Thaw pounding on the door and asking you to come to breakfast, saying that the coffee was getting cold?"

"I don't remember that."

"And did you further tell him at that time that after breakfast Thaw said he wanted to tell you something and asked you to step into your bedroom?"

"No."

"Did you tell him that when you entered the room Thaw, without any provocation, grasped you by the throat and tore the bathrobe from you?...That his eyes were glaring and that he had in his hand a cowhide whip?...That he seized hold of you and threw you on the bed?...That he continued to act like a demented man and beat you very violently there?"

"I did not tell Mr. Hummel that." Each word rang out across the courtroom, clear and distinct in its emphasis. She had regained her self-confidence, and she angrily denied Jerome's accusations.[40]

"Did you tell him that Thaw wanted to injure White and get him in the penitentiary?"

"I told Mr. Hummel," Evelyn conceded, "Mr. Thaw wanted Mr. White put in the penitentiary, yes."

"And that Thaw had begged you time and time again," Jerome asked, "to swear to a written document that he had prepared?"

"No, sir."

"And that these documents," Jerome continued, now referring to the accusation that Thaw had made against Stanford White, "charged this man with having drugged and attacked you?"

"No."

"And that you had told Thaw that this was not so?"

"No."

"And that he had beaten you because you wouldn't sign it?"

"No, sir."

Jerome now offered a single page to the witness, asking her to identify the signature that appeared on the final page of the affidavit he had received from Abraham Hummel. "I show you people's Exhibit No. 76 for identification, and ask you if that is your signature?"

"It looks very much like my signature," she replied hesitantly. She glanced across the room toward the defense attorneys, silently appealing to Delphin Delmas for his assistance, her plaintive expression demanding his intervention—anything to halt Jerome's insistent interrogation.

"Have you any doubt that that is your signature?"

"I don't remember ever signing anything like that."

But there was something curious about the paper that Jerome had offered to the witness, and Delmas realized that the district attorney was asking Evelyn Nesbit to identify her signature on a photographic copy. It was not an original document that Jerome held in his hand but a photograph!

"Is that what counsel means," Delmas demanded, anger and incredulity combined in equal measure in his voice. "Does counsel offer a photograph?"

"Certainly," Jerome replied, turning away from Delmas as if to dismiss the question.

"I submit," Delmas appealed to the judge, "that the question is misleading. When learned counsel asks: — 'Is that your signature?' knowing it is a photograph, the question condemns itself....I submit that the photograph is improper unless the original, its counterpart, is produced, and I object to it."

"I will let her answer," Fitzgerald replied, overruling the objection.

But already Evelyn had regained her composure, and she refused to say that it was her signature at the bottom of the page. It was not possible, she answered, to identify the signature.

"I will have to prove this as an independent fact." Jerome addressed the judge, saying that he wished to call Abraham Hummel as a witness to the affidavit. "I will ask to suspend and lay the ground to offer this in evidence. I wish to adjourn until I can put Mr. Hummel...on the stand."[41]

Jerome had hoped to catch Evelyn Nesbit in a lie, to prove her testimony false, but she had been more elusive in her responses than he had anticipated. Jerome had finished his cross-examination and now he called witnesses in rebuttal. Rudolf Eickemeyer took the stand to testify about the date when he had first photographed Evelyn Nesbit in his studio.

"Were you," Jerome began, "ever connected with Campbell's studio?"

"I was manager for several years," Eickemeyer replied. He had worked at the Campbell Art Studio on Fifth Avenue after moving to New York in 1895.

"Were these taken by you?" Jerome asked, showing Eickemeyer several photographs mounted on cardboard of Evelyn Nesbit.

But Delphin Delmas now reminded the judge that Evelyn Nesbit had not testified on direct examination about the photographs. She had testified only on her conversations with Harry Thaw. The district attorney could call witnesses regarding those conversations, but he could not question Eickemeyer about matters that were not in evidence.

"I desire," Jerome replied, addressing the judge, "to fix the very day on which the photographs were taken." Evelyn Nesbit had said that White raped her on the day after she posed for Eickemeyer in his studio. "I desire to show that on that day Stanford White was somewhere else."

"Your Honor," Delmas interrupted, "has heard my objection."

"Objection sustained," Fitzgerald said.

"That is all, Mr. Eickemeyer." Jerome shrugged his shoulders, as if to accept his defeat. He had hoped to establish an alibi for Stanford White on the night when Evelyn Nesbit said White had raped her; but Delmas had blocked his way.[42]

Could Jerome prove that Evelyn Nesbit had signed the affidavit against Harry Thaw? She had already testified on direct examination that Abraham Hummel interviewed her on her return from Europe in 1903. Hummel had provided the district attorney with a copy of the affidavit, and now he appeared in court to say that the affidavit was genuine.

"When Evelyn Nesbit called on you in October, 1903," Jerome asked, "did she state to you as follows: that Harry K. Thaw had begged her, time and time again, to swear to documents which he had prepared, charging Stanford White with having drugged and betrayed her?"

"Yes," Hummel replied.

Evelyn Nesbit had told him on October 27, 1903, that Harry Thaw had demanded, during their stay in the castle in Meran, that she falsely accuse White of raping her. She had refused his demand and Thaw had beaten her with a whip.

Hummel had dictated the substance of her remarks to his stenographer, and later that same day the stenographer had returned to him a typewritten original and a carbon copy. He gave the original to his notary, Abraham Snydecker, and the next day Snydecker returned the original, now signed by Evelyn Nesbit. He, Hummel, then gave the signed original to her while retaining the carbon copy and a photographic copy of the signature page.

Could Hummel now identify those documents for the

court? "Is People's Exhibit 77 for identification," Jerome asked, showing the witness both the carbon copy and the photograph, "either of those papers?"

"It is," Hummel replied, pointing to the carbon copy of the affidavit.

"Examine People's Exhibit 78, for identification," Jerome instructed, now showing Hummel the photographic copy of the signature page, "and state whether or not it is a true and correct representation."

Yes, Hummel replied, he could identify it as a photograph of the signature page of the affidavit.

The notary, Abraham Snydecker, also testified, saying that he had received the affidavit from Hummel, and later that day he witnessed Evelyn Nesbit sign the original copy.

"On October 27, 1903," Jerome asked, "were you a commissioner of deeds in the city of New York?"

"Yes, sir."

"On that day did you see Evelyn Nesbit?"

"I did.... Miss Nesbit had the paper in her hand probably between five minutes and ten minutes, it may have been a little less, and she then signed her name to the paper. Then I asked her whether or not she had read the paper and whether or not she swore to its contents and she said yes, and I then signed my name to it as commissioner of deeds of New York."

"I show you People's Exhibit 78 for identification and call your attention to a signature there and ask you... whether or not the signature there is your signature." Snydecker fumbled for his eyeglasses and peered at the paper that Jerome held in his hand. He studied it carefully before finally acknowledging his signature at the bottom of the page.

"That is my signature," he said.[43]

A sudden hailstorm rattled the windows of the courtroom. The sky outside had darkened and sheets of rain pounded the sidewalk along Centre Street, driving away the crowd that stood at the entrance to the Criminal Courts Building. There were no more witnesses; the trial had now run its course. Delphin Delmas delivered his closing address on Monday, April 8, telling the jury that Evelyn Nesbit had been a truthful witness. It was pitiful, Delmas stated, that the district attorney had relied on the testimony of Abraham Hummel—a convicted perjurer—to contradict Evelyn's account of the rape. Stanford White had raped Evelyn Nesbit, and Harry Thaw had suffered insanity as a consequence. Every man on the jury, Delmas declared, could recognize the illness that had gripped Thaw. "It is a species of insanity which has been recognized in every court in every State of this Union from the Canadian border to the Gulf of Texas. It is that species of insanity which...I ask you to label 'Dementia Americana.' It is that species of insanity which makes every American believe that his home is sacred....It is that species of insanity that makes him believe that the honor of his wife is sacred."[44]

Travers Jerome came next, reminding the jurors that Evelyn Nesbit's testimony had been contradictory and inconsistent. She had described the rape as profoundly traumatic, yet she had continued to see Stanford White alone long after White supposedly assaulted her. Why had she accepted his money? Why had she been unable to tell the court when White had raped her? Delphin Delmas had criticized the state for calling Hummel as a witness, but Delmas had said nothing about the clerk, Abraham Snydecker, and his testimony that Evelyn Nesbit signed the affidavit in his presence.[45]

The judge now addressed the jurors, explaining how they should regard the evidence that each side had presented. It would not be appropriate, Fitzgerald began, for the jury to consider Stanford White's behavior in determining the culpability of the defendant. "The character of the victim furnishes neither excuse nor justification.... He was entitled to the protection of the law, no matter whether his character was good or bad. A personal avenger of private wrongs or of public wrongs is not recognized by our institutions."[46]

The defense claimed that Evelyn Nesbit's account of the rape, told to Harry Thaw in 1903, was the catalyst that caused Thaw to go insane. The jury, in arriving at its verdict, should therefore consider Thaw's state of mind at the time of the murder. The penal code of New York stipulated that the defendant could not claim insanity if he knew the quality of the act and knew that it was wrong. "The settled law of the State is that the test of responsibility," Fitzgerald told the jurors, "is the capacity of the defendant to distinguish between right and wrong at the time of and with respect to the act." The testimony of the defendant's wife was central to the defense, and it was proper, therefore, for the jury to consider her credibility as a witness. "You should weigh her story in its entirety—were its various parts consistent or inconsistent with each other?"[47]

The twelve jurors left the courtroom in single file, walking along a narrow corridor to the jury room. A large rectangular oaken table occupied the center of the room, stretching from one end to the other. Twelve stiff-backed wooden chairs stood haphazardly around the table, and a brown leather settee rested against the far wall, below the windows facing Franklin Street.

The foreman, Deming Smith, took his place at the head of the table, waiting for the other men to take their seats. Smith spoke first, suggesting that they cast votes to learn if they could reach a consensus. He counted the votes as his colleagues looked on: eight men had voted to convict Thaw of murder in the first degree, but four had acquitted him on the grounds of insanity.

"This man is not right in his head," Henry Harney began, explaining why he had voted to acquit Thaw. "I have watched him very closely from the beginning of the trial, and I sat near enough to him to have an excellent opportunity to observe him, and I know he cannot be right."

Wilbur Steele nodded his agreement. He also had observed the defendant during the trial. Who could forget how Thaw had mumbled to himself, one moment frantically scribbling some notes on a pad, the next moment muttering orders to the attorneys seated next to him? He had seemed incapable of sitting still, constantly fidgeting, always appearing agitated, sometimes angry, even seeming on occasion about to rise in his chair to denounce the district attorney.

Another juror, Malcolm Fraser, reminded his colleagues that several witnesses had described Thaw's expression immediately after the murder. Thaw had had an unnatural look in his eyes, a fixed glare during those moments when he walked through the audience holding his gun above his head. There was a reasonable doubt, Fraser added, that Thaw had known that his act in killing Stanford White was wrong, and on those grounds he would vote to acquit him.

But George Pfaff, one of the eight jurors who had voted to convict on a charge of first-degree murder, could find nothing in such arguments that might persuade him to change his mind. One witness, Clinch Smith, testified that he had talked with Thaw immediately before the shooting, and that conversation, on the stock market, and on Thaw's upcoming trip to Europe, contained nothing to suggest that Thaw was insane. Thaw had deliberated before shooting White, and his actions immediately afterward had given every indication that he knew the import of his act. He had held the gun above his head to show the audience that he intended no further harm, and he had calmly told the duty fireman, Paul Brudi, the reason for the murder.

Smith held a second ballot at six o'clock that evening before adjourning for dinner, but the result was the same. The jurors voted a third time at ten o'clock, but still there was no agreement. The crowds no longer lingered around the courthouse, waiting for a decision, and Thaw's relatives—his wife, his mother, his brothers and sisters—had all abandoned the vigil, returning to their rooms at the Hotel Lorraine.[48]

A reporter for the *New York Herald,* catching sight of Jerome as he left the Criminal Courts Building, buttonholed the district attorney to ask if he would seek a second trial if the jury could not reach a verdict.

"In the event of a disagreement," the reporter asked, "will Thaw be speedily placed on trial again?"

"Not speedily," Jerome replied. There were many other homicide cases on the docket, and there would probably not be another trial until the end of the year. "There is no reason why Thaw's should take precedence over the cases of other Tombs prisoners who are yet untried."[49]

The next morning, shortly before eleven o'clock, a rumor spread through the Criminal Courts Building that the jury had asked to return to the courtroom, and crowds started to gather in the hallways, expecting to hear the verdict. But the jurors only wished to hear again the statements of those witnesses who had seen the shooting. There were two more ballots that afternoon; eight men still voted for a murder conviction and four held fast for an acquittal.

All twelve agreed that Evelyn Nesbit had been an admirable witness, selflessly testifying on behalf of her husband, and her account had been truthful—White had raped her, they believed—but her testimony bore no weight in their deliberations. White's behavior toward Evelyn Nesbit, they agreed, could not justify Thaw's act in killing him. Their verdict would rest only on their judgment of Thaw's mental condition during the murder: if Thaw had been insane, incapable of knowing that his act was wrong, he could not be held responsible for the murder.[50]

One juror, John Dennce, changed his vote on the second

day, now saying that Thaw was insane, but it brought the jury no closer to agreement. Harry Brearley, hoping to break the deadlock, suggested that they compromise by voting to convict Thaw on a lesser charge, manslaughter in the first degree. A conviction for manslaughter would spare Thaw from the electric chair while ensuring that he would receive some punishment for his crime.

But George Pfaff rejected the proposal, saying that he would not change his mind. "You can all vote as you please," Pfaff declared defiantly. "I am going to keep on voting for a conviction in the first degree."

Wilbur Steele spoke next, saying that he too would not change his vote. Harry Thaw was insane, he added, and he could not contemplate any punishment for a man who was so evidently unbalanced.

The next day, Friday, April 12, Smith spoke to the judge, and that afternoon, at four o'clock, the jurors returned to the courtroom, taking their seats on the benches near the front. The spectators searched their faces in vain, looking for some sign that might betray a verdict; and the jurors, in turn, looked out over the courtroom. Every seat was occupied, and the crowd seemed curiously hushed. Thaw sat in the front row, whispering in the ear of one of his attorneys; Evelyn sat directly behind, her left hand resting on her husband's shoulder. Mary Thaw, her veil covering her face, sat next to her daughter-in-law, and Harry's siblings, Margaret, Alice, Josiah, and Edward, looked hopefully at the twelve jurors.

"Gentlemen of the jury," William Penney called out in a loud voice, "please answer to your names."

Each man answered in turn, rising slightly from his seat in acknowledgment of his name.

"The defendant will rise," Penney commanded.

Thaw, his left hand resting on the table in front of him, rose to his feet, the legs of his chair scraping backward against the floor. He looked anxiously at Penney, waiting for the clerk's command, his face set in a grimace, a frown upon his forehead.

"Jurors, look upon the defendant; defendant, look upon the jurors." Penney paused, waiting for the jury to turn toward Thaw.

"Gentlemen of the jury, have you agreed upon a verdict?"

"We have not," Deming Smith replied.

The crowd let out a sigh of disappointment. Thaw, still standing, seemed to stagger slightly before slumping backward into his chair, and Evelyn reached out to comfort him, her hand resting on his arm as she whispered some words of encouragement. Delphin Delmas was already shuffling some papers on the table before him, waiting only for the judge to dismiss the jury before making his exit.

"Gentlemen," Fitzgerald began, his gaze fixed on the jurors, "I have kept you together for a long time and have deemed it my duty to do so as long as there seemed any possibility of your being able to reach a verdict. I have now arrived at the conclusion that this is not possible. . . . I am going to discharge you from further consideration of this case."[51]

There would be a second trial.

Portrait photographs at the turn of the century usually took the form of cabinet cards. Such photographs, typically produced either on gelatin bromide paper or on matte collodion, measured 4¼ by 6½ inches and were often sold commercially to the public or used as illustrations in popular magazines. Evelyn Nesbit posed for a series of cabinet cards, including these five photographs, in 1902 at the Sarony Studio on Fifth Avenue. *(Theatrical Cabinet Photographs of Women [TCS 2], Harvard Theatre Collection, Houghton Library, Harvard University)*

6

SECOND TRIAL

January 6, 1908–February 1, 1908

"HAVE YOU BEEN ILL LATELY, MRS. THAW?"

The lawyer leaned forward, appearing almost to bow before the witness, and Mary Thaw nodded in return, as if to show her appreciation for his words.

"I have," she replied, speaking in a quiet voice, "since early in November.... But I am now well—almost; sufficiently recovered," she added.[1]

She had awaited this moment anxiously, aware that her testimony would determine her son's fate. The attorney, Martin Littleton, had convinced the family that there were no longer any grounds for complacency, no reason to believe that a jury would necessarily acquit Harry Thaw. The jurors in the first trial, Littleton reminded Mary Thaw, had all disregarded Evelyn Nesbit's testimony about the rape, each one telling the newspapermen that he had voted only according to his judgment of Thaw's mental state at the time of the murder.

It would be foolish, Littleton argued, to claim a second time that the rape of Evelyn Nesbit provided sufficient justification for the murder of Stanford White. Their best strategy, their only strategy, according to Littleton, was to persuade the jury that Harry had been insane when he killed White, that he had been mentally incompetent since childhood, and that he was still impaired now. The judge would commit him to an asylum, but eventually, sooner or later, the lawyers would seek his release, arguing that he had regained his sanity.

"When was your son, Harry K. Thaw, born?" Littleton asked.

"February 12, 1871."

"What was the condition of health of Harry shortly after his birth?"

"For three months he was normal—that is, in average good health. Then he had an attack of congestion of lungs, which involved the brain and caused one spasm."

"And then after that what was his condition?"

"A condition of the most remarkable sleeplessness that I have ever known in an infant."

"How long would he sleep during twenty-four hours?"

"I should not think it was one-third what a child should sleep.... We were worn out sitting up with him."[2]

Harry's childhood, from infancy to adolescence, had been punctuated by frequent episodes of excitability, outbursts of anger and ill temper, typically occurring without any ostensible cause. He had been a nervous, irritable child with few companions, and his erratic behavior had lasted until he was fourteen years old. The doctors had variously diagnosed Harry's condition, attributing it to one cause or another, but their advice had not produced any noticeable improvement.

Mary Copley Thaw, shown here with her daughter Margaret, married William Thaw in 1869. Mary Thaw was a devout Presbyterian, contributing thousands of dollars to Presbyterian institutions in Pittsburgh and western Pennsylvania. *(Library of Congress, LC-DIG-ggbain-18581)*

Mary Thaw was a capable witness, speaking each answer as if she had rehearsed it beforehand, occasionally giving an anecdote to illustrate her son's tortuous passage to adulthood.

But the long train ride from Pittsburgh the previous day had left her tired, and her responses came haltingly. The Pennsylvania Railroad express had traveled across the Appalachian Mountains, stopping first at Philadelphia before continuing to New York, a wearisome journey that had lasted more than eight hours.

She also seemed occasionally reluctant, often hesitating, as if she resented the necessity of revealing the shameful secrets that she had never previously told. A tangible sympathy hung in the air for someone so frail and vulnerable, for a woman who seemed crushed by the troubles that had given her so much anxiety.

One year before, during the first trial, she had been a commanding presence, never doubting that the jury would acquit her son, but her self-confidence had now vanished and her expression seemed to foreshadow defeat. Mary Thaw had always triumphed over her adversaries, securing her victories through her determination, but the calamity that had overwhelmed her family, the possibility that her son might die in the electric chair, appeared to have vanquished her.

Nothing could have presented a greater contrast to the mournful appearance of the witness than the ebullient presence of Martin Littleton. The attorney was only thirty-eight years old, yet he had already established his reputation as a lawyer and politician. He had grown up in Texas, working first as a rail-splitter and brakeman on the railroads, then setting type in a printer's office, finally securing a clerical position in the office of the district attorney in Weatherford, a town sixty miles west of Dallas. He studied for the bar, moving to Dallas in 1893 to set up a legal practice, but only three years later he left Texas to move to New York with his wife, Maud.

Littleton joined the Democratic Party and almost immediately obtained a position as an assistant district attorney in Kings County. He was a man who made friends easily, and he secured the support of the Democratic machine, winning the election in 1903 for Brooklyn borough president. Littleton was ambitious for higher office and already, in 1908, he had begun to canvass his allies for the nomination for the upcoming election to the House of Representatives from the First Congressional District.[3]

Harry Thaw hired Martin Littleton as his defense attorney in his second trial. Littleton served one term, from 1911 to 1913, in the U.S. House of Representatives but then failed to win the Democratic Party nomination for election to the U.S. Senate. *(Library of Congress, LC-DIG-ds-10585)*

He was only five feet four inches tall, but his barrel chest and broad shoulders compensated for his lack of height. He had a cheerful disposition and he spoke with a distinctive Texas twang. He had chestnut-brown hair, already gray at the temples, a fleshy, slightly pink complexion, and inquisitive brown eyes. Littleton invariably radiated self-confidence even when his cause appeared hopeless, and now, as Mary Thaw continued to respond to his questions, he attempted to steer her along the path that they had mapped out beforehand.[4]

She told the court, in response to Littleton's questions, that she had first sent Harry away from home in 1881, to study at the Beck School in Lititz, a Moravian community in the interior of the state, seventy miles west of Philadelphia. She had hoped that the experience might improve her son's condition, but it had been an ill-advised move. Harry, then ten years old, was a sullen pupil who intermittently burst into tears for no apparent reason, even occasionally uttering loud howls during class. The principal, Abraham Beck, had written to her, saying that her son was a disruptive presence and asking her to withdraw him from the school. Mary Thaw had written a tearful response, confessing her fear that he was unbalanced and asking for the principal's forbearance, but Harry eventually left the school, returning to Pittsburgh to live again with his mother.[5]

Five years later Mary Thaw enrolled Harry at the University of Wooster, a Presbyterian college in Ohio. Its rural location, in the center of the state, and its small size — only a few dozen students matriculated each year — ameliorated her son's condition: "He did improve . . . he was looking very much stronger." But the faculty at Wooster could not tolerate Thaw's disruptive behavior and expelled him three months after his arrival. Harry then attended the Western University of Pennsylvania, but his studies there were equally lackadaisical.[6]

Harry, according to his mother's testimony, had suffered mental illness for many years, from infancy through adolescence to adulthood. His afflictions were not dissimilar from those that had plagued other members of the extended Thaw family. One of her brothers, Josiah, an uncle of Harry, had experienced an attack of brain fever as a student at Amherst College.

"The brain fever left him very nervous and unstrung. . . . He had three days of violent, acute mania. And then he was taken away to an asylum."

"How long," Littleton asked, "was he away in the asylum?"

"Seven months."

"Did he recover from that afterward?"

"Yes. They discharged him cured."

A second brother, Henry, had been weak-minded as a child, displaying just those symptoms that she had witnessed in her son. Henry would frequently burst into tears, crying for no apparent reason, then relapsing into silence for several hours.

Mental illness had been present also on the other side of the family. Her late husband, William, had a sister who suffered for many years from epilepsy. The attacks would occur without warning and last for prolonged periods.

"She was an invalid," the witness explained, "as long as I knew her, and for many years before, subject to epilepsy."[7]

*   *   *

Several witnesses followed Mary Thaw onto the stand, describing Harry Thaw's irrational behavior. Catherine O'Neil remembered that she had first worked for the Thaw family in 1874, when Harry was three years old. She had remained at Lyndhurst for six years, caring for Harry, dressing him, preparing his meals, playing with him on the estate, and generally arranging his daily schedule. It was a demanding task, made more difficult because Harry threw frequent temper tantrums, screaming and yelling, occasionally speaking gibberish, finally collapsing in exhaustion.

"He used to have awful spells," O'Neil told the court. "He used to throw himself on the floor and holler and yell and stamp until he was exhausted.... He learned very slow and poorly."

"How old was he then?" Littleton prompted.

"Well, these conditions continued from the age of five until the age of seven."

"Was he able to speak or use words intelligently during his early childhood?"

"No, not until he was seven or eight years old."[8]

Abraham Beck, the principal of the Beck School in Lititz, remembered that Harry Thaw appeared excessively nervous when he first came to the school in September 1881. The boy resisted the attempts of the staff to introduce him to the other pupils. He seemed always alone, invariably standing apart from the other children at playtime, refusing any invitation to join their games. Beck, now sixty years old, white-haired, slightly stooped, with a kindly demeanor, painted a heartbreaking picture of a lonely child, morose and withdrawn, a boy who made no friends while attending the school.

"During the time Thaw was at your school," Littleton asked, "did you observe him daily?"

"Yes," Beck replied, remarking parenthetically that the passage of thirty years had not erased his memories.

"Was your attention attracted to him during school hours?"

"Yes," Beck answered. "The quiet of the study room would be broken by a sudden, wild, passionate cry from Harry Thaw. It was the cry of an animal.... He would repeat these howlings and keep them up for twenty minutes at times, and would then lapse into a fit of abstraction. They would cease as suddenly as they started, like the turning off of a fountain jet."[9]

He had written to Pittsburgh, asking Mary Thaw to remove her son from the school. She had replied a few days later, confiding her dread that Harry was unbalanced and pleading that he stay at least until the end of the school term. Beck had reluctantly agreed; but it had been an unpleasant experience, the most trying ordeal he had faced in his long career as a schoolteacher.

Charles Koehler, a former instructor at the University of Wooster, also recalled Harry Thaw as a moody pupil. Koehler had taught mathematics at Wooster in 1886, when Thaw first arrived at the college.

"Do you know the defendant, Harry K. Thaw?" Littleton asked.

"Yes," Koehler replied, glancing toward Thaw, seated among his attorneys in the front row of the courtroom. "He was under my immediate instruction for about a period of three months."

"How old was he?"

"About sixteen or seventeen."

"What was his appearance?"

"He had a nervous gait and walked in a zigzag manner.... His eyes were fixed and staring much of the time; frequently the muscles of his mouth would twitch, and when he walked his gait was unsteady. On some days he was moody and on others more cheerful. His moods alternated. One day he would be more playful and the next deeply depressed."

"What progress did he make in his studies?"

"Very little progress; scarcely any that was perceptible.... His capacity for concentration was so weak that he was utterly unable to follow an ordinary demonstration in mathematics."[10]

Other witnesses followed, all testifying to Harry Thaw's irrational behavior. Amy Gozzett, a nurse, told the court that she had been working in 1897 on the Côte d'Azur in France for her employer, Price Mitchell, an American physician, when she first encountered Harry Thaw. Many expatriates spent the season at Monte Carlo, and she frequently cared for wealthy British and American patients who had taken ill. Thaw had been unwell for three weeks, running a high fever, and she spent that summer caring for him, gradually nursing him back to health. He was an unusual patient who would often refuse his doctor's orders, occasionally rising from his bed, dressing himself, and leaving the hotel for two or three hours before returning to his room. Gozzett recalled that, even after Thaw recovered, he seemed irrational, mumbling to himself, moving jerkily and awkwardly, sitting motionless for long periods, staring into space.[11]

Sydney Russell Wells, a physician at St. George's Hospital in

London, remembered his alarm when he first saw Harry Thaw as a patient in 1899. Thaw, then staying at Claridge's in Mayfair, had been walking about the hotel in his pajamas, brandishing a large stick and shouting obscenities at the staff. Wells had committed Thaw to the Devonshire Nursing Home, a private clinic in the capital, holding him until he recovered his sanity, eventually allowing him to return to the hotel.[12]

Physicians elsewhere, in other European cities, could recall similar episodes. Frederick Burton-Browne, a doctor at the British embassy in Rome, saw Thaw in August 1902. Burton-Browne remembered that Thaw had been feverish, with a slow pulse and dilated pupils, and recalled that his patient's eccentric behavior seemed symptomatic of a maniacal outburst. Finally, Maurice Gauja, the house doctor at the Hôtel Palais d'Orsay in Paris, told the court that he had attended Thaw in 1904 when he, Thaw, had taken poison in an apparent suicide attempt. Thaw had been desperately ill, drifting in and out of consciousness, occasionally vomiting blood, and Gauja had immediately applied a stomach pump. Gauja returned the next day to check on his patient and found Thaw rested and alert, apparently oblivious to his brush with death.[13]

Evelyn Nesbit testified also, repeating the account that she had given the previous year at the first trial. Travers Jerome had already appealed to the judge, Victor Dowling, to hold the second trial *in camera,* with no reporters present, saying that the salacious nature of Evelyn's testimony was not suitable for publication in the newspapers. Dowling was sympathetic; he agreed with the district attorney that the publication of the testimony in 1907 had been deeply shocking, an affront to public morality. But what, he asked, was the point in trying to prevent publication when everything had already appeared in the newspapers? In any case, Harry Thaw had a constitutional right to a public trial, and he, Dowling, could not abrogate that right on account of a concern for public decency.

"The federal constitution," Dowling ruled, "provides a man shall have a speedy and public trial. The civil and criminal codes of this State provide likewise.... It is the Court's opinion that whatever harm might be caused the morals of the community by the printing of certain revolting details and testimony is more than compensated for by the safeguards thrown

This photograph shows Evelyn Nesbit on the witness stand in the Criminal Courts Building. Harry Thaw's attorneys persuaded Evelyn to testify twice on her husband's behalf, first in 1907 and again in 1908. *(Library of Congress, LC-DIG-ggbain-07120)*

around the constitutional rights of the defendant. I therefore decline the appeal of the District Attorney."[14]

Evelyn told her story a second time, but her account of the rape no longer had the force that it had possessed one year before. It played out exactly as it had the first time, but the recitation now seemed shopworn and stale. There had been no change in Evelyn's appearance—she seemed not to have aged even a single day, and she was just as attractive as before—but there was a hardness in her voice, a glint in her eyes, a self-assurance in her bearing that had not existed in 1907. Jerome tried again to intimidate her, to bully her into submission, to confuse her on the details, occasionally comparing her answers to the responses she had given in the first trial, but she fought back relentlessly, matching him point by point, never allowing Jerome to win an advantage.

Her testimony during the second trial was remarkably precise, corresponding exactly, in every particular, to her testimony in the first trial. She added only a few details to the account that she had given previously, details that aimed to convince the jury that Harry Thaw had been insane long before he murdered Stanford White.

She remembered that Harry had returned to New York from Europe in December 1903 to learn that Stanford White had told her that he, Thaw, was a cocaine addict. Other men, friends of White, had confirmed the rumor, adding also that Thaw had whipped and brutalized young girls in his apartments.

He had denied everything, telling her that there was no truth in such gossip, and Evelyn eventually reconciled with

Harry, moving with him in January 1904 to an apartment in the Grand Hotel on Broadway. But the episode had caused Harry great distress. Stanford White had attempted to renew his relationship with Evelyn, telling her all sorts of stories, and Thaw could no longer feel confident that she would remain faithful to him. That month, Evelyn told the court, Harry had fallen into a deep depression. He brooded over the situation, worrying that she would abandon him, fearing that her love for him would evaporate.

"He said," Evelyn recalled, "that his life had been ruined, and that White . . . and his friends were constantly circulating unpleasant stories about him and hurting him in every way possible."[15]

One afternoon, without warning, Harry blurted out that his life had become unbearable — the pain of his existence was too much and he intended to kill himself. There was no way to prevent Stanford White from harming his reputation, and there was no reason for either of them, Harry or Evelyn, to live. They should both commit suicide that afternoon.

"I did not know what to do," Evelyn testified. "He was in a wild state. . . . He said that there was no use living: too many things had happened. He said that he was going to commit suicide. . . . He said he thought he would take laudanum and that I should take it, too. He thought we should go together."[16]

But, remarkably, his mood seemed to lighten as they talked, and gradually Harry became less fretful. He started to relax, he spoke less excitedly, he stopped pacing about the apartment, and his expression no longer seemed so anxious. Evelyn was able to change the subject, to engage him in his plans for their journey to Europe later that year, and soon Harry had forgotten about his threat to commit suicide.

His depression would reappear intermittently, Evelyn testified, but there had been only one other occasion when Harry repeated his intention to kill himself. They had traveled to Paris in March 1904, staying in a suite of rooms at the Hôtel Palais d'Orsay in the Seventh Arrondissement. They had intended to remain only a few days in the capital before taking the train south to Monte Carlo, and Harry had proposed that they then travel through Europe by motorcar.

One evening, shortly before their departure for Monte Carlo, Harry had gone for a stroll along the path that ran beside the Seine. He returned within an hour, abruptly entering the living room, walking hurriedly to the settee where Evelyn was reading a book. His face was white, the color of chalk, and he walked rigidly toward her as though something inhibited the movement of his arms. He announced that he had finally done it; he had swallowed a bottle of laudanum, and he would soon die from the poison.

His appearance seemed to confirm the truth of his declaration: his face was deathly pale; his eyes were fixed with a glassy stare; he started to choke as though the poison had begun to work its malign effect. A telephone stood nearby, on a small table by the window, and Evelyn dialed the front desk, asking the concierge to send a doctor to the apartment. The physician, Maurice Gauja, acted immediately, using a stomach pump to flush away the poison, giving Thaw some morphine to calm his nerves, finally waiting until his patient was asleep in bed before leaving the apartment.[17]

★　　★　　★

Harry Thaw's suicidal impulses, according to the psychiatrists, were congruent with the diagnosis that he suffered from manic-depressive insanity. Charles Wagner, the superintendent of Binghamton State Hospital, testified for the defense that Thaw's behavior alternated between two polar opposites: he would be deeply depressed, sitting motionless for hours at a time, sunk in a deathlike torpor, yet on other occasions he would behave excitedly, frantically engaged in some task to the exclusion of everything else.

"Symptoms of excitement and depression are characteristic of manic-depressive insanity," Wagner explained. "Suicidal attempts often mark these cases. . . . Quick, irregular habits of speech, nervousness and restlessness are all characteristic."

"Have you an opinion," Martin Littleton asked, "of the soundness of mind of the defendant at the time of the commission of the act?"

"Yes. The defendant was of unsound mind, and in my opinion he did not know the nature and quality of the act, and did not know that it was wrong."

The judge, Victor Dowling, interrupted the witness, leaning forward in his chair to ask Wagner about his diagnosis. Harry Thaw had killed once; was it possible that he might kill again?

"Is it not a fact," Dowling asked, turning in his chair to look directly at the witness, "that attacks of manic-depressive insanity are likely to recur?"

"It is," Wagner replied.

"Is there any certainty or way of telling when they will recur?"

"No...."

"Is there any guide by which you can establish when lucid intervals will recur?"

"No."

Dowling leaned back in his chair, a look of irritation on his face, indicating with a motion of his hand that he had no further questions. It annoyed him that Wagner had not been more forthcoming in his responses. It might be necessary to confine Thaw indefinitely—but Dowling would be able to make that decision only on the basis of the psychiatric testimony.

The next witness, Smith Ely Jelliffe, was more accommodating, giving Dowling a better sense of the nature of Thaw's condition. Jelliffe agreed that the defendant had a medical condition that psychiatrists classified as manic-depressive insanity, and the judge again inquired about the diagnosis.

"Do you mean," Dowling asked, "[that] patients are apt to commit assaults?"

"Oh, yes," Jelliffe replied. "They are apt to knock around and tear their clothes, rush through the streets or the wards of institutions they are confined in and do other maniacal acts."[18]

The psychiatrists for the defense—Wagner, Jelliffe, and a third expert, Britton Evans—agreed that Thaw was chronically insane. He had suffered manic-depressive insanity since childhood, and his condition was likely to persist for some time.

But Travers Jerome, in his cross-examination, reminded the witnesses that they had all testified for the defense in the first trial, one year previously, and on that occasion they had told the court that Thaw had been insane only at the moment when he shot Stanford White. They had claimed that Thaw experienced a sudden derangement, a brainstorm, on seeing White at the theater, and in that moment of madness he had drawn his revolver and killed the architect.

But now, in the second trial, the psychiatrists offered a diagnosis of Thaw's condition that could not be reconciled with the first. They claimed now that Thaw had always been irrational, unable to distinguish between right and wrong, and that he was unaware of the nature of his acts, insane in both a medical and a legal sense of the term. The expert witnesses, psychiatrists with extensive experience in treating mental illness, had thus followed the defense attorneys in lockstep fashion, abandoning their previous diagnosis for one that would better support Martin Littleton's claim that Thaw had been insane since childhood.

It was preposterous, the district attorney exclaimed, that the experts should so readily alter their medical opinions to fall in with the attorneys. How could the three psychiatrists claim professional integrity as scientists if they could so effortlessly change their diagnosis?

Travers Jerome called Britton Evans to the stand, eyeing the witness with a look of contempt as Evans made his way across the front of the courtroom.

"Dr. Evans," Jerome demanded, "did you testify at the last trial that Thaw killed Stanford White while suffering from a brain storm?"

"I can only say," Evans replied, speaking cautiously, "that [it] was not a disease, but a phase of his mental condition. My recollection is that during a brainstorm he did the act, but that was not his disease."

"Answer the question, yes or no," Jerome snapped. "Was it your opinion that he killed Stanford White while suffering a brain storm?"

"Yes." Evans seemed to shrug as he gave his answer. "I testified that he had a brainstorm."

"That's all." Jerome abruptly turned away from Evans, signaling to the judge that he had no more questions for the witness. He also interrogated Charles Wagner and Smith Ely Jelliffe that afternoon, demanding that each man acknowledge that, in now claiming that Thaw suffered from chronic insanity, he had contradicted his testimony from the previous trial.[19]

Everyone had anticipated that Jerome would introduce expert witnesses in rebuttal; but Jerome, turning to address the judge, now informed Dowling that the state would close its case. It was an odd decision by the district attorney. The defense had entered a plea of not guilty by reason of insanity. The burden of proof of guilt lay on the prosecution to show that Thaw had been sane at the time of the murder; yet Jerome had decided not to offer any psychiatric testimony. What could it mean? Some observers speculated that Jerome was signaling to the jury that he no longer sought to send Thaw to the electric chair and that he might now be satisfied with a verdict that would send Harry Thaw to the asylum.

Martin Littleton, in his closing address, jubilantly interpreted the absence of psychiatric evidence as an admission by Jerome that he could not prove that Thaw had been sane when he shot White. "New York is filled with doctors and scientists

and neurologists and specialists and experts," Littleton proclaimed. No city in the United States, not even Philadelphia or
Boston, could rival New York in the prestige of its medical
community; yet the district attorney had not offered any sci-
entific evidence. "Why did he not call the names of the city's
pick of insanity experts? Where, oh, where, is this assembled
genius of the profession of New York?"[20]

The burden of proof lay with the state — there was a pre-
sumption of innocence in the American courts — yet Jerome
had failed to make his case. On that basis alone, Littleton concluded, the jury should acquit the defendant.[21]

But the available evidence, Jerome replied in his closing
speech, showed that Harry Thaw had indeed been sane on the
day of the murder. That same afternoon, a few hours before
he shot White, Thaw had played poker with some friends at
the Whist Club before returning to the Hotel Lorraine. He
left the hotel around six o'clock with Evelyn Nesbit, taking a
cab downtown to meet Truxton Beale and Thomas McCaleb
at Café Martin. They had walked across Madison Square after
dinner, arriving at the theater in the middle of the first act of
Mamzelle Champagne.

Jerome faced the jury as he spoke, seeming to address each
of the jurors in turn, leading them through the events of the
day of the murder. It was the culmination of the trial, and a
large crowd had squeezed into the courtroom to hear Jerome's
closing address. Josiah Thaw, seated next to Evelyn Nesbit,
was there to support his elder brother, but neither Harry's
mother nor his sisters were present. Thaw's attorneys, Martin
Littleton, Russell Peabody, and Daniel O'Reilly, sat in the

front row, not bothering to take notes while Jerome talked, but Harry Thaw, seated among his lawyers, occasionally scribbled some notes on a large pad of paper.

No one expected either Stanford White's widow, Bessie, or his son, Lawrence, to be in court, but Charles Hartnett, White's private secretary, was there, seated alone in a corner of the room, trying to be as inconspicuous as possible. A few actors could be seen, scattered among the crowd: Cecilia (Cissy) Loftus, the vaudeville star; Robert Hilliard, reputedly the most handsome man on Broadway; George Nash, then appearing in *The Witching Hour*, playing the role of the district attorney; and William Collier, the comic actor who had made his reputation with Eddie Foy's touring company. The impresario Charles Dillingham, one of Stanford White's closest friends, sat in the center of the room, in the same row as the author Richard Harding Davis. The heiress Aimée Crocker had known White well, and she too had come to court, hoping to hear Jerome denounce the assassination of her friend. Finally, a few politicians were also among the spectators: Joseph Corrigan, a Democratic Party stalwart and city magistrate, and Patrick McGowan, the president of the Board of Aldermen, were both in the audience.[22]

There was a hush in the courtroom as Jerome continued to describe Thaw's movements on the day of the murder. Was it not strange, Jerome asked rhetorically, that the defense had failed to call those witnesses who could testify to Thaw's behavior on that fateful day? One witness only, Christopher Biggan, the steward at the Whist Club, had appeared in court. Biggan said that Thaw had been nervous when he played bridge with other members of the club; but the defense had not called the cardplayers to testify. Charles Schwab, the president of the Bethlehem Steel Company, and John W. Gates, the principal shareholder of the Republic Steel Company, had both played bridge with Thaw a few hours before the murder; but neither man had appeared in court. "Do you think," Jerome said, "that these gentlemen whose names I have mentioned would sit down and play cards with a lunatic?" Martin Littleton could have issued a subpoena, compelling their testimony, but neither Schwab nor Gates had given evidence. "Not one of these gentlemen has been called."[23]

Thaw had spent the evening with Truxton Beale and Thomas McCaleb, dining with them at Café Martin before going to the theater, yet the defense attorneys had called neither Beale nor McCaleb to the witness stand. One witness, Clinch Smith, had appeared for the prosecution, describing his conversation with the defendant at Madison Square Garden; but everything about that conversation indicated that Thaw had been sane.

There was certainly ample motive for Thaw to kill Stanford White, Jerome continued. Thaw believed that the architect had raped his wife. He had learned that White had been gossiping about him, spreading malicious lies around New York that he was a cocaine addict who frequented prostitutes. There was reason for Thaw to think that White hoped to reignite the relationship that he, White, had enjoyed with Evelyn several years before. "White was a man whom this defendant," Jerome paused dramatically, pointing directly at Thaw a few feet away, "wanted to put in the penitentiary. White was a man who had wronged this defendant's wife.... This defendant believed that White was circulating stories about him, charging him with the basest of practices. If all this does not constitute a motive then I don't know what men are made of."[24]

The weapon used by Thaw, a blue-steel double-action revolver, lay on a table at the front of the courtroom, and Jerome, still speaking, stepped three paces to his left, taking the gun in his right hand. "The defendant walked about the roof garden," he declared. "He saw the man he had the most intense reason to hate, and then and there walked to where White sat at the table, leaning his head on his hand, and he shot three bullets into White's body." Jerome held the gun at arm's length, aiming it at an imaginary victim, pulling the trigger to snap the hammer. Once, twice, three times, the sound, a loud click, reverberated around the silent courtroom. "He turned from his victim and, with his arm raised, he held the gun on high broken—a sign to the crowd that he had accomplished his vengeance." Jerome also had now broken the gun and, holding it high above his head, turned about as if to show everyone the weapon.[25]

Thaw had acted throughout with deliberation and intent and was therefore guilty of first-degree murder. There was not a scintilla of evidence in any of his actions to show that he had been insane. On the contrary, he had been aware, at every moment, of the import of his actions, carefully shooting at point-blank range, aiming to kill his victim. He had not afterward resisted arrest, telling his wife as she stood near the elevator that he had acted to protect her, calmly walking with the sergeant along Madison Avenue to the police station on Thirtieth Street.

Jerome turned again to face the jurors, reminding them that they had sworn an oath to uphold the law. They could not accept the defense plea if they believed that Thaw had known, at the time of the murder, the difference between right and wrong, if he had known the nature of his act, and if he had known that it was wrong. "Your oath requires you," Jerome said in conclusion, "to find this man guilty if you believe that he knew it was Stanford White he killed."[26]

The jurors left the courtroom, walking along a narrow corridor, each man taking his seat in the jury room. They had lived together at the Knickerbocker Hotel on Forty-second Street during the trial, and their shared experience had created a sense of solidarity among the twelve men. One or two had grumbled about their privation, complaining that they would not see their families during their confinement, but most felt privileged to play a part in such a sensational drama as the Thaw trial. They ranged in age from thirty-eight to sixty. The majority were married men with children, and they were generally well-to-do, each man having made his mark in his profession—in real estate, shipping, dry goods, banking, and the like. The foreman, Charles Gremmels, a ship broker, married with two children, was the youngest man in the room, but he had already given his comrades an impression of good sense, the conviction that he would organize their discussions in a purposeful manner.[27]

But the first ballot, taken shortly after noon on Friday,

January 31, seemed to foretell that the jurors would never agree on a verdict. Eight men voted to acquit Harry Thaw on the ground of insanity; four, including Gremmels, voted to convict on the charge of murder. One juror, William Doolittle, an auditor for the New York Central Railroad, changed his vote on the second ballot to join the majority, but three men still remained steadfast in their conviction that Thaw was guilty.[28]

There was a brief snowfall that afternoon and a chill wind blew through Centre Street. The crowd outside the Criminal Courts Building gradually dispersed, taking refuge in the saloons along White Street. The two sets of attorneys, Jerome and Garvan for the state, Littleton, Peabody, and O'Reilly for the defense, spent the afternoon drinking together in Pontin's Restaurant on Franklin Street, waiting for the verdict.

Some reporters arrived at the Tombs around two o'clock to interview Thaw in his cell, asking the prisoner if he expected a favorable decision. He had always anticipated an acquittal, Thaw replied, and he had no reason now to change his mind. "I think the jury is a good jury," he answered. "I hope they finish the matter this time.... I deserve to be acquitted.... The result is finally going to be in my favor."[29]

The warden, Billy Flynn, interrupted their conversation to report that a visitor, Raffaele Cascone, was waiting in the outside corridor, and Thaw, pleased that his friend had come to the prison, suddenly ended the interview. Cascone had spent several months as a prisoner in the Tombs, in an adjacent cell, and the two men had become close friends, talking together every day. They seemed to have little in common: Cascone, a leader of the Black Hand, had been indicted for the murder of a rival mobster in 1903. Cascone's subsequent legal odyssey had given Thaw hope that he also would soon be free: Cascone had spent almost three years on death row in Sing Sing Prison, but his lawyers had won an appeal. Remarkably, after several witnesses had refused to testify against the defendant, the jury acquitted him of murder in his second trial.

Later that day, shortly before six o'clock, the jurors returned to the Knickerbocker Hotel for dinner. They had spent the day discussing the murder, combing through the evidence, and now they ate in silence, each man keeping his thoughts to himself. There had been no progress through seven ballots — three jurors were still holding out for a conviction on the murder charge — and no one was optimistic that they would soon reach a decision.

But that evening, after they had returned to the Criminal Courts Building, Charles Gremmels changed his vote. It was possible, he now admitted, that Thaw's medical history, his nervous temperament, might have predisposed him to a sudden derangement and he may have become insane on seeing Stanford White at the theater. Gremmels joined the majority, voting on the eighth ballot to acquit Thaw. Now only two jurors, John Holbert and Frank Howell, still held out for conviction.

The next morning at ten o'clock, Evelyn Nesbit arrived alone at the courthouse. She had slept fitfully, full of anxiety that there had been no word from the jury. "Why can't they agree?" she asked plaintively, speaking to a cluster of journalists waiting in the hallway. "I don't see what keeps them out. A disagreement may mean a third trial, and that would be awful." She gave a heavy sigh as she contemplated appearing as a witness for a third time. "Poor, poor Harry!"[30]

Travers Jerome arrived half an hour later. A reporter for the *New York World* called out a question to the district attorney, asking if he would put Thaw on trial a third time, but Jerome ignored the question, saying only that he had hoped for a decision the previous day. "I guess," he replied, walking to the elevator, "it will be another disagreement. Too bad!"[31]

Shortly before one o'clock Jerome reemerged, appearing from the elevator, striding across the main hall toward the courtroom. There was a bustle in the hallways and corridors, a sudden stirring among the crowd as word spread that the jurors were about to enter the courtroom. Two bailiffs stood by the doorway, watching as the onlookers surged toward them, each spectator rushing forward to get a seat before the doors slammed shut.

Victor Dowling stepped onto the stairs that led to the bench, and simultaneously the jurors walked into the courtroom in single file, each man expressionless, his eyes looking directly ahead.

The voice of the clerk rang out—"Harry K. Thaw to the bar!"—and Thaw, his shoulders square, his face white, a slight smile on his lips, stepped forward, moving one pace away from the defense table. He glanced over his shoulder, nodding first to his wife and then to his brother, before turning to face the jury.

"The jury will rise." William Penney paused, waiting as the jurors rose from their seats. "Jury, look upon the defendant. Defendant, look upon the jury.

"Gentlemen of the jury," Penney continued, "have you agreed upon a verdict?"

"We have," Charles Gremmels answered, a touch of anxiety in his voice.

"How say you, gentlemen of the jury, do you find the defendant at the bar, Harry K. Thaw, guilty as indicted or not guilty?"

"We find the defendant," Gremmels replied, glancing sideways at the other jurors, seated on his left, as if to seek their support, "not guilty on the ground of his insanity at the time of the commission of the act."[32]

For a fraction of a second, no more, there was a hush, a sudden silence, and then the sound of a man clapping shook the spectators from their trance. The judge banged his gavel on the bench, signaling the bailiffs to arrest the offender, and the crowd watched as the officers escorted the man from the room. Harry Thaw, a triumphant grin on his face, had turned to look at his wife, hoping to catch her eye, but Dowling had already started to speak, and everyone's attention was on the judge's words.

"An obligation," Dowling began, "now devolves upon the Court to discharge its duty....Upon the testimony in this case, apart from any other consideration that might arise, the Court is satisfied that the enlargement of the defendant would be dangerous to the public safety....It is ordered that the said

Harry K. Thaw be detained in safe custody and be sent to the Matteawan State Hospital, there to be kept in said hospital until thence discharged by due course of law."[33]

The grin had already faded from Thaw's face, and he looked at his attorneys, expecting them to intervene. The lawyers had held out hope that the judge would allow the family to send Harry to a private sanatorium, but Dowling had defied their expectations, committing Harry to Matteawan, the state hospital for the criminal insane. A deputy sheriff, John Breitenbach, moved to escort Thaw from the courtroom, and the attorneys Martin Littleton, Russell Peabody, and Daniel O'Reilly all followed, walking in single file to the sheriff's office at the rear of the building.

Only now, after Thaw had left the courtroom, did he understand that he would travel that evening under armed guard to the Matteawan asylum. The sheriff had already made the necessary preparations; a train on the Central New England Railway would leave Grand Central Terminal at five o'clock, arriving at Fishkill Landing two hours later. He told the attorneys that he would allow Thaw to cross back to the Tombs to collect his belongings, but there would be no delay otherwise.

"You never told me," Thaw shouted, angrily turning on his lawyers, "he would send me to Matteawan. I will not go to Matteawan." How could he live with the lunatics, the criminal insane? The Matteawan asylum, an institution with a fearsome reputation, contained hundreds of violent criminals, including some of the most notorious murderers in the state. The legislature had never provided sufficient funds for its operations, and the asylum attendants, overworked and under-paid, were not reluctant to use violence against troublesome inmates. It was impossible, unthinkable for him to spend even a brief period of confinement in such an infamous place.

"Where did you think he would send you, Harry?" Daniel O'Reilly, his patience stretched to its limit, refused to tolerate Thaw's petulance any longer. "Did you think he would send you to Rector's or Martin's?"

Martin Littleton stepped forward, seeking to reassure Harry, trying to persuade him that there was no alternative. "You must go," Littleton said. "There's such a thing as public senti-ment in this town." Public opinion would not tolerate the immediate release of a man who had murdered another man before hundreds of witnesses. Many New Yorkers had viewed the shooting as justified and had favored Harry Thaw during the two trials; but the public was fickle, and he could lose sym-pathy just as easily as he had won it.[34]

That afternoon the heavy gates at the rear entrance of the Tombs suddenly swung open and a large black sedan edged its way through the waiting crowd. Several constables, each hold-ing a wooden club, walked alongside the limousine, pushing people back, striking out at any onlookers who stood in the way. The car accelerated along Lafayette Street, and Harry Thaw, seated between two deputies, watched as the crowd fell back, hooting and yelling in its disappointment. The sheriff had allowed Evelyn Nesbit to travel with her husband as far as Grand Central, but she said nothing, only looking out at the stores as they traveled north along Broadway. The car left

Broadway at Twenty-third Street, turning onto Fourth Avenue, and there, on the left, they could see Madison Square Garden, its great bulk looming over the neighboring buildings.

Neither Evelyn nor Harry made any remark, seeming not to notice the place where Harry had killed Stanford White, and ten minutes later the limousine arrived at Grand Central. Evelyn tearfully embraced Harry as they stepped away from the car, whispering her affection, promising to visit him at the asylum early the next week. She stood watching, tears in her eyes, as the deputies escorted Harry into the terminal, waiting until she could see him no longer, and then she turned away, solitary and alone, finally disappearing into the crowds of passers-by on the avenue.[35]

7

ASYLUM

February 1, 1908–August 17, 1913

A DOZEN PHOTOGRAPHERS STOOD WATCHING THE TRAIN AS IT
entered the station. Some passengers stepped onto the platform
and the photographers moved closer, the flashbulbs of their
cameras suddenly flaring, the bright lights casting shadows in
the evening darkness. Several reporters shouted questions at
Harry Thaw as a deputy sheriff, Joseph Bell, escorted the prisoner to a waiting cab. It was a short ride, slightly less than three
miles, from Fishkill Landing to the state asylum, a large redbrick building on the heights above the Hudson River.

The asylum — the Matteawan State Hospital for the Criminal Insane — had first opened in 1892. Its main building, three
stories high, contained administrative offices and residential
quarters for the doctors and nurses. Several large dormitories,
constructed on the Kirkbride plan, in an echelon pattern that
allowed each dormitory to receive sunlight, extended outward on either side of the administration building, along a
ridge that overlooked the Hudson.[1]

The bucolic location, in the open countryside, three miles from the nearest village, could not have been more agreeable; but conditions within the asylum had sharply deteriorated since the turn of the century. The asylum had opened with a capacity for 550 patients, but in February 1908, when Harry Thaw first arrived, there were more than 700 inmates. The staff had squeezed additional beds into the wards and placed more in the corridors, but the cramped conditions led inevitably to fights among the patients.

State Hospital, Matteawan, N. Y.

The Matteawan State Hospital for the Criminal Insane opened in 1892 with a capacity for 550 patients, but by February 1908, when Harry Thaw entered the asylum, it had more than 700 inmates. *(Dr. Robert Matz Collection, New York Academy of Medicine Library)*

The attendants, men and women recruited from nearby villages, had scant loyalty to the institution. They worked long hours for low pay, and they received neither any provision for disability nor any pension. There was a lack of discipline among the staff, and even the doctors, overworked and under-paid, had little sympathy for the men and women in their care. Violence and abuse were commonplace.[2]

The superintendent, Robert Lamb, had already indicated that there would be no special treatment for the new inmate. Harry Thaw would spend his first week in an observation ward to determine the character of his illness. The physicians would then assign him to the appropriate ward for the remainder of his time at the asylum. "He cannot have any special quarters," Lamb remarked in an interview with a reporter from the *New York Herald*, "for all the patients here are treated alike. During the day he will associate with the men and dine at the table in the main dining-room. Thaw will be given no special work to do."[3]

Lamb assigned Thaw to a dormitory in the North Ward, a large, narrow rectangular room designed to accommodate fifty inmates. A row of beds, each bed only three feet from its nearest neighbor, ran along both sides of the dormitory, and a small wooden dresser stood at the foot of each bed. Each morning at six o'clock a loud bell sounded for reveille, and at seven o'clock all inmates, except for those in the isolation wards, gathered for breakfast — oatmeal, milk, and coffee — in the main dining hall.

There was little organized activity during the day; inmates could read in the library or play checkers and chess in the rec-reation room. Occasionally a choral society or theater group from one of the nearby villages would perform in the auditorium. There was a pervasive torpor, an unavoidable tedium that had taken hold of daily life in the asylum. A bell sounded at noon for lunch in the dining hall and the inmates gathered again at six o'clock for dinner—bread and butter, cold meats, stewed prunes, and tea—before going to bed at nine o'clock each evening.[4]

Thaw was sullen and withdrawn during his first day at Matteawan. He had no access to either cigars or alcohol—an intolerable imposition, he protested—and he regarded the other inmates in his dormitory with foreboding. Quimbo Appo, a triple murderer, occupied an adjacent bed, and Appo was the first inmate to approach Thaw, asking for his assistance in an escape plan. Other inmates, resentful at their treatment in the asylum, welcomed any opportunity to speak to a newcomer, and they too buttonholed Thaw, telling him their complaints. Thaw, who regarded himself as sane, unhappily shared his dormitory with rapists, arsonists, and murderers. It was a distressing experience, made palatable only by his expectation that he would soon be released.[5]

His attorneys Daniel O'Reilly and Russell Peabody had accompanied Thaw on the train journey from New York, telling him that he would quickly win his freedom. It was necessary only, O'Reilly confided, that the superintendent of the asylum sign a certificate of recovery to testify that Thaw had regained his sanity. Alternatively, Thaw could petition the courts for a writ of habeas corpus, claiming that, since he was no longer insane, there were no grounds for his continued detention.

There had been a recent precedent in the case of Richard

Preusser, a stockbroker who had shot and killed a gambler, Myles McDonnell, during a quarrel. Preusser's lawyers had persuaded the jury at his trial in June 1906 that he was insane. His behavior in the courtroom had been appropriately eccentric; his wife had testified to his peculiarities; and expert witnesses had all claimed that Preusser was a paranoiac. The jury had agreed with the diagnosis and the judge had committed Preusser to Matteawan, but he remained in the asylum for only five weeks, the superintendent, Robert Lamb, agreeing almost immediately to sign a certificate of recovery.[6]

There was no reason why Harry Thaw should not also win his freedom in like manner. Thaw's murder of Stanford White had been more noteworthy on account of the celebrity of his victim, and Thaw had shot White before hundreds of witnesses; but it was necessary only to allow public interest to subside for Thaw to quietly leave the asylum. It required patience on Thaw's part, his lawyers told him, an acknowledgment that a certain amount of time must pass to avoid the suspicion that his wealth had unfairly purchased his freedom, allowing him to evade justice.

Evelyn Nesbit, accompanied by Daniel O'Reilly, visited her husband for the first time on Monday, February 3, arriving at Fishkill Landing on the midday train from Manhattan. O'Reilly had arranged for them to have lunch at a nearby hotel, Holland House, before continuing on to the asylum; but news of their arrival spread rapidly through the village, and a crowd of sightseers trailed behind as they walked along the high street, not abandoning the pursuit until Evelyn entered the hotel.

It was a chilly day, with temperatures close to freezing; there had been a light snowfall the previous evening, and the carriage ride to the asylum, winding along backcountry roads, seemed interminable. But suddenly their destination appeared above them, on the brow of the nearest hill. It was an incongruous sight: the massive redbrick buildings, stacked together on top of the ridge, stood alone in open country. There were no other carriages on the road, no nearby houses, no signs of life, not even any birdsong to break the silence, but only an endless snowy-white expanse stretching out on all sides. The asylum was not, as Evelyn had anticipated, a melancholy place, gloomy and forbidding. The compact redbrick construction seemed rather to promise efficiency and resolve, a determination to cure the afflictions of the inmates who resided within its walls.

Harry had been waiting expectantly for her visit, and he held her in his arms, kissing her affectionately. He had arrived on Saturday evening, almost forty-eight hours before, and already he had become more accustomed to his surroundings. The food was surprisingly edible, he told Evelyn, and the superintendent allowed inmates to order meals from the village. Harry had entertained himself that morning by playing the piano in the recreation room, and he expected soon to join the orchestra. It was unfortunate, of course, that the superintendent had banned smoking; but several of the attendants were more accommodating, and it was possible to sneak a

cigarette in the courtyard at the rear of the building. The
other inmates were certainly an eccentric lot—no one could
deny that—but the truly dangerous men were kept in the isolation wards, Harry said, and his companions in the open
wards seemed harmless.[7]

But Evelyn was incredulous that Harry could be so noncha-
lant about his changed circumstances. The chief physician,
Amos Baker, had greeted her at the main entrance, escorting
her along the central corridor to a room adjacent to the observation ward, and everywhere she had observed the patients
mumbling to themselves, one man furiously scratching himself, another waving his arms frantically to no purpose, a third
standing motionless against a wall, a fourth, his face twisted
in rage, mouthing silent curses. Other inmates shuffled aimlessly in their slippers, clutching protectively at their blue flannel gowns, casting suspicious looks in her direction, evidently
unaccustomed to the sight of an attractive woman in their
midst. Even the young patients, the men in their twenties,
Evelyn thought, seemed forlorn, hopelessly lost to their afflictions, their vacant expressions signaling their mental deterioration.

Amos Baker chatted politely with Daniel O'Reilly while
Evelyn continued to talk with her husband; and then, as she
turned away, indicating that she was ready to leave, Baker
offered to show his visitors around the women's wards. Most
of the female patients suffered from dementia praecox, and
the medical staff, Baker said with obvious pride, had succeeded in curing several women, enabling them to return to
their families. Baker continued to talk as they made their way

through the wards, occasionally pausing to exchange words with the nurses. He stopped before a heavy metal door and waited as an attendant searched for the key to the lock. "When we enter the next ward," Baker warned, "keep directly behind me as we walk down the center of the room.... Don't be frightened."[8]

They entered a long rectangular room, stepping onto a strip of carpet that ran from one end to the other. There was a stirring in the half light and Evelyn suddenly realized that several dozen women, some in blue flannel gowns, a few entirely naked, were chained to the floor on either side of the windowless room. An unpleasant odor hung in the air, and Evelyn could see that one or two women had soiled themselves. There was no furniture, no tables or chairs, nothing on which the women could sit or rest, and the gray, grubby walls were bare, without any decoration. An attendant led the way, walking along the strip of carpet toward a second metal door at the far end, and the women, awakened by their entrance, shuffled across the floor toward them, screaming and cursing, lunging at them, only to be held back by the chains. Soon the visitors passed safely through the second metal door.[9]

It had been a terrifying experience, made more disquieting by the impression that the physician seemed to regard her obvious discomfort with amusement. It was an episode that reinforced Evelyn's determination that Harry should be freed from the asylum as soon as possible. The lawyers were disinclined to act, counseling patience, but Evelyn was alarmed, fearing that the conditions of Harry's incarceration would cause his mental deterioration. "What a terrible place!" she exclaimed to the reporters waiting at the asylum entrance. "I would be crazy myself if I stayed here for a week. I hope never to look again upon the sights that I saw to-day. All around my husband were grinning men, some of them counting their fingers, some of them murmuring endless tales to themselves. It is not right that he should be confined in such a place."[10]

Mary Thaw had not yet visited her son, but she too believed that it was unjust to compel Harry to live with the criminal lunatics at Matteawan. If the authorities would not release him, she remarked to reporters, they should either allow the family to pay for his care in a private sanatorium or transfer him to a state hospital with a more tolerant regimen. "I don't care where he is sent," she stated, "just so we are permitted to aid in his recovery. I only know that Matteawan means slow but certain death to my son."[11]

But the superintendent, Robert Lamb, had no intention of signing a certificate of recovery to allow Thaw to leave the asylum. Lamb, thirty-eight years old, had worked in the state asylums since his graduation from the Albany Medical College in 1891. It had been an opportune time for a young doctor who hoped to establish his career in the treatment of the criminal insane: the Matteawan State Hospital had opened in 1892 and a second asylum, the Dannemora State Hospital, had opened in 1900. Robert Lamb had first worked at Matteawan, initially as a junior physician, subsequently as the chief medical officer, leaving the asylum in 1900 for an appointment as the superintendent at Dannemora. It was a challenging assignment: the Dannemora asylum held those prisoners convicted of a felony, and the inmates, almost all of whom had committed violent crimes, were relentlessly disruptive, attacking the staff and attempting to escape. Lamb nevertheless proved to be an able administrator, managing an impossible task well, and in 1904 he returned to the Matteawan State Hospital to serve as superintendent there.[12]

Lamb had established his reputation within the state asylums and had no wish to harm his career by allowing Harry Thaw his freedom. The newspapers would whip up a storm of protest against Thaw's release; the public would believe that Thaw had cheated justice on account of his wealth; and condemnation would fall exclusively on the shoulders of that individual who had permitted Thaw his liberty.

There would be the suspicion that the Thaw family had bribed Lamb to sign a certificate of recovery. It might never be proved that there had been a bribe; there might never be any evidence to support the accusation, and Lamb could claim that he had signed the certificate in good faith; but no one would believe him, and he, Lamb, could never prove that he had not accepted a bribe. There was, in short, no good reason why the superintendent would be so foolish as to allow Harry Thaw to leave the asylum.

Lamb might refuse to sign a certificate of recovery, but according to Thaw's attorneys, an application for a writ of habeas corpus, requiring the state to show the grounds for Thaw's incarceration, was more likely to succeed. The New York newspapers would kick up a fuss, of course, but who would contest the writ? There was little likelihood, for instance, that any of Stanford White's relatives or acquaintances would challenge an application for habeas corpus. Stanford White's widow, Bessie, now lived abroad, only occasionally returning to the United States, and she could hardly be expected to return from Europe to oppose the petition.

Dutchess County would oppose Thaw's petition, challenging his release from the asylum; but Mary Thaw had already instructed her lawyers that she was willing to spend any amount necessary to secure her son's freedom. She would underwrite the campaign with her money, even petitioning for successive writs until she had won Harry's freedom. Would Dutchess County be willing to devote its limited resources to keeping Thaw in the asylum? Could the county sustain the expense of a prolonged legal battle, one that might last for years?

The initiative to free Thaw began on April 20, when Joseph Morschauser, a judge on the Supreme Court of New York, allowed the request by Thaw's lawyer, James Graham, to apply for a writ of habeas corpus. There was no basis, Graham claimed in his application, for Thaw's continued detention at Matteawan. The jury in the second trial had acquitted Thaw because of his insanity at the time of the murder. But there had never been any inquiry into Thaw's present mental condition, and the judge, Victor Dowling, had not considered any evidence that might have demonstrated that Thaw was now sane. "He stands before the court," Graham declared, "an innocent man, with no charge against him and with no adjudication of insanity."[13]

It seemed quixotic to claim that Thaw had recovered his sanity. His attorneys during the second trial, less than three months before, had maintained that Thaw had been mentally unbalanced since infancy, and it appeared far-fetched to assert that he had already recovered. Nevertheless, the judge issued the writ of habeas corpus, saying that he would hold a hearing in Poughkeepsie the following month.

Most observers predicted that the hearing would last several weeks. Francis Garvan, the assistant district attorney, expected it to last at least a month, perhaps longer, and claimed that it would be ruinous for the taxpayers of Dutchess County. The expense of a hearing would likely amount to $30,000, and other asylum inmates, moreover, might follow the precedent set by Thaw in demanding a writ of habeas corpus. The county would soon be forced into bankruptcy as a consequence. "How would the people of this county like it," Garvan inquired, "if under this new precedent every one of them insisted on a hearing here?"[14]

The hearing opened on May 14 but, remarkably, lasted only four days. Thaw's attorney, James Graham, had too little acquaintance with the details of the case, and he came ill-prepared. Travers Jerome had the advantage of long experience with Harry Thaw, and Jerome, moreover, could present one witness whose testimony seemed incontrovertible. Amos Baker, the chief medical officer at Matteawan, had observed Thaw since his arrival at the asylum, often talking with him about the murder of Stanford White. Thaw's behavior, according to Baker, had been consistently eccentric. On one occasion he had ordered two hundred chocolate éclairs from a local bakery, saying that he had bought them for the hospital attendants, and on another occasion Thaw had announced his intention to decorate the wards with Easter lilies. He frequently violated the regulations, smoking cigars on the ward, refusing to permit the physicians to examine him, and demanding that the staff allow him to drink whiskey with his meals.

"Did you," Jerome asked, "regard his conduct, appearance and language as abnormal?"

"I did," Baker replied.

"Is it in your experience that lunatics often show a subtle cunning?"

"It is."

"Do you regard him as insane at this time?"

"I do."

"Do you think he has a form of insanity which would make him dangerous and a menace if released?"

"I certainly do," Baker answered.

Later that month Morschauser dismissed the writ of habeas corpus, ruling that Thaw would remain in the asylum. "I am satisfied," the judge declared, "that the mental condition of Harry K. Thaw has not changed.... The safety of the public is better insured by his remaining in custody and under observation until he has recovered or until such time as it has been reasonably certain that there is no danger of a recurrent attack.... I find that he is now insane, and that it is so manifest as to make it unsafe for him to be at large."[15]

Mary Thaw had failed to anticipate that Morschauser would deny the writ, and she now realized, for the first time, that the struggle to free Harry might not end quickly. There would be a second attempt, of course, but it could not be done in haste. Her lawyers would need time to prepare.

She had never reconciled herself to her son's marriage to Evelyn Nesbit, and now she began to prepare the groundwork for their divorce. She had always believed her daughter-in-law to be the cause of Harry's troubles. Evelyn had entrapped her son, gradually casting a spell over him, luring him to his doom. Harry would have had no reason, other than his infatuation with Evelyn, to kill Stanford White, and there would have been no scandal if he had never met her.

It mattered not at all to Mary Thaw that Evelyn had testified on her son's behalf in 1907, and again in 1908, and that she had thereby saved Harry from the electric chair. It mattered not one jot that Evelyn had sacrificed her reputation for Harry's sake, telling the world about her scandalous liaison with a married man three times her age. Mary Thaw regarded Evelyn Nesbit as no better than a strumpet who had played her part on the Broadway stage, and she now bitterly regretted that she had ever allowed her son to marry a cocotte.

She had tolerated her daughter-in-law these past eighteen months solely because Evelyn had been so willing to testify in Harry's defense; but Evelyn's testimony was no longer needed. It was now necessary only for the psychiatrists to demonstrate that he had recovered his sanity, and it would serve no purpose for Evelyn to tell her story again.

Private detectives had shadowed Evelyn for several months, surreptitiously watching her, taking notes on her acquaintances, sending weekly reports to Mary Thaw on her movements. In 1907 Evelyn had moved, at Harry's expense, from the Hotel Lorraine to a house on Park Avenue between Fifty-sixth and Fifty-seventh Streets, and detectives watched the entrance night and day, secretly recording her visitors.

There was little to report, but Mary Thaw felt nevertheless that she had sufficient information to provide Harry with a dossier listing those occasions when her detectives had seen Evelyn with a male companion. The New York newspapers, breathlessly reporting Evelyn's movements about town, also played their part in stirring Harry's jealousy into a frenzy; and soon the breach between Harry and his wife had become irreparable.[16]

Attorneys for the Thaw family were quick to propose a settlement: Evelyn would file for an annulment of the marriage, telling the newspapers that she alone was responsible for the initiative. She would receive an immediate payment of $15,000 in cash and an annual payment for life of $12,000. She would agree to abandon any other claims on Harry for support, and she would make no request for alimony.

It was a happy end to an unpleasant situation — but Evelyn soon learned that her adversary had attempted to deceive her. She had received three checks from Mary Thaw, each for $5,000, drawn on the Union National Bank of Pittsburgh, but the bank had refused payment, saying that there were insufficient funds in the account. It had all been a despicable trick, and Evelyn withdrew her lawsuit on May 26, telling the court that she no longer wished to have the marriage annulled.[17]

From time to time Harry sent her small amounts of money, fifty dollars one week, seventy-five the next, but she knew that his generosity might end peremptorily, without any warning. His payments on the rent for the Park Avenue house stopped that summer, and Evelyn moved to a studio apartment at 31 West Thirty-third Street, behind the Waldorf Hotel. She lived a bohemian existence, seeing friends from her Broadway days, taking the occasional literature course at Columbia University, going to Pittsburgh once a year to visit her mother; but she made no plans for the future, not even attempting her return to the stage.[18]

Harry Thaw renewed his application for a writ of habeas corpus in 1909, but his second attempt seemed no more likely to succeed than the first. Isaac Mills, a judge on the Supreme Court for the Ninth Judicial District, granted the application, scheduling the hearing to begin on July 13 in White Plains, a village in Westchester County, just north of New York City. The attorneys for the state, having heard of the rift between Evelyn and her husband's family, issued a subpoena for her appearance, but she proved a reluctant witness.

Evelyn, wearing a blue serge jacket and holding a gold mesh pocketbook, appeared in court on the first day of the hearing. She seemed relaxed, almost languid, as if she had become accustomed to testifying under oath; but her outward appearance masked an inner turmoil. She was alone, without any allies, without even any legal counsel who could give her advice. Her mother-in-law, Mary Thaw, seated directly behind the attorneys, was indignant that Evelyn should testify against her son, and her face was tense with rage and anger. Harry's sisters, Alice and Margaret, sat next to their mother, their distress written in their expressions, their hostility toward Evelyn evident in every glance. Harry alone seemed to bear her no ill will, and he regarded his wife almost dispassionately, as if her testimony could have no effect on his campaign to win his freedom.[19]

The deputy attorney general, Roger Clarke, stepped to the front of the courtroom, standing directly before the witness. Clarke had heard rumors that Harry Thaw had threatened his wife, but he knew nothing more substantial, and he had had no opportunity to talk beforehand with Evelyn Nesbit about her testimony.

"Your full name?" Clarke asked.

"Evelyn Nesbit Thaw."

"You are the wife of Harry K. Thaw?"

"I am."

"You recall Mr. Thaw's commitment to Matteawan?"

"Yes."

"Did you go there and see him?"

"Yes."

"Do you recall an occasion when you went there some months ago with Mr. Daniel O'Reilly?"

"Yes."

"Did Harry K. Thaw on that occasion say anything to you in the nature of a threat to kill you, Mrs. Thaw?"

"I don't wish to answer—I don't want to answer."

Clarke turned to address the judge. There was no reason, he said, why the witness should refuse to answer his questions.

She had not claimed that her answers would incriminate her. There was a subpoena compelling her to testify, and she would otherwise be in contempt of court.

"Your Honor," Clarke stated, "as Mrs. Thaw does not claim any privilege, I must ask that she be instructed to answer."

"Unless you claim a privilege, madam," warned Mills, "it is your duty to answer."[20]

"When you visited Mr. Harry K. Thaw shortly after his commitment to the Matteawan State Hospital," Clarke continued, "did you hear Harry Thaw say 'When I get out of here I shall have to kill you?'"

Evelyn turned pleadingly to the judge. "Now I've got to answer that question?" she asked. She could not, she would not, testify against her husband. She knew too well his vindictive nature; she knew too well that he would harbor a grudge against her, and she was fearful of the consequences if she should be the cause of his continued imprisonment in the Matteawan asylum.

"You must answer it, madam," Mills insisted.

"But Your Honor, you see I am here under a subpoena from the State. I came here against my will." Evelyn spoke frantically, her words coming in rapid bursts as if the urgency of her speech might force the judge to acknowledge her dilemma. "I'm frightened and terribly afraid of him. If I answer I'll earn Thaw's everlasting enmity and hatred. . . . He will refuse to support me any more and I can't live without anything. And besides, I'm still married to him."

"I appreciate your position thoroughly," Mills answered. He spoke with a gentleness that reflected the sympathy he felt for her. "It is a very distressing situation, but I don't see what I can do. What you have said makes no difference in the eye of the law, and you must answer."

"But I'm still married to him, still married to him. These people already hate me, and if I answer he will hate me always. I don't want to answer. I'd rather not. Is there no way out of it?"

"You must answer."

She had no choice; she could not evade the question. Evelyn, now resigned to her fate, turned to face the deputy attorney general with a defiant expression on her face, resolute in her determination not to acknowledge the hostile looks of Harry Thaw's mother and sisters.

"Yes, he did," Evelyn testified, finally. "He said: 'When I get out of here, I suppose I shall have to kill you, next.'"[21]

Harry Thaw, speaking afterward to a reporter from the *New York World*, denied that he had threatened Evelyn. His attorneys, Thaw claimed, would show that Evelyn had written to him affectionately long after her visit to the asylum. He had continued to support his wife, providing her with a generous allowance, but it was never enough, and Evelyn constantly clamored for more money.

"That was always the cry," Thaw complained ruefully, "more money; more money! If we gave her a million tomorrow she'd be back for more in a week." Evelyn had no self-restraint, no ability to temper her extravagance; she often purchased the most fanciful items on a whim. "Evelyn will be taken care of," Thaw promised. "She will receive regularly her $70 every week and her $200 every month, no matter what happens. She cannot say she has been abandoned or thrown on her own resources."[22]

Other witnesses testified during the hearing, some for the state, some for Harry Thaw, some to say that Thaw was still insane, others to claim that he was rational. The psychiatrists repeated their testimony, explaining to the court how the available evidence supported their various diagnoses. Travers Jerome played his customary role, cross-examining the witnesses and reading into the record the transcript of the testimony given at the second trial, testimony that Thaw had been irrational almost since birth.[23]

It had all become so painfully familiar to those observers who had followed the twists and turns of the Thaw saga over the previous three years. The same evidence had been presented so many times. Was there anything that had not already been said so often before?

There was nothing to indicate, on the morning of July 28, that the testimony that day would be any different. The attorneys for the state chatted together, waiting for the judge to take his place on the bench; Harry Thaw, on the other side of the aisle, whispered some remarks to his lawyer, Charles Morschauser, turning occasionally to say a few words to his mother, Mary, and his sisters, Margaret and Alice; and the spectators, scattered haphazardly around the half-empty courtroom, waited in drowsy expectation. It promised to be another hot July day, sticky with humidity, and the bailiffs had opened the windows wide to allow a faint breeze to blow across the room.

The first witness appeared, taking the oath before sitting in the high-backed chair at the front of the courtroom, and the New York reporters exchanged quizzical glances, as if to demand her identity. She was between forty and forty-five years old, a short, stocky woman, her raven-black hair tucked unobtrusively beneath her bonnet, her coal-black eyes darting nervously around the courtroom. She had been attractive twenty years before, but she was now obese; her round face had a fleshy appearance, and her flabby cheeks quivered slightly as she spoke. She wore a dark-blue skirt and a blue jacket; there was a white handkerchief in her left hand, gripped tightly between her pudgy fingers; and her jewelry—silver bracelets on each wrist, diamond rings on her fingers—sparkled in the morning sunlight.

Harry Thaw stared in amazement at her unexpected appearance. His face flushed crimson red, and he quickly bowed his head, looking neither right nor left, his gaze fixed on the documents lying before him on the defense table. His attorney whispered in his ear, asking him to identify the witness, but Thaw remained mute, struck dumb with embarrassment.

Few spectators noticed that Jerome had quietly taken a leather satchel from a chair by his side. He removed a whip from the satchel, placing it on the table in front of him, before returning the empty satchel to the chair. The district attorney remained motionless, looking down at the whip for a few seconds before speaking to his witness.

"Do you know Harry K. Thaw?" Jerome asked, his rasping voice suddenly breaking the silence of the courtroom.

"I certainly do," Susan Merrill replied cheerfully. She smiled as she looked across the room at Thaw, almost as if she were expecting him to acknowledge her presence, but Thaw continued to stare down at the documents before him.

"Tell us how you came to know him," Jerome continued.

"When I took a place of my own, at No. 241 West Forty-third street, he engaged rooms from me."

"For what did he say he wanted the rooms?"

"He said he wanted them for the theatrical business. That was in the fall of 1903. He said he was in the business of engaging and placing young ladies from all over the country on the stage. He came there mostly in the daytime to meet the young ladies who called for him." The girls, Merrill continued, had come to the house in expectation of an audition for a position in the theater; but Thaw had straightaway taken each girl to an upstairs room at the rear of the building.

"Now, Mrs. Merrill." Jerome seemed suddenly solemn, as if to impress upon his witness the gravity of the occasion. "Did you ever notice any unusual occurrences in those rooms which Mr. Thaw rented from you?"

Susan Merrill hesitated, turning in her chair to face the judge. "Must I tell everything?" she appealed.

"Yes," Isaac Mills replied abruptly, "everything."

"I did see many unusual things there; many very strange things. Mr. Thaw had a great many visitors, a great many. Most of them were young women, very young girls, not over fifteen or sixteen years old, many of them, though some were older.

"There is one incident I recall very well. A very young girl had gone up to Mr. Thaw's rooms and soon I heard a great hollering from there. I rushed up and went through the parlor into the bedroom and found he had been beating her. She had great welts on her limbs and neck and was crying out that he was trying to murder her."

"What was his position when you entered the room?"

"Why, he was bending over her with a whip in the act of striking her. He put down the whip when he saw me and went out."

"Is this the whip?" Jerome asked. He showed her the whip, allowing her to take it in her hands. It was a sidesaddle horse-whip, about three feet long, with a whalebone stock and an ivory grip inlaid with gold filigree.

"Yes, that is the whip," she replied. "At least that's one of his whips. He had three or four different kinds.

"I heard the screaming and found him just in the act of striking her with the whip. When I went in there was a lot of fussing and she cried a lot, and then when he was gone I saw the whip on the table."

She had comforted the girl before returning downstairs. Thaw was still in the house, standing in the parlor, smoking a cigar, listening as the girl upstairs continued to cry and sob. Merrill had ordered Thaw to leave her house, berating him, demanding to know why he had beaten the girl. He had answered her defiantly, explaining that the girl had been truculent in her manner, saying that he had tried to teach her how to behave.

Thaw called again at the house a few days later, offering to pay compensation to the girl for her injuries and promising that the episode would not recur. Susan Merrill, according to her testimony, relented, allowing Thaw again to have rooms in the house; but she caught Thaw a second time in the act of striking a young girl.

"The very same thing," Merrill said, "happened again in a day or two, over and over again."

"How often," Jerome asked, "did you actually see him strike girls with a whip?"

"Well, three different girls on different occasions."

"What did he ever tell you about his reasons for whipping these girls?"

"He answered me that they'd been bad girls, that they weren't smart and he'd had to beat them to teach them something.... He would say he couldn't make the girls learn stage work properly without he got angry with them and whipped them."[24]

Thaw returned to the house many times, each time attacking some unsuspecting victim. Merrill remonstrated with Thaw, and he would invariably express regret, promising each time that he would never again attack anyone.

Travers Jerome seemed content to end his direct examination, indicating to the judge that he had no further questions. Susan Merrill, despite her initial anxiety, had been an excellent witness, providing detailed descriptions of Thaw's behavior at her house. Thaw had always dismissed the gossip that he whipped young girls as malicious invention, fabricated for the purpose of blackmail, but now, for the first time, a witness had testified under oath that she had seen Thaw in the act of striking a girl. Thaw's attorneys did their best to discredit her testimony on cross-examination, attempting to expose contradictions in her account, but Jerome had taken them by surprise and there was little they could do.

Charles Morschauser reminded Merrill that she claimed to have been horrified by Thaw's violent behavior—yet she had permitted him to return to her house many times. Why had she allowed Thaw to rent rooms when she had repeatedly witnessed his attacks on the girls?

"Why did you keep him with all these scenes going?"

"He always promised to be good," Merrill replied. She glanced angrily at Thaw as she explained that he had threatened her if she ever reported him to the authorities. "If you want to know, he told me he'd kill me."

Thaw had paid the girls for their silence, bringing Merrill thousands of dollars to distribute to his victims. After his arrest in 1906, while he was in the Tombs, he had fretted that the girls would testify against him. Thaw's lawyers at the time, Russell Peabody and Clifford Hartridge, had often come to her house to give her money for the girls.

"It went for their expenses and to keep them silent," she added.

"How much?" Morschauser demanded.

"Oh, it was vast sums, vast sums of money," Merrill replied airily, giving a sweeping motion with her hand as if to indicate the sacks of money that Thaw had provided. "It was always cash, always cash; money, money, money." She looked around the courtroom and her gaze fell on Mary Thaw, sitting bolt upright, her face pale, her lips pursed with anger; and Susan Merrill, contemplating that the matriarch had unknowingly provided the money for her son, gave a short, sardonic laugh.

One girl, she remembered, had received $7,000 for her trouble. There had been many girls, perhaps as many as two hundred in the years since Thaw first rented rooms from her, and all of them had received similar sums.

"Any receipts?"

"No, indeed." Merrill smiled. "No receipt asked or needed, one way or the other."

"Recall any other sums you paid out?"

"Yes, there was two little girls that came from Atlanta, Ga., to see Thaw. I gave them $3000 or $4000. These two were very young girls, I recall."[25]

The hearing lasted almost two more weeks, until August 8, but no other witness could compete for dramatic effect with Susan Merrill. Harry Thaw issued a statement to the press denouncing her testimony as perjury, saying that such stories were attempts to extort money from his family, but his lawyers were unable to produce any evidence that Susan Merrill had ever attempted to blackmail Thaw.

Merrill's testimony served not only to blacken Thaw's character but also to remind the reporters that Jerome had previously introduced an affidavit, allegedly signed by Evelyn Nesbit, stating that Thaw had whipped her to coerce her to testify that Stanford White had raped her. Evelyn had denied that she signed the affidavit; but could she have been lying on the witness stand to save her husband from the electric chair?

Was her subsequent account, that White had drugged and raped her, false, an elaborate fiction invented to protect Harry Thaw?

Amos Baker, the chief physician at Matteawan, testified on Tuesday, August 3, saying that he had observed Thaw carefully during his confinement, taking detailed notes on his deportment and behavior since he had first arrived at the asylum. Thaw had often appeared restless and uneasy; his memory was defective, his intelligence below normal, and his judgment faulty; he was careless about his appearance, leaving his shoes unlaced and his hair unkempt; and he had gained weight, as much as fifteen pounds, since his committal. Thaw habitually responded to requests from the medical staff with insolence, refusing to submit to any physical examinations, and he frequently upbraided the other patients, calling them idiots and donkeys.[26]

Isaac Mills scribbled notes as Baker continued to talk, only occasionally glancing at the witness. Baker, having concluded his testimony, was about to step away but the judge stopped him, indicating that he wished to ask him some questions.

"I consider you a very important witness," Mills began. "You are a public official, charged with the administration of public affairs in a just and equitable manner. . . . You have had full charge and care of Harry K. Thaw, is not that so?"

"Yes, sir; I have," Baker replied.

"Do you take the position after your observation of Mr. Thaw," Mills said, leaning forward slightly, adjusting his eyeglasses as he spoke, "that he is insane or that he is not?"

Thaw had been at Matteawan nearly seventeen months, Baker replied, but there had been no improvement in his condition. "My position is that this man is insane."

"Do you consider that his enlargement would be a menace to the public peace and safety?"

"Yes, sir; I do."

"Thank you. That is all."[27]

The evidence, Isaac Mills announced in his verdict on August 12, 1909, led inexorably to the conclusion that Harry Thaw was insane. Susan Merrill's testimony, that Thaw had used her apartments to violently assault young girls, was credible. Thaw's accusations against Stanford White, the judge declared, were delusions that existed only in his imagination, delusions that he had employed to justify the murder of the architect. Baker, moreover, had been emphatic in his warning that Thaw would again commit acts of violence if he were released.

"The Court is disposed to pay great respect to the opinion of the hospital authorities," Mills read in his decision, denying the writ of habeas corpus. "All such authorities are public officers, with no conceivable motive except to do their duty.... Dr. Baker has been entirely frank and sincere in his conduct and testimony.... He is clearly of the opinion that the prisoner is now insane to the degree that his discharge would be dangerous. The enlargement of Harry K. Thaw," Mills concluded, "would be dangerous to the public peace and safety and therefore cannot be permitted.... The writ therefore must be dismissed upon the merits."[28]

It was a bitterly disappointing verdict. Mary Thaw had

expected to win her son's freedom, but the hospital administration had opposed the writ. The superintendent, Robert
Lamb, had sent his chief medical officer, Amos Baker, to testify that Thaw would be a danger to the public, and Baker had
provided a wealth of detail to convince the judge that Thaw
was insane. Lamb had refused to sign a certificate of recovery,
and he appeared resolute in his determination to keep Harry
Thaw at Matteawan.

It was necessary, Mary Thaw now realized, to somehow
remove Lamb from his position as asylum superintendent, to
replace him with someone more malleable, someone who
would listen to her entreaties; but how could she accomplish
such a seemingly impossible task?

The firemen arrived shortly after midnight on January 13, 1910,
a few minutes after receiving the alarm, and quickly extin-
guished the flames. The fire had spread from a ground-floor
apartment to the second story, but there had been remarkably
little damage to the structure, an apartment house at 248 Seventh Avenue in the Park Slope section of Brooklyn. There had
been no injuries and there was no obvious cause for the blaze;
the fire marshal, Thomas Patrick Brophy, wrote in his report
later that night that the fire had started in a coal bin at the front
of the house.

The fire, a minor episode in the daily rhythm of the city,
was soon forgotten until, five weeks later, on February 22, an
unemployed copywriter, Norman Lees, entered police headquarters on State Street, saying that he had set the blaze that

night. His conscience had been bothering him, Lees claimed, and he needed to make a full confession.

No one at the police station knew anything about a fire on Seventh Avenue, but Lees, thirty-seven years old, a recent immigrant from Britain, seemed strangely insistent that he had set it and appeared almost relieved when the desk sergeant eventually arrested him. Later that year Lees appeared in court on a charge of arson in the first degree, and his lawyer, saying that Lees was irrational, asked the jury to accept a plea of not guilty on the grounds of insanity. Lees, disheveled and unkempt, frequently muttering to himself, often staring vacantly into space, seemed unable to recognize the gravity of his situation, and the magistrate, James Tighe, committed Lees to the Matteawan asylum.[29]

Lees remained at Matteawan for five months, winning his freedom in August 1910 on a writ of habeas corpus. He met with Mary Thaw a few days after his release, telling her that the scheme had worked as she had anticipated. He had had access to many inmates, even those in the women's wards; he had closely observed the attendants and their interactions with the patients; and he had kept detailed notes on every aspect of daily life in the asylum. There was enough material in his notes, Lees claimed, to condemn Robert Lamb as a superintendent who tolerated violence and abuse against the patients in his care.

Later that year several inmates, all claiming to be sane, applied for writs of habeas corpus. Norman Lees was their sponsor, arranging for lawyers to represent each patient, contacting relatives, making sure that the newspapers had sufficient information to report on each case.

Dora Schwam, an orphan, had first come into the care of the state after the death of her mother in 1906. The authorities had sent Schwam, then thirteen, to a reformatory, the Training School for Girls, but she had been a disruptive presence, swearing and cursing at the teachers, fighting with the other girls, even attempting on one occasion to escape. She had remained at the reformatory until February 1910, when the principal of the school arranged her transfer to the Matteawan State Hospital. It was a puzzling decision: Dora Schwam had committed no crime, and there was no evidence that she was insane, yet she now languished in a hospital for the criminal insane.

She might have remained at Matteawan for the rest of her years—except that Norman Lees had discovered her during his stay at the asylum, and he now applied for her release on a writ of habeas corpus. "I saw this girl a number of times while I was detained," Lees told a reporter for the *New York World*, "and I thought it outrageous that one of her youth, against whom there was no charge of ever having committed a crime, should be kept in such an institution under conditions that are absolutely vicious and tend to make her a criminal and immoral character."[30]

Dora Schwam remained at the asylum until February 18, 1911, when the judge at the hearing on the writ ordered her immediate release. Everyone agreed that it was a mystery why she had ever been sent to Matteawan in the first place. Schwam, now seventeen, was remarkably pretty, neat in appearance, in good health, with excellent manners and intelligence.[31]

Norman Lees wasted no time in arranging an interview with the *New York World* to allow Schwam to describe her experiences at Matteawan. It had been a nightmare, the girl recalled, from the first day to the last. The nurses in the women's wards had been violent and abusive, frequently hitting and beating patients for no apparent reason. "We were struck and knocked about continually," Schwam remembered. "A woman might be standing in the way of the nurse making a tour of the ward. Instead of being asked to move, the nurse would slap the patient on the side of the face, or hit her in the back or side with closed fist." The attendants had used a variety of restraints, often tying patients to their beds with ropes, using straitjackets, even occasionally drugging patients to render them insensible.

The staff displayed hostility or indifference toward the patients but never kindness, and there was little attempt to cure the individuals in their care. "I never saw one of the women attendants who apparently felt a spark of pity or sympathy for any patient," Schwam said bitterly. "The doctors were mostly just indifferent.... They were all alike, all in a league to have the easiest time possible for themselves."[32]

More revelations emerged later that year as Lees, using money provided by the Thaw family, filed applications for writs of habeas corpus on behalf of other inmates. Myrtle Lapp, twenty-eight, the daughter of a clergyman, had been sentenced in 1907 to a term of four years on a charge of bigamy and sent to Auburn Prison. Lapp, believing that conditions in a state asylum would be more tolerable, had feigned mental illness, winning a transfer to Matteawan in 1910. She had expected that she would leave the asylum the following year, at the end of her sentence, but was shocked to learn that she might now be held indefinitely, until the superintendent signed a certificate of recovery. Fortunately for Lapp, Norman Lees arranged for her to appear in court on a writ of habeas corpus, where she complained bitterly about her treatment, saying that the attendants had frequently attacked her, beating and choking her for minor infractions of the regulations.[33]

Mary Mullen, twenty-five, originally from the state of Virginia, had lived a peripatetic existence, drifting from state to state, committing one misdemeanor after another. She had spent most of her life in reformatories and prisons, serving time for various offenses, including vagrancy and theft, but few places in her experience, she declared, had been as chaotic and as brutal as the Matteawan asylum. Mullen claimed that the hospital attendants had frequently been intoxicated on the wards, even occasionally drinking whiskey in front of the patients.[34]

Inmates who applied for a writ of habeas corpus seemed always to succeed in winning their liberty. Norman Lees was a ubiquitous presence, counseling the petitioners, speaking to the newspapers, castigating Robert Lamb for his mismanagement of the asylum, and occasionally appearing in court as a witness. Mary Thaw, always taking care to avoid the limelight, provided financial support, giving Lees the money to continue his campaign, hiring attorneys and psychiatrists, even paying writers to insert favorable articles in the New York magazines.

The drumbeat of scandal grew steadily louder, the complaints of each inmate reinforcing a sense that Robert Lamb had ceded control of the asylum to the attendants and nurses. George Cobb, a Republican state senator, expressed the shared sense of dismay among the legislators at the apparent collapse of discipline in the asylum. "That's one of the worst places we have in the State," Cobb complained. "It's worse than the State's prisons." The state legislature, Cobb promised, would not remain passive but would soon establish a committee to investigate conditions at Matteawan.[35]

Nothing more starkly exposed the chaos that apparently reigned at the asylum than the circumstances surrounding the death of John Nugent on Friday, February 3, 1911. Nugent had left his ward the previous Wednesday in an attempt to escape. A duty nurse, seeing Nugent in the assembly hall, sounded the alarm, and three attendants seized Nugent, dragging him along a corridor and up some stairs, eventually locking him in an isolation cell on the second floor. Two days later, early on Friday morning, an attendant discovered the lifeless body of Nugent lying on his cot.[36]

Amos Baker, the chief medical officer, stated that Nugent had escaped from his ward by crawling through a transom window. Nugent had fallen from the transom, hitting his head on the concrete floor, and subsequently died from injuries sustained in his fall. There were no bruises on his body, Baker claimed, and no signs that anyone had mistreated Nugent.[37]

But the coroner's physician, Howell Bontecou, determined that there had been a rupture of the left renal artery, resulting in hemorrhage, a finding consistent with blows from a blunt instrument. Later that month Joseph Seery, a patient at the hospital, told an assistant district attorney, Edward Conger, that he had witnessed two attendants holding Nugent by the arms while a third had struck him about the face and body. "I was following them up the stairs," Seery told Conger. "Nugent gave a groan when he was struck."[38]

The controversy over Nugent's death led various state and local authorities to establish inquiries into conditions at Matteawan. The State Commission in Lunacy, an oversight body established by the legislature in 1894, began an investigation one week after Nugent's death, sending its agents to the asylum to interview both staff and patients. The governor of New York, John Alden Dix, acting under the authority of the Moreland Act, established a committee of psychiatrists and laymen to report on the treatment of patients. The district attorney of Dutchess County, John Mack, suspecting foul play, interviewed patients on Nugent's ward and the medical staff who had had care of Nugent.[39]

Finally, the state legislature also initiated an inquiry: Louis Cuvillier, a Democrat in the New York State Assembly, brought forward legislation in April 1911 for an appropriation of $20,000 to investigate the hospital administration, while a freshman senator from Dutchess County, Franklin Delano Roosevelt, proposed a companion bill in the state senate, asking also for an investigation into conditions at the Dannemora State Hospital.[40]

The state superintendent of prisons, Cornelius Collins, announced that his staff would cooperate with the inquiries, saying that he would welcome the prosecution of any employee who had abused patients. "If the conditions as reported," Collins declared, "that patients were being abused or maltreated, were true, and...if one had died from the effect of such maltreatment," then a crime had been committed. But Collins, superintendent of prisons since 1898, was already out of favor with the governor. Earlier that year, Dix, the first Democratic governor of New York since 1894, had initiated a comprehensive investigation of the prison system, and the committee of inquiry had uncovered fraud in the management of Sing Sing Prison and Clinton Prison. The chaos within the Matteawan asylum gave Dix another reason to replace Collins, a Republican appointee, and Collins, realizing that he had no future in a Democratic administration, obligingly resigned his position on April 26.[41]

The furor over conditions at Matteawan seemed likely to claim Robert Lamb as its next victim. The investigations into the asylum continued through April and May, each inquiry uncovering one scandal after another. Norman Lees, busily working at the behest of Mary Thaw, continued to file petitions on behalf of the inmates, claiming that as many as sixty patients at Matteawan were sane and should be released.

Lamb fought back valiantly, defending his management of the asylum, telling anyone who would listen that Harry Thaw was behind Lees's campaign, but his position had become increasingly untenable. In June yet another inmate, Severn De Angelis, applied for a writ of habeas corpus, his attorneys claiming that Lamb had tampered with court documents in an attempt to deny De Angelis his liberty. The judge, Arthur Tompkins, had been initially skeptical, but both Lamb and Amos Baker eventually admitted the truth of the accusation.[42]

The new superintendent of prisons, Joseph Scott, eager to start his tenure with a clean slate, demanded Lamb's resignation. Lamb, in an interview with the New York newspapers, attributed his departure in July 1911 to the recent death of his father—"I am called upon to take charge of my father's estate"—and a concern with his own health. "I wanted a vacation," Lamb said. "I needed a rest badly, and this had much to do with my action. The alleged charges against me and the administration of the hospital had nothing whatever to do with my action."[43]

A few weeks later the chief medical officer, Amos Baker, also resigned. Baker had always opposed Harry Thaw's release, testifying twice that Thaw was insane, and Mary Thaw was jubilant that Baker had now resigned his position. "It was with thanksgiving," she told a reporter from the *New York Sun*, "I learned...how Dr. Lamb's resignation had been followed by that of his assistant." Lamb had always behaved in a vindictive manner, punishing Harry for trivial infractions of the rules and restricting his access to his attorneys, and she was thankful that Lamb would no longer be able to torment her son. Harry was sane, she declared, held in the asylum against his will as a prisoner, and she was hopeful that there would soon be a new superintendent at the asylum who would be more responsive to her requests.[44]

But what had happened to Evelyn Nesbit? There had been no news of her for almost three years, nothing since 1909, when she was in White Plains for the second hearing on habeas corpus. There was gossip among her New York friends that she had moved to Europe. Edward Thomas, a wealthy American banker living in Paris, had frequently dined with an attractive woman in the French capital, and the newspapers speculated that his companion was Evelyn Nesbit. But it was only a rumor, and nobody seemed to know with any certainty Evelyn's whereabouts.[45]

Evelyn Nesbit gave birth to a son, Russell, in October 1910 when she was living in Berlin. It was fashionable at the time to wear a hat with a bird motif, and here Evelyn is wearing a casque, a close-fitting hat without a brim, with feathers covering a cloth body and glass eyes serving as real eyes. The Migratory Bird Treaty Act, passed by Congress in 1918, ended the millinery trade in bird feathers, and the fashion died away soon afterward. *(Library of Congress, LC-DIG-ds-10584)*

The *New York Herald* broke the news first, reporting on May 13, 1912, that Evelyn was the proud mother of a boy, Russell, now almost two years old. Evelyn had become pregnant in February 1910. Wanting to avoid publicity, she had secretly traveled to Germany with a friend, the actress Lillian Spencer, to live in Bad Harzburg, a spa town sixty miles southeast of

Hanover. Later that year, Evelyn moved to Berlin to give birth in a private clinic near Unter den Linden.[46]

She returned to New York with her baby several months later, to live uptown, moving into a house at 220 West 112th Street. Evelyn had no desire to attract attention, and only a few of her acquaintances even knew that she had returned to the United States. But inevitably someone gossiped, and the *Herald* was the first newspaper to print the story, splashing the sensational news across its front page.[47]

She insisted that Harry Thaw was the father. She had often spent time alone with Harry during her visits to the asylum, Evelyn said. "One only has to look at the little darling," she cooed, "to know who its father is. . . . Harry is my husband and the father of my child. I love my baby and am going to see that it is justly treated by relatives of my husband."[48]

But Harry Thaw ridiculed Evelyn's claim as preposterous. He had separated from his wife in 1908, shortly after his arrival at the asylum, and Evelyn filed for an annulment of the marriage later that year. She subsequently withdrew the suit, but their marriage had effectively ended. She had stated that the birth occurred in October 1910, but she had last visited him in the asylum nearly a year before that, on the Thanksgiving holiday in 1909. "This is a trumped up deal," Harry said. "A hundred persons can deny the possibility of such a thing being true." Some other man, a companion living in Europe, was the father, Harry speculated, and Evelyn was cynically hoping to lay claim to the Thaw estate by falsely naming him as the father. There was not a shred of evidence for her assertion, and the Thaw attorneys would, if necessary, go to court to protect the family's interests.[49]

That summer, in June 1912, Evelyn and Harry again crossed paths when she testified at a third hearing on habeas corpus. Evelyn had previously been reluctant to bear witness against her husband, but now she had no inhibitions in speaking about her marriage. She had given up so much for Harry's sake—her dignity and her reputation—and she had received nothing in return. Harry's attorneys at the first trial had persuaded her to testify that Stanford White had raped her, and she had been too young to understand the consequences for herself. Only now, at twenty-six, did she realize how wickedly those attorneys had manipulated her, and she was now resolute to chart her own course.

Harry Thaw, according to Evelyn's testimony in 1912, was obsessed with young girls, often talking over newspaper reports of assaults and rapes. On several occasions she discovered, among his papers, pen-and-ink sketches depicting a man whipping a girl. In 1907, on a visit to the Tombs, as she handed her husband a volume from his library, a sketch of a naked girl fell from the book onto the floor of the prison cell.

"Describe it," Travers Jerome suddenly interrupted.

"It was a picture of a nude woman. . . . Thaw had drawn himself as standing over the woman with a whip in his hand. There were marks on the woman's back to show where she had been whipped."

"Did Thaw frequently talk to you," Jerome continued, "about little girls being drugged and attacked?"

"Yes, very often," Evelyn replied. "He would talk about the youth and virginity of girls."[50]

It was another peculiar obsession of her husband that he could not bear the thought that someone might disregard his wishes. He was mercurial, unpredictable in his moods, frequently throwing a tantrum if, say, a servant did not comply exactly with his commands.

"Did Thaw ever talk to you about obedience?" Jerome asked.

"I should think he did," Evelyn replied. "He had a mania on that subject."

"Did Thaw ever talk to you about beating you?"

"Yes; he said that was the trouble with me — that I needed a good beating."

"Did he offer to give you one?"

"Yes, he did."[51]

Evelyn had testified unapologetically about her marriage, providing damning information about her husband; but she refused to speak again about the rape in Stanford White's town house. She had already testified twice about that night when White drugged and assaulted her; but only to save Harry from the electric chair, and she would not tell the story a third time. Evelyn bitterly regretted that she had so naïvely allowed Thaw's attorneys to deceive her, and there was no reason for her now to repeat her testimony.

Clarence Shearn, an attorney hired by Thaw a few weeks before, hoped to discredit Evelyn's testimony by asking her about the rape; but she refused to respond.

"I will not go over this again," she snapped. "I don't propose to answer your questions any further."

"I shall try," Shearn continued, "to avoid unpleasantness—"

"You had better," Evelyn interrupted, "for if you go into those things I won't answer you. It was bad enough for Thaw to hide behind my skirts in his two dirty trials without permitting you to go over this now. Don't you ask me a single question about it for I won't answer."[52]

The judge, Martin Keogh, saying nothing, looked first at the witness, then at the attorney, and again at the witness. Evelyn Nesbit had taken an oath and she was obliged to answer the lawyer's questions; but her expression—defiant, angry, hostile—told Shearn that it would be futile to continue his interrogation. He shrugged his shoulders, as if to acknowledge his defeat, and turning to Keogh, he said that he would read her previous statements, those given at the first trial, into the record.

"You'd better," Evelyn exclaimed angrily. "You won't read them while I am in the room."[53]

It was a moment of triumph for Evelyn, an episode that told the world that she had achieved her independence. She was no longer the chorus girl who had sought sanctuary in a marriage with Harry Thaw, and she now neither expected nor desired to depend on the charity of her husband's family. Her future was uncertain—she had no income; she now had a child to support—but Evelyn was steadfast in her determination never again to allow anyone to manipulate her. She would make her own way in the world; she would determine her life on her own terms; and her success would shield her from the vengeance of her husband and his mother.

Harry Thaw lost his third attempt to win his freedom

through a writ of habeas corpus. The judge, Martin Keogh, stated in his decision that Thaw was likely to commit a violent assault again similar to the murder of Stanford White. "Harry K. Thaw," Keogh declared on July 27, "is still insane and...his discharge would be dangerous to the public peace and safety."[54]

Mary Thaw, listening to the judge's decision, blamed Evelyn Nesbit for this latest defeat. No one could have heard Evelyn describe her husband without concluding that Harry was a violent psychopath, and Keogh's verdict seemed certain to condemn Harry to spend the remainder of his days in the asylum. There had never been any possibility of a reconciliation between the Thaw family and Evelyn Nesbit; and the events of that year—Evelyn's claim that Harry had fathered her child; Evelyn's testimony against Harry in the courtroom—had strengthened Mary Thaw's resolve to cast her daughter-in-law out of the family circle as soon as possible. But that task would come later. For the moment she was too preoccupied with securing Harry's release to bother about Evelyn.

Mary Thaw had finally, after great effort, succeeded in removing Robert Lamb from his position as the superintendent of the Matteawan asylum, and John Russell, a graduate of the Albany Medical College, had been appointed in January 1912 in his place. She had already made cautious inquiries, and she had been pleased to learn that the new superintendent would be considerably more receptive to her pleas than his predecessor.

John Russell sat waiting in an easy chair in the hotel lobby, idly watching the bustle of guests at the entrance. The Astor House, built in 1836 in the Greek Revival style, had once been the most fashionable hotel in New York, but its reputation had declined in tandem with the deterioration of the neighborhood near City Hall. The hotel still retained the features that had once given it distinction—the courtyard enclosed by a glass dome; the curving mahogany bar, almost fifty feet long; the half-dozen private dining rooms—but the area west of the hotel, a warren of narrow streets, had become disreputable, notorious for its brothels and saloons.

Russell, the superintendent of the Matteawan asylum, frequently visited New York, usually staying uptown at the Savoy Hotel on Fifty-ninth Street. He had chosen the Astor House for the rendezvous that day because it offered anonymity. Few New Yorkers, not even the clerks working in the financial district nearby, took their meals in the hotel's ornate dining room, and most patrons were out-of-towners—traveling salesmen and businessmen.

He had waited only ten minutes when he saw John Anhut appear at the Broadway entrance. Anhut, wearing a light gray suit and a four-in-hand purple tie, looked impossibly young, no older than twenty, but he appeared self-confident beyond his years. His youthful appearance was slightly misleading—Anhut was then twenty-nine—but already he had amassed a wealth of political experience in his home state, Michigan, winning election in 1909 to the state senate. He had recently moved to New York, intending to practice law in the city, and somehow, immediately upon his arrival, he had become enmeshed in the scheme to free Harry Thaw.[55]

The two men exchanged greetings in the lobby, and Russell

escorted Anhut upstairs to a private dining room overlooking Barclay Street. Anhut spoke first, telling Russell that he had met with Mary Thaw two days before. She was prepared to reward the superintendent if he would only sign a certificate of recovery for her son. There would be no need for Russell to obtain the consent of the psychiatrists or any of the medical staff, Anhut claimed: Russell could sign the certificate on his own authority, and Harry Thaw would be free to leave the asylum.

"How much did Thaw give you?" Russell suddenly interrupted, his voice betraying his impatience.

He had received $25,000, Anhut replied. One of Thaw's sisters, Margaret, had endorsed stock certificates in the Consolidated Gas Company to the value of $20,000, and Mary Thaw had provided $5,000 in cash. But the full payment, Anhut added, would be made only if Russell released Thaw by the end of the year. One half of the amount would be forfeited if Thaw remained in the asylum after January 1, 1913, and further delay into the summer was unacceptable. "All this money," Anhut warned, "goes back if I don't get Thaw out."

Russell hesitated. He would risk his position at Matteawan by releasing Thaw. It would stir up tremendous controversy, and inevitably there would be an inquiry into the matter.

"I will give you twenty thousand if you discharge Thaw," Anhut said, adding that he, Anhut, would receive $5,000 for his part in the scheme.

"I wouldn't do it for a cent less than $20,000," Russell replied, speaking with indignation, as if even that amount was far less than he had expected. What would he do if there was an outcry against Thaw's release and he, Russell, was forced to resign his position as superintendent? He had made his career within the state system of asylums, and there was little likelihood that he would ever again obtain a comparable post.

"If you lose your position," Anhut said reassuringly, "Thaw will pay you $10,000 a year until you are established."

It was a generous proposal; still Russell hesitated, saying only that he needed time to consider the offer. But later that month, a few days before Christmas 1912, Russell mentioned the scheme to a colleague, William Clark, asking for his advice. It all ended predictably: Clark confided his knowledge of the proposal to some close friends; and soon the New York journalists had caught wind of the scheme, hinting in their reports at the rumor that Thaw might soon leave the asylum.

Anhut's attempt to bribe the superintendent was revealed publicly two months later, after a new administration had taken office in the state capital. The governor, William Sulzer, had won election the previous November with the support of the Democratic Party machine, but he quickly proclaimed his independence, declaring at his inauguration that he would end corruption in New York. He was true to his word, removing Tammany officeholders and appointing several commissions to investigate graft in state politics.[56]

A committee of inquiry into the state prisons held hearings in February 1913. John Russell appeared as a witness, testifying that John Anhut had attempted to bribe him to release Harry

Thaw. Russell denied that he had ever accepted any money, but he did admit that he had not informed Joseph Scott, the state superintendent of prisons, about the bribery attempt.

Mary Thaw had pinned all her hopes on Russell in a final effort to win her son's freedom, but her scheme had collapsed in spectacular fashion, and soon all the protagonists in the affair had lost their positions. Russell, unable to explain why he had neglected to tell his superior officer about the bribe, resigned his post as the Matteawan superintendent on February 28. Joseph Scott left office two weeks later, on March 13, after the committee of inquiry determined that he had failed to exercise oversight over his department, allowing theft from the state prisons to go unchecked. Scott had never held his staff to account, and thus, according to the committee of inquiry, he had been at least partially responsible for the Thaw debacle.[57]

John Anhut appeared in court in May 1913 on an indictment charging him with bribery. Anhut denied the accusation, saying that Russell had initiated the bribe, but the jury found him guilty of the charge, and the judge, Samuel Seabury, sentenced him to a term of four years in Sing Sing Prison.[58]

It seemed ironic that Harry Thaw should entirely escape punishment; but how could the state prosecute an individual who was confined to the Matteawan asylum because of his insanity? An insane man could not knowingly commit a crime, and the attorney general, Thomas Carmody, was unlikely to seek an indictment. But Thaw had, nevertheless, suffered a defeat that now seemed to end forever any possibility that he would leave the asylum.

Harry had always rejected the suggestion that he might

attempt to escape. In 1908, at the end of the second trial, his brother Josiah had planned for gangsters to overpower the guards on the train journey to Matteawan. Harry could then have escaped across the state line before his arrival at the asylum. But Harry had refused the offer, telling Josiah that he would eventually win his freedom by legal means in the courts. Why should he live the life of a fugitive, Harry asked, when he was a sane man?[59]

But now, five years after he had first entered the asylum, there seemed little possibility that he would ever leave Matteawan. The courts had repeatedly rejected his writs of habeas corpus, saying that he still posed a danger, and no superintendent of the asylum was ever likely now to sign a certificate of recovery. It seemed impossible for Harry to imagine that he might spend the rest of his days as a prisoner, locked away in the asylum. He must leave; but how?

8

ESCAPE

HARRY THAW, HIS HANDS IN HIS POCKETS, HIS BACK AGAINST THE wall, stood inconspicuously in the shade, watching the guard hut on the far side of the courtyard. It was still early, seven thirty in the morning, but some other patients had started to appear after breakfast, and they stood chatting together in small groups at the rear of the asylum. There had been no rain since June, and Harry noticed that the patches of grass in the yard had started to wither and die in the summer heat. The ground was sandy brown, baked by the sun, and now almost indistinguishable from the weathered redbrick walls of the asylum that enclosed the courtyard on three sides. A stockade fence, twelve feet high, constructed from rough lumber pilings, with a heavy wooden gate at the center, completed the enclosure.

A bell sounded by the gate to signal the milk delivery, and Harry waited as a guard, a large metal key in his right hand, emerged from his hut, walking in the sunlight along a path toward the fence. Harry also began to step cautiously in the direction of the gate, moving almost parallel to the guard as both men, separated by a distance of almost ten yards, advanced toward the fence.

The guard, Howard Barnum, turned his key in the metal lock and slid back a heavy iron bolt, slowly pulling the gate inward on its metal rollers. The dairyman, Bill Hickey, urged his horse forward, guiding the milk cart between two large pillars, one on either side of the gate, maneuvering the cart through the narrow space into the yard.[1]

At that moment, as Hickey edged his cart forward, Harry Thaw squeezed his body into the gap between the cart and the gatepost. The space seemed impossibly narrow, less than three feet, but Harry made his way through, catching his jacket on a hook at the rear of the cart before breaking free.

A black six-cylinder Packard touring car, its engine running, stood twenty yards ahead, at the bottom of an incline that led from the gate of the asylum to the road. Two men waiting by the car sprang to their feet, watching Thaw as he ran across the grass toward them. Thaw, winded by his quick sprint, jumped into the rear seat and the car roared to life, accelerating in an easterly direction, turning south at Stormville, crossing a bridge over Fishkill Creek, and heading directly toward the Connecticut state line twenty-seven miles away.[2]

There was nothing to indicate the boundary between New York and the neighboring state of Connecticut, no sign to tell travelers when they had left New York, but thirty minutes later, when the car reached Danbury, in Connecticut, Harry Thaw knew that he was safe. The jurisdiction of the New York authorities ended at the state line, and no one, not even the governor of the state, could now take him back to New York without first submitting a request for his extradition.

Richard Butler, sitting in the front passenger seat, introduced himself, telling Thaw that they would drive north through Massachusetts and New Hampshire, entering Vermont close to the northern border before crossing into Canada. Butler, a member of the Gophers, one of the gangs from the Hell's Kitchen neighborhood on the west side of Manhattan, was well known in the city as a fixer with influence among the labor unions. Ten years before he had won election on the Democratic ticket to the state assembly; but he had soon abandoned politics, preferring to spend his time with friends in the Hell's Kitchen saloons.[3]

The Gophers had received part of their payment, Butler reminded Thaw, and they expected the remainder, according to the agreement with the family, once they crossed the border into Canada. The driver, Roger Thompson, said nothing, his eyes fixed on the road ahead, his attention focused on the signposts that indicated the route north; but a third man, Michael O'Keefe, seated next to Thaw in the rear, occasionally interrupted, prompting Butler to include those details of their itinerary that he had forgotten.[4]

Soon they had left Connecticut, driving north through Massachusetts. They stopped at Lenox, pausing for lunch, before continuing on to Pittsfield, entering New Hampshire close to the Connecticut River.

Richard Butler had chosen their route with care, intending to cross into Canada from the northeastern corner of Vermont in a remote, sparsely populated area west of the White Mountains. Neither the United States nor Canada had installed border controls in that region, allowing unrestricted travel between the state of Vermont and the province of Quebec, and there was consequently no requirement to show any identification to pass from one country to the other.

But their limousine, a Packard Dominant Six luxury model, would attract a great deal of attention in the villages and hamlets of rural Vermont and New Hampshire. It would be impossible, Butler decided, to drive such a car without being noticed. They would instead travel the remainder of their journey by train, taking the Grand Trunk Railway on the line that connected Portland, Maine, to Montreal.

That afternoon, shortly after four o'clock, they abandoned the car in Rochester, a town in eastern New Hampshire, to take a train on the Boston & Maine line as far as Littleton to connect to the Grand Trunk Railway. They had made good progress since leaving Matteawan, traveling unnoticed through four states, and very soon, in less than two hours, they would be in Canada. Harry Thaw, watching the passing countryside through the train window, could not have been more satisfied. His companions were in the smoking car, playing cards, and he sat alone, daydreaming, as the train hurried on its way across New Hampshire.

A large heavyset man, around forty years old, boarded the train at Lancaster, making his way down the center aisle of the carriage, searching for an empty seat. Burleigh Kelsea, the deputy sheriff of Coos County, had spent the day in Lancaster, the county seat, and now he was on his way home to Colebrook.

He nodded a greeting as he sat down opposite Harry Thaw. but neither man said anything and Kelsea started to read his newspaper. He glanced up as the conductor came through the carriage, checking the tickets, and he looked again, more closely, at Thaw, seated opposite him.

"I know who you are," Kelsea said suddenly. "You are Harry Thaw. I feel pretty sure you are Harry Thaw. Aren't you?"

Thaw hesitated, reluctant to confirm his identity, but then he started to talk.

"You're right," he confessed, "but I am a perfectly free man here."

He had left New York, he explained, and there were no grounds for his extradition from New Hampshire. The jury at his trial had acquitted him of the murder of Stanford White, he said, and he had not, therefore, been convicted of any crime.

"Nobody can hold me," he added, a note of defiance in his voice, "for they haven't anything on me. I was acquitted of that murder, and they can't extradite me."

"No, I guess not," Kelsea replied.

"How did you recognize me?" Thaw asked.

Kelsea pointed to his paper. "From the picture in the newspaper which I am now reading," he said. There, on the front page, was a photograph of Thaw along with an account of his escape from Matteawan.

"Where are you going?" Kelsea asked.

"I'm on my way to take a boat at Montreal for England," Thaw replied, saying that his sister lived in London and that he expected to stay there for some time.[5]

The train started to slow down as it approached Colebrook. Kelsea rose from his seat, collecting his belongings, saying that he had arrived at his destination, and wishing Thaw a pleasant journey.

He had thought about arresting Thaw on the spot—but on what charge? Harry Thaw was correct in saying that the jury had acquitted him, and it was true that, in the eyes of the law, he had not committed a crime. He had walked away from the Matteawan asylum, but it was not evident that he had thereby broken the law. And anyway, did Kelsea have the authority to detain Thaw? He had no warrant for Thaw's arrest, and Thaw had committed no crime in New Hampshire.

Thaw had indicated, during their conversation, that he believed he was traveling on the through train from Portland into Canada as far as Montreal. But he was mistaken: only two trains each day made the journey into Canada, and Kelsea knew that this train would end at Beecher Falls, a small town just inside the United States, about eight miles from the border. There would be no more trains traveling that night into Canada, and Thaw would be stranded, unable to complete his journey. Kelsea planned to drive to Beecher Falls from Colebrook, notify the local police, and surprise Thaw before he could cross into Canada.

But Kelsea was too late. Thaw and his companions, alighting from the train at its terminus, had realized their mistake and hired a driver and his car at Beecher Falls. No one saw them enter Canada—the border crossing was unmanned—and later that night, they reached Saint-Herménégilde, a small village in the province of Quebec.

*　　　*　　　*

Mary Thaw was gleeful that her son had finally escaped. "I thank God he has gone!" she exclaimed. "It is time the travesty was ended. My boy ought never to have been sent to Matteawan in the first place." Some newspapers speculated that the family had arranged his flight, paying gangsters to spirit him away, but she denied the accusation. "None of the members of the family had anything to do with his getting away," she protested, "but I am glad that he is out." She had had no inkling that Harry was planning his escape. She had arranged to visit Harry at the asylum on Monday, August 18, and his departure caught her by surprise.[6]

Evelyn Nesbit was horrified that Thaw had escaped. He had threatened to kill her, and she had no doubt that he was capable of carrying out his threat. She had recently begun a vaudeville engagement at the Victoria Theatre, and she would perform, she informed the manager, Willie Hammerstein, only if he provided her with a police escort. "You know Harry's history," she exclaimed to the reporter from the *New York Herald*. "One drink of liquor and he is as mad as ever....So long as Harry Thaw is alive and free I shall never close my eyes in peace."[7]

Thaw had also threatened the psychiatrists who had given evidence against him. Both Austin Flint and Carlos MacDonald had testified that Thaw suffered from an incurable condition, and their evidence had prolonged his imprisonment. Flint had repeatedly warned that Thaw might try to escape, but his statements had been ignored, and this disaster was the sorry consequence. Both psychiatrists predicted that Thaw would commit a violent act if he remained long at liberty, and it was only a matter of time before he assaulted someone. "He will immediately return to all of the vices to which he was addicted," MacDonald stated. "The moment that he takes a drink of whisky or a bottle of wine he at once will...single out any one of the many persons whom he believes have wronged him."[8]

No one could say if Thaw intended to make good on his threats, but he had almost certainly left the state. Raymond Kleb, the asylum superintendent, had sent out cars in pursuit, but the trail had quickly gone cold. Frederick Hornbeck, the sheriff of Dutchess County, also raised the alarm, sending telegrams across the state to inform neighboring counties of Thaw's escape, and John Riley, the state superintendent of prisons, announced a reward of $500 for the recapture of Thaw. The police in Manhattan informed their counterparts in other cities throughout the northeastern states, transmitting a description of Thaw and asking for assistance in his capture.[9]

Reports soon arrived that several men, one of whom resembled Harry Thaw, had boarded a launch at Roton Point, a harbor on the Connecticut coast. The launch had carried its passengers out to sea, to a large yacht, *Matchgard II*, which had then sailed out into Long Island Sound, disappearing from view. A second account claimed that a group of men had stopped at the Hotel Green in Danbury to ask directions to Massachusetts, indicating by their questions that they planned to drive north to Canada. Other witnesses reported seeing Thaw at various towns in New England. Two men, one of whom resembled Thaw, had supposedly stayed the night in a hotel in Lenox. A building contractor at Bellows Falls, a small town in Vermont, claimed that two large cars, each carrying several men, one of whom might have been Thaw, had stopped him to ask for directions to Newport, a town close to the Canadian border.[10]

But even if the authorities knew Thaw's eventual destination, it was not evident that they could easily compel his return to New York State. The jury in the second trial had not convicted him of a crime, determining only that he had been insane at the time of the murder; there were, therefore, no grounds for his extradition. Thaw, by crossing the state line, had put himself beyond the reach of New York, and it was not likely that he would ever return. John McIntyre, a prominent criminal lawyer, cogently expressed the consensus that Thaw had won his liberty and there was nothing anyone could do about it. "Harry K. Thaw is not a fugitive from justice," McIntyre stated, "nor a person convicted of a crime, nor a person under indictment, nor an escaped convict. Under the law he is simply an insane patient who has escaped from a State hospital. I cannot see any possible ground on which he could be extradited." Charles Whitman, the district attorney for New York County (Manhattan), was keen to see Thaw back in the asylum, but he also regarded any attempt to recapture him as futile. "The act of acquittal," Whitman claimed, "abolished any indictment against Thaw in New York county for crime. Consequently he cannot be extradited."[11]

The authorities might have had grounds for Thaw's extradition if he had committed a crime in order to accomplish his escape; but he had not assaulted any of the guards, and there was no evidence that he had attempted to bribe the hospital staff. Edward Conger, the district attorney for Dutchess County, had already executed a warrant to charge Thaw with conspiracy to leave the asylum. But the State of New York had held Thaw on account of his insanity. Could the authorities legitimately charge him with conspiracy? How could an insane man knowingly participate in a conspiracy?

Herbert Parker, a former attorney general of Massachusetts, believed that Thaw had done nothing that would permit that state to send him back. "The New York authorities," Parker stated, "might ask the police here to hold him on some charge such as being a vagrant, pending a request for extradition, but it does not seem to me that such a thing is at all likely. To extradite a man you must accuse him of some crime, and that the New York authorities cannot do."[12]

Thaw's escape had exposed New York to ridicule. Raymond Kleb, the superintendent of the asylum, bitterly complained that he had done everything possible to prevent an escape, but the courts, by allowing Thaw and other patients to confer privately with their lawyers, had given Thaw the freedom to arrange his escape and to make the payments to the men who had provided the Packard limousine. "It is no secret," Kleb said, "that Harry Thaw hated me. He knew my attitude toward him, and his lawyers knew how I felt." The manner of Thaw's escape, the ease with which it had been accomplished, left little doubt in Kleb's mind that Thaw had bribed the hospital attendants. "At least one of my employees has not been faithful," he complained, "and if I find that any money has been spent to make possible this escape I shall go to the full limit of prosecution."[13]

Howard Barnum, the Matteawan gatekeeper, protested his innocence, saying that he had known nothing about the affair—"I stood in the opening....Suddenly Thaw made a dash past me"—but the sheriff, Frederick Hornbeck, had him arrested nevertheless.[14]

The governor of New York, William Sulzer, hinted that his enemies in the state legislature had somehow engineered the escape in order to embarrass his administration and to hasten his downfall. John Riley, the superintendent of prisons, one of Sulzer's most important allies, had responsibility for oversight of the state asylums, and any accusation of incompetence against Riley would also be an accusation against the governor who had appointed him.[15]

Dawn was breaking as Burleigh Kelsea, accompanied by the village constable, Jean Boudreau, approached the inn, a two-story building set back from the main street. He had picked up Thaw's trail at Beecher Falls, tracking him into Canada as far as Saint-Herménégilde. The local police chief had issued a warrant, sending one of his men with Kelsea to make the arrest.

Harry Thaw was already awake, standing in the kitchen in his shirtsleeves, watching the innkeeper, Ben Cadieux, prepare breakfast. He stepped back a pace as Kelsea and Boudreau entered, moving toward the door that led to an outside courtyard, but already the constable had seized hold of his wrists.

"I arrest you, Harry Thaw, as a fugitive from justice."

The innkeeper, a frying pan in his hand, stood by the stove, looking on in astonishment, but Thaw had already recovered from his surprise. It was a case of mistaken identity, he told the constable. He had arrested the wrong man.

"Why, I'm not Thaw," he exclaimed. "How do you know I am the famous Harry Thaw?"

"By the photographs," Boudreau answered, "in the daily newspapers." He had expected that Thaw might resist arrest; he was surprised that his prisoner remained so calm.

"You had best beware of arresting," Thaw retorted. "You know, there is a punishment for false arrest."

"We'll take the chance, all right," the officer answered, his hand gripping the prisoner's wrist more tightly.[16]

Later that day, Alexis Dupuis, a justice of the peace, listened as a court official, Hector Verret, read the charge against Thaw that he had escaped from the penitentiary at Matteawan. Dupuis remanded the prisoner into custody, ordering that he remain in the county jail in Sherbrooke, a town twenty-three miles to the north. It was a specious indictment; but its purpose was to hold Thaw until immigration inspectors could determine his status. Thaw's lawyer, William Shurtleff, protested the order, telling the judge that his client had not broken any law in walking away from the asylum, saying that he would petition for a writ of habeas corpus at the earliest opportunity.

But the government had recently passed legislation that greatly restricted entry into Canada, and few observers believed that Harry Thaw would be able to remain in the country. Several thousand Japanese had entered western Canada to complete the Grand Trunk Railway, and thousands of eastern

Europeans had crossed the Atlantic in search of work in the eastern provinces, and the House of Commons had started to respond accordingly to demands for immigration restriction. The Immigration Act of 1906 had provided the government with the power to exclude several categories of immigrants, including those who were likely to become a public charge, those convicted of a crime, those involved in prostitution, and crucially for Thaw, those who were insane or who had been insane within the previous five years. Subsequent legislation in 1910 had strengthened the discretionary power of the federal government to exclude certain groups of immigrants, including political radicals, and enabled a board of inquiry to deport anyone who had lived in Canada for less than three years. A federal board of inquiry could refuse entry or deport anyone on any credible evidence, and the courts could neither review the decisions of a board nor hear appeals.[17]

William Shurtleff had criticized the decision to detain Thaw, but already the Bureau of Immigration had sent inspectors to Sherbrooke to establish a board of inquiry to determine if Thaw could enter Canada. The result seemed inevitable: Thaw, who had been in an insane asylum since 1908, would surely be returned to the United States just as quickly as he had arrived.[18]

But would the authorities return him directly to New York or to some other state? Thaw had entered Canada from Vermont, and he could reasonably expect the immigration inspectors to return him there. But New Hampshire could also claim the privilege of receiving Thaw. His arrest had arisen from a complaint by Burleigh Kelsea, the deputy sheriff of Coos

County, in New Hampshire. It was also possible that the board of inquiry would determine to return Thaw to his native state, Pennsylvania, a decision that would effectively stymie his extradition back to New York.

The New York authorities, anxious to recapture Thaw as soon as possible, were quick to assert their claim. Officials from Dutchess County, the jurisdiction in which the Matteawan asylum was located, soon arrived in Canada. Edward Conger, the district attorney, and Frederick Hornbeck, the sheriff, went first to Montreal to meet with government officials, later traveling to Sherbrooke for the immigration hearing. John Riley, the state superintendent of prisons, wired the American consul in Ottawa, asking for his assistance and suggesting that the Canadian government deport Thaw to Rouse's Point, a border crossing directly south of Montreal.[19]

William Shurtleff filed a writ of habeas corpus on August 20, saying that Thaw had not committed any offense in Canada and the arrest, in any case, had been improperly executed. There were, Shurtleff claimed, no grounds for the continued detention of his client.[20]

But Shurtleff realized his error almost immediately. The immigration inspectors had already gathered in Sherbrooke for the hearing that would decide Thaw's fate. The board of inquiry could meet, however, only if Thaw was available to answer questions; and he would not be available if he remained in jail in Sherbrooke.

It was obviously necessary for Shurtleff to withdraw his petition for a writ of habeas corpus. Thaw would then remain in jail until his trial on the original charge, and the board of inquiry could hold an immigration hearing only when that process had run its course. Thaw needed time, as much time as possible, to marshal his resources, to prepare his case, and his best option was to postpone the immigration hearing far into the future. It would be possible to nullify the writ of habeas corpus by petitioning the court to grant a second writ, a writ of discontinuance.

On August 27, crowds of sightseers from Sherbrooke and the neighboring villages started to gather outside the courthouse to witness Harry Thaw's appearance in support of his counsel's attempt to quash the petition of habeas corpus. Even Thaw was surprised at the enthusiasm of the well-wishers who applauded his short journey from the Sherbrooke jail to the courthouse. Hundreds of Canadians, waving hats and handkerchiefs, lined Winter Street as Thaw, sitting in an open carriage, accompanied by four guards, appeared at the front gate. An immense crowd applauded as Thaw, waving in acknowledgment, passed along Dufferin Avenue, turning onto Wellington Street, finally stopping in front of the courthouse. A squad of constables ran down the steps to shield Thaw from the surge of his supporters who pushed forward, threatening to overwhelm him. The police forced a passageway through the crowd, escorting Thaw through the doors of the courthouse.[21]

The judge, Arthur Goblensky, left no doubt in anyone's mind that he favored Thaw's petition. The lawyers for New York had no standing in the case, Goblensky announced, and he refused to hear their pleas. Harry Thaw, he continued, had asked to withdraw the writ of habeas corpus, and it would be absurd for the court to compel the writ. "It is the petitioner's right to have the writ withdrawn," Goblensky concluded. "No court can force it upon him. . . . Therefore his request is granted, and he is hereby ordered to be returned to jail."[22]

His supporters pushed forward to shake Thaw's hand and to congratulate him that he would now return to jail. A crowd of spectators cheered the prisoner as he appeared on the courthouse steps, waving their hats as his guards escorted him back into custody.

No one was more popular than Harry Thaw. He stood alone against the might of the United States, and every Canadian could applaud his courage. New York had sent its representatives to Sherbrooke, arrogantly assuming that the Canadian courts would bow to its demands, but Thaw had struck back and had emerged victorious.

Few Canadians knew the details that had previously emerged about Harry Thaw. They knew only that Thaw had killed a man who had raped his wife; but they had heard nothing about the accusations that he had assaulted and whipped young girls. The murder of Stanford White, in the opinion of many Canadians, had been an act of valor, and Thaw's continued incarceration in Matteawan had been unjust and unfair. He had sought refuge in Canada, but New York continued its persecution by attempting to return him to the asylum. Who would not wish Harry Thaw well in his fight against such injustice?

The applause for Thaw inside the courtroom and the cheers that greeted his appearance outside shocked the New York lawyers who had traveled to Sherbrooke. They had expected to travel back to New York with Harry Thaw; but now they would return empty-handed. Thaw would not now appear in court again until October, and who could say what might happen in the interim? His attorneys had hinted that he might seek to obtain bail; and then he would be free to slip away again, perhaps to Europe.

Most of the officials and lawyers from New York, reluctant to spend any more time waiting in Sherbrooke, returned home, but Jerome remained in Canada, seeking to deliver Thaw into the hands of the immigration inspectors, unwilling to leave before he had explored every option. "Thaw reminds me just now of a rat in a blind hole," Jerome remarked, "outside of which a cat is waiting." Would Alexis Dupuis, the judge who had remanded Thaw into custody on the original warrant, be willing to release him? The warrant had been faulty—everyone knew that—and Dupuis could act on his own initiative to free Thaw. But Dupuis was reluctant to assume such a burden, and his wife, Sophia Dupuis, was adamant that her husband should not be the cause of Harry Thaw's downfall. "I am for Thaw. He did the manly act when he shot White," she said to reporters. "Harry has been hounded by the New Yorkers.... He has been unjustly treated since the time he shot White." Alexis Dupuis endorsed his wife's statement, saying that he would allow the judicial process to run its course.[23]

Jean Boudreau, the constable who had arrested Thaw at Saint-Herménégilde, had committed him to jail on a charge— "escaping from a penitentiary at Matteawan"—that was flimsy at best. Thaw had escaped from an asylum, not a penitentiary, and in any case, there was no legal statute in Canada that applied to such an act in the United States. It had been a false arrest, and Boudreau, after discussing the matter with Jerome, realized that Thaw could sue him for damages. Boudreau could resolve his dilemma, Jerome suggested slyly, by petitioning for a writ of habeas corpus to release Harry Thaw from jail, and so, later that week, on Saturday, August 30, Boudreau applied for a writ on behalf of the prisoner.

W. H. McKeown, another attorney for Thaw, denounced Boudreau's writ as preposterous. Jerome had masterminded the affair, and Boudreau was the stalking horse. "Habeas corpus proceedings," McKeown stated, "must be instituted by a person acting for the prisoner." Harry Thaw had no intention, McKeown said, of holding the constable liable for damages, and Boudreau had nothing to fear. "Boudreau is in no danger of being sued by the Thaw family. Fancy a person of Thaw's wealth trying to recover from a country constable. Boudreau is only a tool and used as such by the New York men."[24]

The judge, Matthew Hutchinson, scheduled the hearing on Boudreau's petition for September 2, saying that he would hear arguments on the writ in private chambers. There would be no scenes in his courtroom, Hutchinson announced, similar to those that had occurred on Thaw's previous appearance, and he would allow only the parties involved, along with their lawyers, to attend.[25]

But again crowds of sightseers started to converge on Sherbrooke from the neighboring villages. Thaw's attorneys returned, gathering at the Hôtel Royal to debate their court-room strategy. The officials from New York, optimistic that this time they would triumph, boarded the train once more for the long journey north. Journalists and reporters from across the northeastern United States and from Canada also appeared, seeking accommodation wherever they could find it.

Thaw's supporters held an open-air meeting on the day of the hearing, the speakers denouncing the noxious presence of the New York authorities, one firebrand suggesting that Jerome should be tarred and feathered. Popular enthusiasm for Thaw appeared undiminished, but now, on his second appearance in court, there was an awakened determination on the part of the Canadian authorities that the matter end as quickly as possible. Lomer Gouin, the attorney general of Quebec, signaled the resolve of the provincial government, sending a representative from Quebec City to campaign against Thaw. "Our jails are not public boarding houses," Aimé Geoffrion declared. "It is the Attorney General's desire that this matter be settled instanter by the liberation of Mr. Thaw. . . . If he is not liberated on the writ other means will be taken. Thaw must not be harbored in the Canadian jail."[26]

The federal government also acted, sending a battalion of immigration inspectors to Sherbrooke. No one could predict if the judge would grant Boudreau's petition and release Thaw from jail; but the board of inquiry would be prepared to hold a hearing on Thaw's status at the earliest opportunity, just as soon as he was available.

Jerome also had marshaled his resources in anticipation of Thaw's release from jail and subsequent deportation. Deputy sheriffs from Dutchess County, along with several attendants from the Matteawan asylum, waited across the border in Vermont, ready to seize Thaw. The immigration hearing would last only a few hours, Jerome predicted, and his men would then take hold of Thaw at the border crossing, driving in a fast car to New York State to forestall any chance that the prisoner might claim refuge in Vermont.[27]

Even Harry Thaw now seemed resigned to his expulsion from Canada, packing his possessions into a large steamer trunk, posing in his cell for the newspaper photographers, and wishing his guards good cheer.

Matthew Hutchinson delivered his decision on Wednesday, September 3. He believed that the prisoner was being held illegally on an erroneous warrant, and he would therefore grant the writ of habeas corpus for his release. "The jailer," Hutchinson proclaimed, "has no authority to hold Harry K. Thaw in custody. He is hereby liberated and discharged from his present detention."[28]

E. Blake Robertson, the deputy superintendent of immigration, moved to the front of the courtroom, placing his right hand on Thaw's shoulder. "You are under arrest," he said, as two Dominion constables, distinctive in their blue uniforms, took hold of Thaw, one on either side, shepherding him toward a side entrance. Four more policemen suddenly appeared to escort Thaw to a waiting automobile, and within minutes a convoy of four cars had left Sherbrooke, driving south to Coaticook, a small town a few miles from the United States border.[29]

Immigration inspectors for the Dominion of Canada pose with Harry Thaw in this 1913 photograph. Thaw had entered Canada illegally on August 17, 1913. His attorneys were confident that he would be able to remain in Canada, but the Bureau of Immigration was determined to deport Thaw at the first opportunity. (Library of Congress, LC-DIG-ds-10591)

The Bureau of Immigration now took custody of Thaw, confining him to rooms above the Coaticook railroad station on Rue Lovell, and on September 4, the board of inquiry began its interrogation of the prisoner. There was little doubt that Thaw had entered Canada illegally, and it seemed probable that the board of inquiry would find additional grounds for his deportation on account of his previous status as an insane patient at Matteawan. Théophile Maréchal, a representative of the federal government, arrived later that week from Ottawa to press the board of inquiry to deport Thaw immediately. "Canada will have no more of Thaw," Maréchal stated. "The Government does not want him here. He is undoubtedly an undesirable alien. . . . He cannot override the immigration laws of the Dominion, and under them we will deport him."[30]

Even Thaw's lawyers in Canada seemed resigned to his fate. The board of inquiry would announce its decision later that afternoon, on Friday, September 5, and no one believed that Thaw would be able to stay in Canada. "It is only a matter of hours," William Shurtleff predicted, "when Harry Thaw will have to go back to the United States."[31]

That morning, as the immigration inspectors met with Thaw in their offices, a small group of newspapermen whiled away their time playing poker on the sidewalk outside, using a large suitcase as an impromptu card table. One reporter beckoned to Jerome, standing a few feet away, suggesting that he try his luck. It was all good fun—everyone knew that Jerome liked to roll the dice—and the district attorney accepted some cards, putting several pennies on the table as a wager.

Jerome lingered for only a few minutes, playing a couple of hands before making his way along Rue Lovell to his hotel. But a passer-by, Wilford Aldrich, a mill hand, walking on the other side of the street, had spotted Jerome placing his bets, and later that morning a constable, John Andrews, approached Jerome as he sat sunning himself on the porch of his hotel.

"You are under arrest," Andrews announced, "for gambling on the highway." Andrews drew back his shoulders, standing erect before the district attorney, his right hand clutching a warrant for Jerome's arrest. "I am a constable of Coaticook," he continued, "and as a representative of His Majesty's law I order you to come with me."

A small crowd, attracted by the presence of the constable, had gathered in front of the hotel, and as Jerome started to descend the steps, some catcalls rang out.

"Walk along quickly," Andrews commanded.[32]

Jerome, the interloper from New York, the persecutor of Harry Thaw, was the most despised man in Coaticook, and the constable was delighted that he could play his part in the drama. Jerome seemed to take the arrest in his stride, calmly following the directions of the constable, ignoring the jeers of the crowd, as they walked together toward the town hall.

It was too improbable, too ludicrous, that Jerome, who had fought so tenaciously as district attorney against the gambling dens in Manhattan, should now sit in a jail cell for illicit gaming. Hector Verret, an attorney in Canada for the New York authorities, obtained bail for Jerome later in the day, winning his release that afternoon, but the episode, a source of great entertainment for Thaw and his supporters, had embarrassed the Canadian government. Jerome remained unruffled, saying only that he suspected that the Coaticook police had detained him in order to hinder his efforts to capture Harry Thaw.

The arrest of Jerome was only a sideshow to the main event. At half past three, Blake Robertson emerged to announce that the Canadian government would deport Thaw immediately on both counts against him: that he had entered Canada illegally, and that he had been insane when he crossed the Canadian border.

Thaw's attorneys in Coaticook had been conspicuous by their apparent acquiescence in the proceedings of the board of inquiry, and even Thaw had been uncharacteristically taciturn, refusing invitations by New York reporters to comment on his approaching deportation. His cause appeared hopeless, and it seemed to casual observers that even his attorneys had deserted him, leaving him defenseless against the authorities.

But appearances were deceptive. Two of the best lawyers in Canada, Napoléon Laflamme and James Greenshields, both King's Counsel, had spent that morning in Montreal arguing Thaw's case before the Court of Appeals, asking the court to grant Thaw a writ of prohibition against an adverse decision by the board of inquiry. Now, just at that moment when the immigration authorities announced that they would send Thaw back to the United States, Greenshields arrived in Coaticook on a special train, triumphantly waving the writ from the Court of Appeals. The Bureau of Immigration could not deport Thaw, not yet, Greenshields announced: Thaw's attorneys had secured him an appearance in Montreal on September 15, before the Court of King's Bench.

Greenshields threatened that Thaw's attorneys would seek to challenge the 1910 legislation that allowed the government to restrict immigration. "We can keep the fight in the highest courts for an indefinite period," he predicted, "and perhaps knock out certain paragraphs of the present law."[33]

Théophile Maréchal, the federal representative, indignant

that the courts had foolishly granted Thaw a reprieve, railed angrily at the decision before leaving Coaticook to travel to Montreal to meet with Charles Doherty, the minister of justice in the Conservative government. "Thaw will gain some respite," Maréchal said as he boarded the train, "but his case will not be allowed to lag. If a man in his position can upset our laws we are no longer safe."[34]

The news that Thaw's lawyers had halted his deportation spread quickly through Coaticook. The immigration inspectors had confined Thaw to a set of rooms above the railroad station, and crowds of sightseers from Coaticook and the surrounding villages began to gather to cheer their hero. Thaw, who had access to a balcony overlooking Rue Lovell, reciprocated their enthusiasm, appearing on the balcony to wave to the crowds and to acknowledge their hurrahs. Thaw had brought prosperity to the town, and on Saturday, September 6, the citizens of Coaticook held a parade to honor their benefactor. The Coaticook Fife and Drum Corps stepped out proudly at the head of the demonstration, playing "The British Grenadiers" and other popular marching songs, while several dozen townsfolk paraded behind with signs in support of the prisoner.[35]

Three days later a train carrying a regional dramatic society stopped briefly at Coaticook. The company was destined for Sherbrooke to stage performances of *The Pink Lady,* a musical comedy that had had a successful run in New York. The actors, including a dozen chorus girls, took advantage of the interruption in their journey to serenade Thaw, laughingly telling him that they expected him to come see the show when he eventually won his freedom.[36]

Harry Thaw had never felt more confident that he would remain safe in Canada. His lawyers had advised him that they would continue to appeal his case through the courts, even taking their appeals to the Privy Council in England. The federal government had greatly expanded its power to exclude immigrants on the basis of vague and arbitrary clauses contained within the immigration laws of 1906 and 1910, and Thaw's appeals, according to his lawyer James Greenshields, would challenge the constitutionality of this legislation. The government had provided boards of inquiry with the authority to exclude immigrants while simultaneously ensuring that the courts could not review decisions of the boards; and Thaw's appeals would challenge this provision also. "Thaw's chances of ultimate freedom," Greenshields remarked, "are better now than they have been at any time since he was first arrested. The Immigration act is full of holes and is a disgrace to Canada."[37]

Nothing could have occasioned more alarm within the Conservative government than the remarks attributed to Greenshields. The Conservatives had won the 1911 federal election by appealing to national pride and by promising to restrict Asian immigration into western Canada. Neither the prime minister, Robert Borden, nor the minister of justice, Charles Doherty, could afford to tolerate Harry Thaw's challenge to the immigration laws. A weak response would imperil the electoral prospects of the Conservatives. But what could be done? Thaw's attorneys had threatened to continue their appeals indefinitely, and no one doubted that the Thaw family would be willing to spend their millions in support. Could the federal government somehow thwart Thaw's challenge, or would the legal process continue, perhaps for many more years?

Harry Thaw lay in bed half-asleep, listening to the early morning birdsong outside his window. He could hear the murmur of voices below as the commuters, quietly chatting among themselves, waited on the station platform for the first train to Sherbrooke. He expected to take the train to Montreal, later that day, for the hearing before the Court of King's Bench, and he congratulated himself that, once again, he had evaded the net that had tightened around him.

The door to his bedroom suddenly opened with a loud crash. He recognized the familiar figure of Blake Robertson, the deputy superintendent of immigration, and watched, still half-asleep, as Robertson started to walk toward him. Four policemen, distinctive in their blue jackets and steel-tipped helmets, crowded into the room, waiting expectantly as Robertson pulled back the bedclothes.

"Thaw, get up!" Robertson shouted. "I have an order to deport you immediately." He held a piece of paper in his right hand, thrusting it impatiently into Thaw's face. "Here is an order signed by the Minister of Justice commanding deportation to the United States. You must come at once — there is an automobile waiting down stairs."

"But you can't take me," Thaw protested as he got out of

bed. He stood in his bare feet, his eyes wide in surprise as he gazed at the piece of paper that Robertson held out before him. "I am to go to Montreal."

"Hurry up! Don't talk," Robertson snapped, returning the paper to his pocket as he reached out to seize his prisoner. "Get up and get dressed. You will be taken to the border in a motor car."[38]

The two men stood only inches apart; yet somehow Thaw managed to move a few paces to his left, grabbing a water tumbler that stood on his bedside table. He stepped quickly away, skipping around the bed as he threw the tumbler at Robertson's head. It missed its intended target, smashing through a window and sending a shower of glass onto the station platform below.

"I'll see you all in hell!" Thaw shouted to his tormentors. "My lawyers will take care of this."

Already he had reached a second window, taking hold of the casement to call down to the startled commuters below.

"They are kidnapping me! Don't let them get me!"

But two policemen had seized him, one man pulling him away from the window, the other man clasping his hand over Thaw's mouth. They dragged him back into the center of the room, stripping him of his pajamas, pulling on his shirt and trousers, fastening his shoes, tightly holding his wrists as they pushed and pulled Thaw toward the door, carrying him along a narrow hallway, down the stairs, and to a waiting car.

The commuters watched in amazement as the four policemen carried Thaw in midair, his legs and arms thrashing helplessly as his captors pushed him into the limousine. Thaw continued to appeal for assistance, shouting against his abduction, but the spectators stood motionless, not daring to interfere, silently watching the car as it drove away in a cloud of dust.

The car headed directly south, crossing the unguarded border twenty minutes later, stopping inside the United States on a deserted backcountry road one mile from the village of Norton's Mills. Robertson, a grin on his face, turned to address Thaw.

"You may get out here," he said, nodding to one of the policemen to push Thaw out of the car.

"Where are we?" Thaw asked, looking around.

"You are in the United States," Robertson replied, "and you are a free man so far as Canada is concerned. Do not return to Canada."[39]

The car door slammed shut behind him as Thaw stumbled into the road and watched the limousine drive away, back to Canada. He waited, standing in the middle of the road in the morning sunshine, expecting to flag down a passing car; but there was no traffic at such an early hour. It was not yet nine o'clock, and he suddenly realized that he had had nothing to eat that morning. He searched his pockets, hoping to find his wallet, but he found only a few dollar bills. There was no collar to his shirt, and he had left Canada without a necktie; his trousers, missing a belt to hold them in place, sagged awkwardly around his waist.

Not a single car had passed in either direction in ten minutes; and then, with a sudden jolt, Harry Thaw realized the peril of his position. He was now back in the United States, in either Vermont or New Hampshire. Jerome had threatened to seize him at the border, saying that he would take Thaw back to New York in a fast car. Jerome would learn that he had left Canada and his men would soon be scouring the backcountry roads, searching for him. He had to get away as quickly as possible; but how?

9

FINAL VERDICT

September 11, 1913–July 16, 1915

HE SPOTTED THE MOTORCAR IN THE FAR DISTANCE, ITS ENGINE rattling as it struggled up a steep hill. The car disappeared from view and then, just as suddenly, it reappeared, turning a corner, heading directly toward him. Harry Thaw recognized Frank Elser, a correspondent for the Associated Press, and he waved, watching as the car came to a halt. Elser jumped out to shake Thaw's hand, telling him that the reporters had all left Canada, scattering across northern Vermont in search of him.

Elser could not help Thaw in evading capture, he said, and he could neither give him money nor provide him with directions; but, he added slyly, almost as an afterthought, he would have no objection if Thaw commandeered the car on his own initiative.

Harry Thaw gladly accepted the suggestion, ordering the chauffeur to drive east, toward New Hampshire. There was no sign of Jerome, no indication that the New Yorkers even knew that he had left Canada, but Vermont is contiguous on its western border with the state of New York, and Thaw had no desire to give Jerome any opportunity to find him.

They paused for breakfast at a farmhouse near Averill, a village in eastern Vermont, before crossing the Connecticut River into New Hampshire. From time to time Thaw, hoping to speak to his attorneys in Montreal, would stop the car at a wayside inn, asking to use the telephone; but already the wires were busy with the news of his departure from Canada, and the operator could never make the connection.

It was eleven o'clock when they saw, on the road to Stewartstown Hollow, a black sedan driving toward them. The car slowed as it approached, its occupants carefully scrutinizing Thaw, and suddenly one of the passengers motioned for them to pull alongside.

"Stop! I'm the Sheriff of Coos county," the man called out, stepping from the car. Holman Drew introduced himself, saying that an alarm had gone out across the state that morning.

"I want you, Harry Thaw," Drew commanded. "You must come along with us."

"You can't touch me," Thaw replied defiantly. "I'm a free man and you have no warrant for me."

He did not need a warrant, Drew replied. He moved toward Thaw, his hand almost touching the revolver in his holster, and he paused, waiting for his deputies to surround Thaw, nodding to one man to step to the front of the car to prevent its departure.

"You better come with us to Colebrook," he said.

"Give me a square deal, Sheriff," Thaw pleaded. His resistance had suddenly crumbled and he acquiesced to the sheriff's demand. "They did me dirt in Canada," he complained, walking toward the sedan, a deputy sheriff trailing close behind, "and I hope for better treatment in New Hampshire."

"We will only do what is right," Drew replied.[1]

The news of Thaw's capture sparked a flurry of activity back in New York. Edward Conger, the Dutchess County district attorney, convened a grand jury the next day, September 12, to consider an indictment against Thaw on a charge of conspiracy to escape. Later that evening Conger traveled to the state capital, Albany, to meet with the governor, William Sulzer, to prepare an extradition request to return Thaw to New York. The state attorney general, Thomas Carmody, also met with Conger, telling him that he had asked Travers Jerome to go to New Hampshire to represent the state and to coordinate with the local authorities for Thaw's return.[2]

The governor of New Hampshire, Samuel Felker, had already announced that he would grant any extradition request from New York, provided that New York followed the correct procedure. Neither Felker nor the state attorney general, James Tuttle, had any desire to allow Thaw to remain in New Hampshire. "You can rest assured," Tuttle declared, "that New Hampshire will go the limit to get him back into responsible hands." William Chandler, a former member of the United States Senate from New Hampshire, urged the governor to act as quickly as possible, saying that, under the federal constitution, the state had an obligation to return Thaw to New York. "He killed a man in New York deliberately," Chandler exclaimed. There had been nothing improper in the legal proceedings that had followed the murder, nothing that could justify Thaw in claiming sanctuary in another state, and he had no right to remain in New Hampshire. "Does any one seriously say justice was not done him? When he escaped and came to Canada, was he not fleeing from justice?"[3]

But there could be no extradition of Harry Thaw until a grand jury in New York State had voted for the indictment charging him with conspiracy to escape, and word now reached New Hampshire that the jurors in Dutchess County had refused their consent. There seemed no good reason why the citizens of Dutchess County should burden themselves with the cost of bringing Thaw back from New Hampshire to put him on trial on the charge of conspiracy and to lock him up in the asylum a second time, all at public expense. Thaw's lawyers would then, no doubt, continue to agitate for his release from the asylum, and the taxpayers would again have to bear the burden of legal battles that could continue for many more years.[4]

Harry Thaw was jubilant that the grand jury had refused to vote for the indictment. Travers Jerome had pursued him for many years, always expecting the taxpayers to support his vendetta, and finally the citizens of New York had refused their consent. How could New Hampshire now extradite him back to New York if there was no indictment charging him with a crime? "The attempt is so ridiculous, and so utterly absurd," Thaw declared, speaking of Jerome's quixotic endeavor to extradite him, "that the people of New York should wash their hands of any further obligation for my maintenance."[5]

Once again, just as in Canada, Harry Thaw had captured the public imagination. He had stood alone, against the might of New York State, always refusing to be cowed or intimidated, and he had again triumphed over adversity. He had achieved an almost mythic status as the heroic individual who had succeeded against the odds, and he had emerged victorious. The New Hampshire authorities had moved Thaw to the state capital, Concord, in anticipation of a hearing on extradition, and once again large crowds had appeared, first at Colebrook, then at Littleton, to cheer Thaw on his journey and to demand his release.

He arrived in Concord on September 17, receiving a rapturous reception at the train station, more boisterous than anything he had previously experienced in either Canada or the United States. The mayor, Charles French, called on Thaw at his hotel, welcoming him to Concord and asking the prisoner for his autograph. A crowd of supporters had gathered on Main Street, in front of the hotel, and French invited Thaw to step onto the veranda to say a few words; but Thaw's attorneys brushed aside the request, saying only that he would give a statement at another time.

There was little to indicate, during Thaw's first few weeks in Concord, as he waited to learn if he could remain in New Hampshire, that he was a prisoner. He had secured the largest apartment—a suite of rooms on the fifth floor—in the Eagle Hotel, the best hotel in Concord, where he received the local politicians and dignitaries who came to pay him homage. From time to time he would go sightseeing, visiting some landmark in town or making an excursion into the country-side. St. Paul's School, an elite boarding school, was nearby, and Thaw paid a visit, greeting some of the boys and watching a tennis match. On another occasion Thaw visited the former home of Mary Baker Eddy, the founder of Christian Science, remarking on the attractive appearance of the house but say-ing nothing on the merits of her theology.[6]

He had anticipated that the failure to win an indictment in Dutchess County would force New York State to abandon its demand for extradition. But Travers Jerome was not to be denied, and on October 23, six weeks after Thaw first arrived in New Hampshire, Jerome presented an indictment for con-spiracy to a grand jury in New York County. Several men, members of a West Side gang, according to Jerome, had con-spired with Thaw to effect his escape from Matteawan. They had hatched the plan in a Hell's Kitchen saloon, and it was therefore legitimate, Jerome argued, to convene a grand jury in Manhattan to hear the indictment.

The situation had been reversed in the twinkling of an eye. Seventeen witnesses testified before the grand jury, and the foreman, George Putnam, one of Jerome's closest acquain-tances, called a vote that afternoon. The jurors needed only a few minutes to decide to support the indictment, and the next day, October 24, Jerome, accompanied by Franklin Kennedy, the deputy attorney general, traveled to Albany to meet with the new governor, Martin Glynn, to obtain the requisition for Thaw's extradition. That evening Jerome caught the train to

New Hampshire, arriving at Concord late at night, and the next morning he presented the extradition request to the governor, Samuel Felker.[7]

There had never been any doubt that Felker would honor the request. Several petitions asking him to deny extradition had arrived at the state capital, but the United States Constitution, Felker believed, gave him no choice in the matter. The extradition clause in the Constitution could not have been more explicit—"a person...who shall flee from justice, and be found in another state, shall on demand of the executive authority of the state from which he fled, be delivered up"— and so, on November 8, two weeks after receiving the request, Felker ordered the removal of Thaw back to New York.[8]

But Thaw's lawyers, acting in anticipation of Felker's decision, had already applied to the United States District Court for a writ of habeas corpus; and Thaw would therefore remain in New Hampshire, in the custody of a federal marshal, until the hearing on the writ. Edgar Aldrich, a judge on the District Court, informed the attorneys for both sides that he expected to give a decision on the writ sometime during the following year; but the circumstances of Thaw's extradition, he stated, had raised important constitutional questions. The Constitution of the United States, Aldrich explained, did stipulate that one state should acquiesce in the extradition of an individual who had absconded from custody in another state; but should extradition apply in all circumstances and under all conditions? Was the demand of one state for the extradition of a fugitive absolute upon another state?

The State of New York had confined Harry Thaw for several years as an insane person, yet the extradition request had been made on an indictment charging Thaw with conspiracy. How, Aldrich wondered, could an insane person conspire to commit a crime? Should extradition take place if the request were patently unreasonable or even capricious? He would give his decision, Aldrich continued, but only in expectation that one side or the other would appeal to the United States Supreme Court for a final and more definitive judgment.[9]

Aldrich did decide to grant the writ, eventually issuing his verdict in April 1914 and formally releasing Thaw from extradition, but he left undetermined Thaw's request to be released on bail, thus ensuring that Thaw would remain in Concord in the custody of a federal marshal. "The constitutional right of extradition," Aldrich declared, "does not reasonably apply to such a situation as this. . . . An order will be made sustaining the writ, and that the petitioner be discharged from the extradition process."[10]

The attorney general of New York, Thomas Carmody, called a press conference later that same day. The state, he told the journalists, would appeal the decision to the United States Supreme Court. Only an executive power, in this case the governor of New Hampshire, had the authority to decide to extradite a fugitive, and Aldrich, representing the judicial power, had no constitutional right to influence the matter one way or the other. "No court has the power to assume jurisdiction in the case," Carmody declared. "We will seek to have the appeal determined as soon as possible."[11]

⋆   ⋆   ⋆

The attorneys sat at their desks in silence, waiting for the arrival of the justices, watching the clerks as they prepared for the morning session of the Supreme Court. It had snowed during the night in Washington, D.C., and the temperature outside had dropped almost to freezing; but the senate chamber, heated by four large iron stoves, was uncomfortably warm. The chamber, a large semicircular room in the north wing of the Capitol, was decorated in crimson and gold, but everything seemed slightly threadbare, as if the Treasury had positively refused to spend any more money than necessary on the Supreme Court. The mahogany desks and chairs were nicked and scuffed with age; the carpet, decorated with a pattern of gold stars, had faded almost to oblivion; evidently no one had thought to clean the window drapes in several decades; and even the ink in the inkstands seemed curdled and crusted.

The nine justices, each man accompanied by a clerk, started to appear in the chamber shortly before ten o'clock. Joseph McKenna was the first to arrive, greeting the waiting lawyers with a slight nod of his head; Mahlon Pitney, Joseph Lamar, and Willis Van Devanter, all nominated by William Taft, appeared shortly afterward; and Edward White, the chief justice, entered next, taking a seat at the center of the long table on the dais at the front of the chamber. James McReynolds, nominated earlier that year by Woodrow Wilson, had been on the Supreme Court only since August, less than four months, but already his colleagues despised him for his acerbic temper and mean-spirited disposition, and none of the five justices already in the chamber acknowledged his presence. William Day, one of the more competent and conscientious members of the Court, the author of the recent decision in *Weeks v. United States,* came next, a few minutes after the hour, followed closely by Charles Evans Hughes, the former governor of New York, an intensely ambitious man who was already plotting to win the Republican nomination for the 1916 presidential election.

Oliver Wendell Holmes was the last to arrive, taking his place on the dais beside his colleagues. He was now seventy-three, the oldest member of the Court, with thick white hair, a luxuriant mustache, and clear blue eyes. There was an austere grandeur about him, an old-fashioned majesty in his appearance, an effect magnified by his morning suit, black waistcoat, and striped trousers.[12]

Franklin Kennedy, the deputy attorney general for New York, spoke first, saying that a grand jury had voted an indictment to charge Thaw with conspiracy, and on that basis, the governor of New York had requested Thaw's extradition. There had been nothing improper about the demand, and New Hampshire had indicated its willingness to proceed accordingly. The federal Constitution was unambiguous in mandating the extradition of an individual charged with a crime, and New York should receive Thaw without any further delay.

Later that day, after lunch, the justices listened as Thaw's lawyers, Philander Knox and William Stone, explained that the circumstances were so singular as to destroy any merit in the request for extradition. Thaw had been acquitted on the charge of murder at his trial in 1908, Knox argued, and he had committed no crime in leaving Matteawan. The asylum was in Dutchess County, and an indictment against Thaw properly belonged only to that county, yet the attorney general had presented the indictment to a grand jury in New York County. Last but not least, the State of New York had declared Thaw to be insane yet claimed nevertheless that he was capable of conspiring with others to escape from the asylum.

The next day, on December 12, the chief justice, Edward White, asked Oliver Wendell Holmes to write the unanimous opinion of the Court in upholding the appeal of New York. Holmes had already written ten decisions that term, more than most of his colleagues, but it was not a complicated case and he readily agreed, saying that he would deliver the opinion before the Court adjourned for the Christmas holiday.[13]

Harry Thaw, according to the decision of the Supreme Court announced on December 21, had no standing to remain in New Hampshire. Thaw claimed that the indictment against him had no merit, but this assertion did not thereby give him the right to absent himself from the legal process to be followed in the New York courts. "There is no doubt that Thaw is a fugitive from justice," Holmes wrote. "The Constitution says nothing about habeas corpus in this connection, but peremptorily requires that, upon proper demand, the person charged shall be delivered up. . . . It is for a New York jury to determine whether, at the moment of the conspiracy, Thaw was insane. . . . We regard it as too clear for lengthy discussion that Thaw should be delivered up at once."[14]

*   *   *

It had been sixteen months since Thaw first entered New Hampshire and finally, finally, the State of New York had him once more in its grasp. A boisterous crowd, almost five hundred strong, gathered at the Concord courthouse at eleven o'clock on a chill January morning to witness the transfer of the prisoner into the custody of New York, loudly cheering their support for Thaw as the Dutchess County sheriff, Frederick Hornbeck, escorted him from the courthouse to the Eagle Hotel to collect his belongings.

That afternoon, more than one thousand men, women, and children waited at Union Station on Commonwealth Avenue, hoping to catch a glimpse of Thaw when he boarded the 2:25 p.m. train to leave Concord. Thaw, escorted by three detectives, arrived just in time to catch the train, and the crowd surged forward, pushing and shoving in an attempt to see the prisoner before he left town. One elderly woman, tears streaming down her face, threw herself at Thaw, clutching at his coat, trying to embrace him before his departure.[15]

The Boston newspapers had already reported that Thaw would spend several hours in the city before traveling onward to New York, and that afternoon, January 22, Bostonians started to gather at North Station to greet his arrival. The train came into the station shortly before five o'clock, and a dozen constables surrounded Thaw as he stepped onto the platform. The crowd, numbering almost two thousand, surged this way and that, shouting their support for Harry, but the police, forming a circle around the prisoner, drew their clubs and started to advance. Some roughnecks from the South End stood in their way, at the platform entrance, calling on the crowd to free Thaw, but the constables rushed ahead, pummeling the hooligans with their nightsticks, eventually reaching the station exit.[16]

It was all great fun, and Thaw, the axis around which the world seemed to turn, appeared to enjoy himself enormously. That evening he received visitors at Young's Hotel on Court Street, greeting a stream of local worthies who came to pay their respects. The former mayor of Boston, John (Honey Fitz) Fitzgerald, came to the hotel to welcome Thaw to the city and to wish him well. Fitzgerald, a garrulous extrovert with a passion for baseball, later chatted with reporters in the hotel lobby, giving them his rendition of a popular song, "Sweet Adeline."[17]

The next day, Saturday, January 23, crowds started to gather at South Station in anticipation of Thaw's departure from the city. It was an injustice, everyone believed, that New York continued to persecute Harry Thaw. He had acted in defense of his wife in killing Stanford White, and it seemed outrageous that New York could again imprison him for such a selfless deed.

No one could predict how many persons might be waiting at the station; no one could tell if there might be an attempt to free the prisoner. It would be possible, the sheriff decided, to take Thaw to New York only on the night train, leaving South Station at one o'clock in the morning, at a time when the crowds would have dispersed.[18]

The station was almost deserted, and no one among the waiting passengers paid any attention when Thaw, accompanied by his entourage—Franklin Kennedy, the deputy attorney general; Frederick Hornbeck, the Dutchess County sheriff; Travers Jerome; and two detectives—arrived at South Station shortly after midnight. The journey, in a special carriage provided by the New Haven Railroad, passed without incident, and six hours later, when the train arrived at Grand Central early on Sunday morning, Hornbeck could take his prisoner to the Tombs without anyone realizing that Harry Thaw was once again in New York.

The warden, John Hanley, assigned the new arrival to a cell on the second tier. That morning Thaw attended services in the prison chapel. He was in good spirits, buoyed by the support he had received from the crowds in Boston, and confident that he would soon win his freedom. "I welcome the opportunity to stand trial here," Thaw told a reporter from the *Evening Telegram*. "I have no fear of the result."[19]

The State of New York had finally captured Harry Thaw, and he would again appear for trial in the Criminal Courts Building. New York had been able to extradite Thaw from New Hampshire only on account of an indictment for conspiracy, and there was now an obligation on the state to put the prisoner on trial. But according to Thaw's attorneys, Thaw could not simultaneously be insane *and* guilty of a criminal act; and if he was found guilty, New York would no longer have any claim to return him to the asylum.

Thaw would serve his sentence in the penitentiary—no more than twelve months, according to the statute—and he would then be a free man. The trial, according to John Stanchfield, lead counsel for the defense, would be more a verdict on

Thaw's mental condition than a judgment on his escape from the asylum. "We expect," Stanchfield said at the opening of the trial, "to try the question of insanity before this jury. We will show that at the time Thaw left Matteawan he was sane. We will produce witnesses to show that he was sane, believed that he was sane and had a perfect right to go free."

It would work to Thaw's advantage, therefore, to demonstrate to the jury that he had knowingly planned his escape and that he was guilty of the charge against him; and so on March 11, 1915, Stanchfield called Harry Thaw as a witness to testify against himself.

Thaw, in response to questions from his attorney, stated that he had been in the asylum from February 1908 until his escape in August 1913. He had repeatedly attempted to obtain his release from Matteawan by petitioning the courts on a writ of habeas corpus, but in each instance the judge had denied his application. He had believed himself to be sane, but successive superintendents refused to issue a certificate of recovery to allow him to leave the asylum. The situation had become intolerable, and in 1912 his attorneys advised him that, since he had never been convicted of a crime, he could not be held against his will.

"Was there a time," Stanchfield asked, "when you had conversation with people about your right to leave?"

"Yes."

"Did you see lawyers?"

"I did," Thaw replied. "I was advised that there was no law against my leaving Matteawan so long as I did not do it by violence.... I was exceedingly particular not to commit a crime."

His attorneys had warned him beforehand that he should neither attempt to bribe the attendants nor assault anyone when
leaving the asylum.

He had arranged through an intermediary, Horace Hoffman, to hire Richard Butler to drive him north into Canada,
giving Hoffman $7,000 to pay Butler and to secure a car and a
driver for the journey.

"I intended to go to Pittsburgh," said Thaw. "First I expected
to go through Connecticut to Canada, through Canada to
Detroit, and from there to Pittsburgh, which is my home."[20]

Other witnesses also testified during the trial, but neither
the witnesses for the defense nor the witnesses for the state
provided evidence to contradict the indictment. It was most
peculiar: both sides desired the same result.

The defense, on the one hand, would welcome a guilty verdict as proof that Thaw was sane when he left the asylum. The
judge would, no doubt, give him a custodial sentence, but
Thaw, after spending a few months in the penitentiary, would
then be a free man, and New York would have no further
claim on him.

The prosecution, on the other hand, would welcome a
guilty verdict as the guarantee that the state would eventually
be able to apprehend Thaw. In 1908, at the conclusion of the
second trial, the judge, Victor Dowling, had committed Thaw
to the asylum, and that committal was still in effect. The Matteawan superintendent, Raymond Kleb, would send his attendants to capture Thaw just as soon as he left the penitentiary,
at the moment when he stepped away from the prison gates,
and they would immediately return him to the asylum.

The judge, Alfred Page, instructed the jury not to consider the matter of Thaw's sanity. That question was irrelevant, Page said, to the charge of conspiracy. Had Harry Thaw conspired with others to leave the asylum? If the jurors believed that Thaw had known that he was committing an illegal act in walking away from the asylum, then he would have acted with criminal intent and the jurors should return a guilty verdict.[21]

It seemed almost a foregone conclusion that the twelve jurors would vote to convict; but the first ballot—eight to four for acquittal—signaled the possibility that there might be a hung jury. The next day, Saturday, March 13, the foreman, Frank Bailey, told the judge that the jurors had agreed on their verdict. Ten minutes later they filed into a crowded courtroom.

The clerk, William Penney, called the roll of the jurors, asking each man to identify himself. Penney then called on the foreman to announce the verdict.

"Not guilty," Bailey said, "of conspiracy as charged."

There was a gasp of surprise among the spectators. Frank Cook, the deputy attorney general, jumped to his feet, calling out to the judge, "Your Honor, there are attendants from Matteawan waiting here to take this man back to Matteawan, where he belongs." Two men had stepped forward, away from the crowd of spectators, and Cook motioned with his hand as if commanding them to seize hold of Thaw. The jury had acquitted Thaw, Cook explained, and there was no longer any legal sanction against him. The State of New York would therefore immediately exercise its authority to return Thaw to the asylum.

But Abel Smith, a member of the defense team, also stepped forward, protesting to the judge that New York had no right to interfere with his client in this way. "There are motion papers before Your Honor," Smith shouted above the hubbub, "asking that Thaw be returned to the State of New Hampshire from which place he was extradited." New York had extradited Thaw on an indictment for conspiracy. The jury had absolved him of the charge, and it would be unethical — an act of bad faith — for New York now to attempt to detain him on some other pretext.[22]

Two days later, on March 16, the judge denied the motion that Thaw be allowed to return to New Hampshire, saying that New York did indeed have a right to detain Thaw and to send him back to the asylum. Thaw was now within the borders of New York State and was subject to its jurisdiction. "The motion is therefore denied," Page wrote in his decision, "and the Sheriff is directed to deliver the said Thaw to the proper authorities, to be conveyed to the Matteawan State Asylum for the Insane."[23]

But already Thaw's attorneys had applied for a writ of habeas corpus. The State of New York must now demonstrate the grounds on which it claimed possession of Harry Thaw.

It had always been customary in the New York courts for one judge alone to decide habeas corpus, but nothing in the Code of Civil Procedure foreclosed the possibility that a jury might make the decision, and Thaw's lawyers now asked the judge, Peter Hendrick, to convene a jury to hear the application. Hendrick was quick to adopt the suggestion, saying, however, that the jury would act only in an advisory role. He would listen to the evidence, he would consider the jury's verdict, and then he would make his decision. "The time has come," Hendrick stated, "when the question of Thaw's sanity should be determined by the court, with the aid of twelve men who are not lawyers or doctors, but who are called from the various walks of life to aid the court by their advice."[24]

It was a fateful decision, one that opened up the real possibility that Harry Thaw would finally win his freedom. There had been several previous hearings on Thaw's sanity, but always a single judge had made the final decision, and always that decision had denied Thaw his liberty. But now, for the first time, a jury would help to determine his fate, and that jury seemed more likely to decide in favor of Thaw. Nearly a decade had passed since the murder of Stanford White, but public sentiment in favor of the killer had never ebbed. Thaw had avenged the rape of his wife—nothing else mattered—and everyone agreed that he had acted with justification. The authorities had unfairly persecuted Thaw for nine long years, pursuing him relentlessly, always clamoring to incarcerate him, and he had suffered enough. It was time, most New Yorkers agreed, to end his torment.

John Stanchfield, in his opening address to the court, candidly admitted that his client had suffered temporary derangement when he had seen Stanford White in the audience at the opening of *Mamzelle Champagne*. But Thaw had long since regained his sanity and there was no longer any reason to confine him in an asylum. He had lived peacefully in New Hampshire for almost eighteen months, and nothing had occurred during that time to indicate that he was insane. He had not assaulted or attacked anyone; he had not even displayed any bad temper; and there were no signs that Thaw was likely to kill a second time.

Fourteen witnesses who had known Thaw either in Canada or in New Hampshire testified on June 24; thirteen more witnesses spoke the next day on Thaw's behalf; and three psychiatrists completed the testimony, saying that they had never observed any signs of insanity.

Bert Richardson, a physician who had treated Thaw in New Hampshire after Thaw sprained an ankle, stated that his patient had appeared entirely normal; Oliver Pelren, the manager of the Eagle Hotel in Concord, claimed that Thaw had been the perfect guest, always retiring early and never giving any cause for complaint; and Holman Drew, the sheriff who had accompanied Thaw in New Hampshire, asserted that he, Thaw, had been invariably courteous to everyone he had encountered. Emma Sergent recalled that she had met Thaw at a football game and that afternoon they had discussed the campaign for woman suffrage; she considered him a perfect gentleman, normal in every way. Noel Guillet, a doctor at the state reform school in Manchester, New Hampshire, had given Thaw a tour of the institution, explaining to his guest that the superintendent had banned the use of corporal punishment. Thaw had conversed rationally on the subject, Guillet remembered, saying that he also disapproved of the practice.[25]

There could have been no greater contrast to such testimony than the evidence provided by the first witness to appear for the state. Susan Merrill sat in the witness chair, nervously clutching a black leather purse, occasionally wiping her brow with her handkerchief, all the while glaring angrily at the deputy attorney general, Frank Cook. She no longer lived in New York, having moved to Boston the previous year, and after her appearance as a witness at a previous hearing in 1909, she had wanted nothing more to do with Harry Thaw.

But the lawyers for New York had discovered her hiding place in Boston and had tricked her into returning to the state. They had served her with a subpoena as soon as she crossed the state line, thereby compelling her appearance as a witness in the hearing. "I didn't want to come," Merrill protested, turning to address the judge. "I was brought here.... They brought a policeman, bundled me into an automobile and brought me here."[26]

But nothing she could say, no words of protest, would allow her to escape the obligation to provide the answers that Cook demanded, and she proceeded to recount the same narrative that she had told six years before. Harry Thaw had first rented rooms from her in 1902 when she was working as a housekeeper on West Forty-sixth Street. One day she heard a commotion in an upstairs room, as if someone had overturned a bureau, followed immediately by a series of short, piercing screams.

"I ran to Thaw's room and saw him with a whip raised to strike a girl who had most of her clothes off. Thaw ran out when I went in. The girl was about sixteen years old. Her back was covered with black and blue marks."

Thaw had dropped the whip, leaving the room as she entered. She had comforted the girl, wiping away the blood, bathing her wounds, and giving her a new shirtwaist.

"I asked Thaw," Merrill continued, "why he struck her. He said she was stupid and he was trying to make her learn.

"On another occasion I heard screams and found him beating another girl. His eyes were sticking out, his face was red and his veins were protruding. After he ran out I quieted the girl and gave her some money Thaw left for her."

It had happened so many times after those first occasions in 1902. One or two girls, sometimes more, would call at the house, expecting to audition for a role on the stage. Thaw would escort them upstairs, and very shortly afterward she would hear loud screams. Thaw's victims would be half-naked, their upper bodies covered in blood, with welts on their shoulders and torso. He always promised to change his ways, but the whippings continued nevertheless. She had protested, telling him that he could no longer rent rooms, but Thaw threatened her, saying that he would kill her if she told anyone. In 1905 she moved to a boardinghouse at 208 West Fifty-fourth Street, and Thaw again rented rooms from her, taking three bedrooms at the rear of the building, continuing to assault young girls even after his marriage to Evelyn Nesbit.

"In West Fifty-fourth street I heard the same screams and

when I ran up to Thaw's three rooms I found him with two girls. The back of one of the girls was all black and blue and her arms bleeding. Thaw's face was red, as I have described. She told me she was twenty-two years old."[27]

Susan Merrill, despite her anxiety on the witness stand, had been an excellent witness for the state. Her testimony had damned Thaw as a vicious degenerate who sought a perverse pleasure in attacking his victims; and Frank Cook, the deputy attorney general, could congratulate himself on securing such compelling testimony.

But Cook anticipated even greater success when he called Harry Thaw as his next witness. The defense attorneys had produced thirty witnesses to testify that Thaw appeared rational. But none of these witnesses, Cook believed, had ever conversed with Thaw on the topic that invariably enraged him—the supposed immorality of Stanford White—and Cook planned to question Thaw exclusively on the murder, hoping to provoke him to anger.

Thaw had testified before, in previous hearings to determine his sanity, and he had always behaved erratically, his mood shifting from one moment to the next. He could be angry and indignant, often for no ostensible reason, but his demeanor might suddenly change, again for no apparent cause, and he might be almost excessively pleasant, even cheerful. At other times Thaw could appear supercilious, haughty, even patronizing toward the lawyers; and then, without any warning, as if someone had flicked a switch, he would seem strangely timid, mumbling his answers as though ashamed to speak.

Thaw, dressed in a dark-blue suit, first appeared as a witness on Thursday, July 8, at ten o'clock in the morning. It promised to be another hot, humid day, and the bailiffs had opened the windows, allowing sunlight to fall in rectangular patterns across the courtroom floor. An electric fan, on a small table at the front of the court, made a whirring sound as it rotated from side to side, and the spectators, crowded onto plain wooden pews, watched as Thaw settled into his seat. He crossed his right leg over his left, then reversed himself, crossing his left leg over his right, trying to make himself comfortable. But the noise of the fan, almost directly at his back, was an irritant, and he turned to the judge, Peter Hendrick, to request that an attendant silence the hum.

Frank Cook, tall, thin, bespectacled, with a pale complexion and sandy-brown hair, waited patiently; then he began his attack with his first question.

"Why did you kill Stanford White?"

"Because of the injury he had done Miss Nesbit." Thaw tilted his head backward, at a slight angle, looking up at the deputy attorney general standing above him.

"Then it was not because of these other women you had mentioned?" Cook's harsh voice rang out across the courtroom, waking the spectators from their early morning drowsiness. "Had his conduct toward the other girls anything to do with the shooting?"

"No. I would not have bothered him on their account.

I would not have paid any attention if Evelyn had escaped him."

"What was the date of the killing of White?"

"June 25, 1906."

"You shot Stanford White . . . three years after Evelyn Nesbit told you her story. Why did you wait so long?"

"No answer I can give to it." Thaw had a puzzled look on his face, as if he had never considered the question before. He shrugged his shoulders. "No reason."[28]

"Where had you been on the day you killed Stanford White?"

Thaw recalled that he had breakfasted around nine o'clock with his wife at their hotel. Later that morning he had gone alone to the offices of the steamship company to purchase two tickets for the SS *Amerika,* to travel to Germany. That afternoon he had played cards at the Whist Club, returning to the hotel to dress for dinner. He left the hotel with his wife shortly before six o'clock, and they took a cab to go downtown to Madison Square.

"Did you have a revolver with you all that day?"

There was a sudden silence. Thaw looked down at his hands, appearing to study his fingers, before looking out across the courtroom to stare at the back wall. Cook watched him impassively, waiting for an answer, and Thaw awoke abruptly from his reverie.

"My answer to the question is yes," Thaw finally replied.

"Did you believe, or do you believe now, that Stanford White had hired the 'Monk' Eastman gang to beat you up?"

No one had ever explicitly told him, Thaw admitted, that White intended him harm; but everyone knew the enmity that existed between them. There were rumors, gossip that someone might attack him, and he had purchased the gun as a precaution. "I knew that Miss Nesbit had told Stanford White that it was my desire to put him in State's prison."[29]

"What time did you dine at Martin's the night of June 25?"

Thaw remembered that he had arrived at Café Martin with his wife shortly after six o'clock. They had dined with two friends, Truxtun Beale and Thomas McCaleb, before leaving the restaurant to walk across the park to Madison Square Garden.

But the performance had been lackluster and they had decided to leave early. He started to follow his wife to the elevator but suddenly noticed Stanford White sitting alone at a small table close to the stage.

"There was some sort of aisle leading to the stage. I went down twenty or twenty five feet from the place and then turned around and looked at him. I saw Stanford White sitting there. He was sitting with his head resting on his hand..." Thaw's voice trailed away. He looked away from Cook, his eyes wandering around the courtroom as if searching for something. He resumed his narrative, but the words now came more slowly. "I walked straight up to him and shot him. He looked up—and glared at me and—I—shot—him.

"I turned around and saw that the people were jostling one another and pushing back from me. Holding the revolver so that all could see it, I turned slowly about, hoping to lessen the excitement.... Two men approached me and I asked one of them to take the pistol. I think one of these gentlemen arrested me."

"What did you say to your wife?"

"I said, 'Perhaps I have saved your life,'" Thaw stated.

"What did you mean by that?"

"I meant that with White dead she need not have anything to fear and would be free to live her own life."[30]

Frank Cook had anticipated that Thaw would lose his composure as he talked about the murder. But Thaw, nervous at the outset, occasionally halting and uncertain, seemed to gain in confidence as he continued to speak. There was little sign that he might become irrational or unbalanced on the stand; and Cook suddenly switched to a new line of questioning.

Thaw had attended Harvard University for almost fifteen months, from November 1890 to February 1892, he acknowledged, but he had been an indifferent student, spending his time playing poker and drinking in the saloons on Main Street. He had been conspicuous by his absence from the lecture halls, and he had been a troublesome presence in the town, frequently refusing to pay his bills and getting into fights with waiters, bartenders, and anyone else who happened to cross his path. On one occasion, while playing cards, Thaw had threatened another student with a knife, and on another occasion he had drawn his gun after a dispute with a cabdriver over his fare. Cook now reminded Thaw that the police had restrained him, holding him overnight in a cell and confiscating the gun.

"Do you recollect the trouble with the cabman?"

"Yes. He overcharged me," Thaw replied. "I went up to my room and got my gun. I did grab a shotgun and go down with it after the cabman, and it was taken away from me, but the gun was not loaded."

"Were you drinking that night?"

"I think I was."

There had been persistent rumors that the president of Harvard, Charles Eliot, had called Thaw to his office one day to expel him from the university. Thaw, according to the gossip, had abused a young boy in the town, and Eliot had acted immediately, telling Thaw that he could no longer consider himself enrolled as a student.

"Why did you leave Harvard, Mr. Thaw?" Cook demanded.

Thaw appeared to gasp slightly and he flinched, as if someone had struck him a sudden blow. His eyes searched the courtroom a second time, and the lawyers on both sides stared at him expectantly.

"Did you leave Harvard voluntarily or did the authorities invite you to go?"

But one of Thaw's lawyers, John Stanchfield, interrupted, saying that the question was irrelevant. The court had convened to determine Thaw's present state of mind, and Thaw's presence at Harvard, twenty-five years before, had no bearing on the matter. The judge, Peter Hendrick, upheld the objection, telling Cook that his line of questioning was immaterial.[31]

Susan Merrill had testified only a few days before, and Cook now asked Thaw about their acquaintance.

"You know Mrs. Merrill?"

"I do," Thaw replied tersely.

"You know her quite well?"

"Yes."

Thaw admitted that he had been a few times to the building on Fifty-fourth Street, but he denied that he had ever assaulted any girls.

Did he admit, Cook asked, that he had given money to Susan Merrill to give to the girls whom he had attacked?

Thaw shook his head. It was all false, he said.

"I never paid money to Susan Merrill but only to obtain legitimate information."

"How much did you pay her?"

"Twenty, twenty-five or thirty dollars, a small amount."

He had gone to Fifty-fourth Street only because he was trying to bring Stanford White to justice. White had frequented the building in his insatiable pursuit of young girls. White was paying Susan Merrill to provide him with girls, and Thaw had given her small sums of money in exchange for information that he could use to prosecute the architect.[32]

Frank Cook, speaking to the jurors at his closing on July 14, reminded them that Thaw had lived a dissolute life. He had failed at every task he attempted, except one. "He never completed anything in his life," Cook said, "except the killing of Stanford White." He claimed to have acted in defense of his wife, always asserting that White's misdeeds justified the assassination. Yet Thaw had rented rooms in several locations in Manhattan to assault young girls in the most wicked and depraved manner. Did any of the jurors, Cook asked, have daughters, young girls who might have answered the advertisements that Thaw placed in the newspapers? "This fellow Thaw," Cook exclaimed, pointing his finger at the miscreant, "with his exaggerated ego and his degenerate mind, goes to Madison Square Garden, shoots White and then dispassionately breaks the gun." Thaw's lawyers had manipulated his young wife, persuading her to testify falsely in 1907 and 1908 that White had raped her. It had been a shameful episode, Cook concluded, an indelible stain on the history of the New York courts; and the jurors must end the farce by sending Thaw back to the asylum.[33]

But John Stanchfield, speaking in his turn, reminded the jurors that they were in the courtroom only to judge Thaw's present condition. "There is no doubt," Stanchfield began, "that Thaw was mentally distracted on June 25, 1906. The question is this: Is he sane to-day?" There had been no incidents during Thaw's time in the asylum; there had been nothing untoward during his brief stay in Canada, and there was no record that Thaw had even lost his temper during the eighteen months that he spent in New Hampshire. "It was an honest, sober, upright and decent life that Thaw lived in New Hampshire. Every person who came in contact with him knew he had escaped from a madhouse, and therefore of necessity were particularly on their guard to see if he did not give some evidences of a mind disturbed."

Frank Cook had spoken about events in Thaw's life many years before; but Cook had said nothing about the man Thaw had become. Cook had deliberately omitted any mention of the time spent in New Hampshire, preferring instead to speak of Thaw's student days twenty-five years earlier. "I am submitting this case to you," Stanchfield appealed finally, "with the hope and expectation that you will restore Harry K. Thaw to his citizenship and to his mother and to his family who have stood by him so loyally."[34]

The jury retired shortly before three o'clock that afternoon, but each man seemed instinctively to recognize that there would be no disagreement. One juror, Charles Basil, voted against his comrades on the first ballot, saying that he wished thereby to compel the jury to spend at least a few minutes discussing the evidence; but the second ballot, taken at half past three, confirmed that the verdict would be unanimous.

The clerk of the court, Frank McGurk, waited impassively, watching each juror as he filed into the courtroom. He called the roll, asking each man to identify himself, and then called for the jury's decision.

"Gentlemen of the jury, have you reached a verdict?"

The foreman, David Robinson, a slight man of medium height, half-rose from his seat, handing a sheet of foolscap to McGurk. The clerk, without reading the typescript, passed the single sheet of paper to the judge.

The spectators, almost two hundred souls crowded onto plain wooden benches, waited in hushed silence; the attorneys, their faces turned to the judge, scarcely moved, each man trying to intuit the decision; and the bailiffs, standing guard alongside the walls of the courtroom, silently scanned the room, waiting expectantly to curb any enthusiasm from the crowd.

The judge returned the foolscap to the clerk, indicating

with a slight nod that McGurk could now read the verdict to the court.

"Gentlemen of the jury, harken to your verdict. The question you have been asked is, 'Is Harry K. Thaw sane now?' and your answer is 'Yes.'"[35]

There was a sudden exhalation, as if two hundred spectators had simultaneously released a sigh, allowing their breath to escape from between their lips. The judge reminded the lawyers that the jury's decision was advisory only. He would give the final verdict later that week. "I will reserve decision," Hendrick announced, "until I make up my mind. In the meantime I will remand him."[36]

Hendrick had said that he would delay his decision, but few people had any doubt about the outcome, and two days later, on Friday, July 16, New Yorkers started to gather in Chambers Street in front of the New York County courthouse. The crowd soon filled the street, packed shoulder to shoulder along its length, from Broadway on the west side as far as Centre Street on the east. There was a celebratory mood among the sightseers, confident that Harry Thaw's ordeal would soon be over; but the atmosphere inside the courtroom was more somber, even solemn, as the attorneys waited for Hendrick to announce his decision.

"Gentlemen," Hendrick began, "I have reached a decision in this case and it is based upon my own judgment fortified by that of a very intelligent jury.... It is overwhelmingly founded on the weight of evidence, and I declare as the decision of this court that Harry K. Thaw is sane."[37]

It had been a long ordeal for Harry Thaw and now it was

over. He remained inside the courtroom for only ten minutes, staying long enough to shake hands with the jurors and to take leave of his attorneys, and then he emerged into bright sunlight at the top of the stone stairway that led from the door of the courthouse down to Chambers Street. His broad grin told the waiting crowd that he was a free man, and he lifted his hat in acknowledgment of their cheers. The sheriff, Max Grifenhagen, ordered his men to force a passage for Thaw down the steps to a waiting sedan; and slowly the car edged its way through the crowd as far as Broadway. The sedan accelerated as it turned onto Broadway, and Thaw was soon en route to Pittsburgh to celebrate his freedom.

It had been nine years since the murder of Stanford White and finally it was over. Thaw, by one estimate, had employed forty lawyers and had spent more than $1 million in a legal odyssey that had eventually reached its destination. There had been several distinct legal actions, and each one had engendered its own series of ancillary lawsuits. The State of New York had fought Thaw step by step, blow by blow, spending more than $300,000 in its campaign to convict Thaw and to keep him in the asylum.[38]

Editorial opinion in the New York newspapers was sharply divided. It had been a valiant fight, according to the *Morning Telegraph,* and Thaw's victory had been deservedly earned. He had been insane when he pulled the trigger but he had since demonstrated his sanity. "The average citizen," proclaimed the *Telegraph,* "does not take with much seriousness the conclusions of so-called experts.... There has been little doubt in the minds of most thinking men of Thaw's mental restoration for several years."[39]

The verdict was not unexpected, the *New York World* decided, but it was nevertheless deplorable. Thaw had had the opportunity to win his freedom only because of his family's vast wealth. It was a disgraceful episode that had tarnished the legal system of New York State, and the community had every expectation and hope that Thaw would now disappear from public view. "The Thaw money, operating through lawyers, doctors, experts and legal processes...kept the question of the prisoner's sanity before the courts.... The Thaw money has brought reproach to the medical as well as the legal profession."[40]

Thaw had used the legal system to get the result he desired, the *New York Press* declared. The courts had first absolved Thaw of the crime of murder on account of his insanity and had now restored him to health. The laws of New York, the *Press* stated, had permitted this regrettable travesty. "If you have plenty of money to hire the right kind of legal talent so as to get the right kind of legal action you may kill a man with some inconvenience, but with perfect safety to yourself."[41]

But no one could have felt more dismay and regret at the verdict than Evelyn Nesbit. She had twice testified against her husband, telling the courts that he had threatened to kill her, and she was now terrified that he would take his revenge. "All I ask of him is that he leave me in peace to continue my stage career," Evelyn told the reporter for the *New-York Tribune*. "I do not want his name, and I do not want his money." She had sacrificed her reputation for his sake, saving him from the electric chair, receiving nothing for her efforts; now she wanted only that he leave her alone. She had shared her life with him and she knew his vengeful, vindictive nature. She knew also that Harry was violent and unpredictable: an explosion of rage, an outburst of anger, might occur at any time, for no apparent reason, and she was fearful that she might be his next victim.[42]

10

EPILOGUE

FRED GUMP STOOD ALONE IN THE CENTER OF HERALD SQUARE ON Christmas Eve 1917, watching the passers-by on the sidewalks jostling against one another, each person heedless of his or her neighbor in the rush to get home before the holiday. Macy's department store dominated Herald Square on the west side, and a never-ending stream of shoppers went in and out, triumphantly clutching their packages as they spilled out onto Broadway. From time to time, the Sixth Avenue elevated train clattered noisily overhead, the din drowning out all the other sounds in the square, the shadow of the carriages faintly visible on the roadway below. The *New York Herald* newspaper building, an elaborate confection designed by Stanford White in the style of the Italian Renaissance, stood directly ahead, on the northern edge of the square, and Gump could see through the large plate-glass windows that the printing presses were running full tilt, churning out that afternoon's edition of the newspaper.

Gump, nineteen years old, recently graduated from Central High School in Kansas City, had arrived in New York that afternoon. It was his first time in the East, his first experience of the metropolis, and he was awestruck by the ceaseless tumult, the anthill crowds, the enormous buildings, and the restless urgency of the city. He had taken a cab from Pennsylvania Station to the Hotel McAlpin on the east side of Herald Square, leaving his suitcase with the concierge, and now he was about to go uptown for a rendezvous with his patron, Harry Thaw, at the Century Theatre on Sixty-second Street.

He had first met Thaw thirteen months earlier, in November 1915, in an ice cream parlor in Long Beach, California, where he was on vacation with his parents. Thaw had asked about his plans after graduation, and Gump answered that he might study engineering at college. Did he know, Thaw asked, that the steel magnate Andrew Carnegie had recently established an engineering school, the Carnegie Institute of Technology, in his hometown, Pittsburgh? The Carnegie Institute had been in existence only fifteen years, yet already it had an excellent reputation. Thaw asked Gump for his address in Kansas City, promising to send more information.

Later that month, Gump, thinking nothing of his encounter with Thaw, returned to Kansas City with his parents. But Thaw surprised him, sending him several letters, offering to pay for his education, to give him a monthly allowance, and to act as his guardian during his stay in Pittsburgh. Gump's parents had no reason to question Thaw's motives, and they were keen for their son to accept the offer. They believed, along with most Americans, that Thaw had suffered unjust persecution for taking his revenge against the man who had raped his wife. Thaw, moreover, had earned a reputation, since his release, as a generous philanthropist, contributing thousands of dollars to worthy causes in Pittsburgh.[1]

Fred Gump had taken up Thaw's suggestion, and he had now come to New York to see his benefactor before traveling west to Pittsburgh. Thaw had invited him to a performance of *The Century Girl,* a musical revue presented by Florenz Ziegfeld, and later that evening, after the show, they arrived back at the Hotel McAlpin, where Thaw had reserved a suite of rooms on the eighteenth floor. The Hotel McAlpin, then the largest hotel in North America, with more than one thousand rooms, had been designed to impress, and it did not disappoint. The enormous lobby, constructed with violet-rose Breche marble from Italy and pale-yellow Caen limestone from France, soared three stories and included murals around the walls by Thomas Gilbert White. The McAlpin, the only hotel in New York with a telephone in every room, boasted a ballroom, several restaurants, a Chinese tearoom, a Turkish bath, a grill-room with terra-cotta murals, and a hospital with its own surgical and medical staff. It was more modern than the Knickerbocker, more opulent than the St. Regis, more profitable than the Plaza, and more fashionable than the Waldorf. In short, the Hotel McAlpin could claim to be among the leading hotels in the city.

A bellhop accompanied Harry Thaw and Fred Gump to the eighteenth floor. Their apartment, set apart from its neighbors by its location at the far end of the building, was decorated in the art nouveau style and contained a large sitting room, several bedrooms, two bathrooms, and a parlor. Gump had spent hours earlier that day traveling on the train—he was exhausted—and he readily accepted Thaw's suggestion that he take a bath before retiring.

Half an hour later, as Gump stepped naked from the bath, the bathroom door opened unexpectedly. Thaw stood in the doorway, holding a bathrobe in his left hand. Gump reached for the robe and Thaw suddenly attacked, beating him across his shoulders with a whip. Gump fought back, striking his assailant with his fists, trying desperately to free himself, but Thaw had the advantage of surprise.

"You are my slave now," Thaw cried triumphantly, dragging his victim into the sitting room, forcing him to his knees, and continuing to beat him with the whip. "You will submit to me, won't you?"

Gump pleaded with Thaw to stop, and the whipping ended as suddenly as it had begun. Thaw, holding the whip high above his head, as if to strike again, ordered Gump to swear always to be his slave and to obey his commands.

Thaw, satisfied that he had beaten his victim into submission, eventually went to bed; but Gump, terrified that Thaw would attack a second time, remained awake throughout the night. On one occasion, around two o'clock, he silently tiptoed to the door leading to the hallway, hoping to escape while Thaw slept, but the door was locked and the key was nowhere to be found.

Only the next morning, after breakfast, did Gump manage to slip away. He knew no one in New York, and his only thought was to get out of the city as quickly as possible. The train for Kansas City left Pennsylvania Station at midday, and that evening Gump arrived home and described his ordeal to his parents, showing them the welts on his shoulders and torso.[2]

His father acted quickly, arranging for a lawyer, Frank Walsh, to return with Gump to New York to file a complaint with Edward Swann, the Manhattan district attorney. Swann was also quick to respond, arranging for a photographer to take pictures of Gump's wounds and sending his detectives to the Hotel McAlpin to investigate.

The concierge confirmed that Gump had indeed stayed with Harry Thaw at the hotel on Christmas Eve. But Thaw had already checked out of the McAlpin. He had not left a forwarding address, and the concierge had no idea where he had gone.

The district attorney eventually learned that Thaw had fled to Philadelphia. Swann sent his detectives to Philadelphia, where they fanned across the city, checking the hotels, watching the trains leaving Broad Street Station, and speaking to the car rental agencies. Thaw had stayed at the Hotel Belgra via on Rittenhouse Square for a few days, but he had subsequently disappeared. Had he already left Philadelphia? Could he now be back in Pittsburgh?

Every policeman in Philadelphia had joined the hunt for the fugitive, but no one thought to look for Thaw outside the city's commercial center, an area bordered by the Delaware River on the east and the Schuylkill on the west. Few people would have considered searching for him on the outskirts of the city. But Thaw, acting on the advice of an old Philadelphia friend, had gone to ground under an assumed name in a boardinghouse at 5260 Walnut Street, far from the center of the city, and here he remained, waiting for an opportunity to avoid the dragnet.

He had never been so disconsolate, never so depressed. He had always had an optimistic outlook, even when faced with overwhelming odds, but now he had lost hope. He had read the newspaper reports that Fred Gump's parents were eager to assist the Manhattan district attorney in prosecuting him; he had read that a grand jury in New York County had voted an indictment against him for kidnapping and assault; and Thaw realized that the State of New York would again demand his extradition. There had been public support for his assassination of Stanford White, but there would be only condemnation for his brutal attack on a defenseless nineteen-year-old.

He arose at eight o'clock on Friday, January 12, to take his bath and to dress for breakfast. He moved slowly, bowed down by his depression, every action accomplished only by great effort. His family could not help him and his friends had deserted him. He had no future, no way to escape years of imprisonment in the penitentiary.

A straight razor, with an ivory handle and a carbon steel blade, lay on the washstand. Thaw picked it up, turning it slowly in his hand, the sunlight glinting on the sharp steel edge. He cut himself first on the left wrist, a small incision near his hand, and then he made a deeper gash along his forearm, watching the blood as it spilled into a porcelain washbasin. He cut himself a third time, across the base of his jaw, and then again, across his windpipe, finally staggering backward onto the bed, blood seeping onto the bedclothes.

At that moment his landlady, Elizabeth Tacot, knocked

and, hearing no answer, opened the door to see Thaw, covered in blood, softly moaning, lying sprawled across the bed. Amazingly, and despite his best efforts, Thaw had cut neither the artery in his arm nor the jugular vein in his throat; he was still alive. Tacot ran downstairs to call her doctor, and the physician, S. E. Bateman, arrived a few minutes later, quickly binding up the cuts to prevent further hemorrhaging. It seemed miraculous that Thaw should survive his wounds; but Bateman, speaking to the reporters later that day, claimed that Thaw had fallen in such a way that the bedclothes saved his life. "It is a lucky thing for him," Bateman said, "that he tumbled upon the bed in such manner that the coverlet pressed against both his wrist and neck. Otherwise he would have been dead when found."[3]

Thaw's whipping of Fred Gump, his flight from New York, and his suicide attempt in Philadelphia persuaded even Mary Thaw that her son was mentally unbalanced. The doctors had moved Thaw from the boardinghouse to a private suite in St. Mary's Hospital, in the Kensington neighborhood of Philadelphia, and Mary Thaw visited her son every day, sitting at his bedside each afternoon, while he made a fitful recovery.

She announced to the newspapers that she would no longer contest his commitment to a mental institution, and the next month, while Thaw convalesced in his hospital bed, she petitioned the Court of Common Pleas in Philadelphia to appoint a commission to determine his condition. "I am unable to resist the facts that demonstrate my son's insanity," she announced. "Now I know, as I never knew before, that my son is an irresponsible man whom the law must guard. Therefore to the courts of my State—of his State—I have applied to help a mother protect her son from his infirmities." An attorney for the Thaw family, Frank Johnston, agreed. "The best thing for all parties," Johnston argued, "would be to keep him under restraint." Did the State of New York wish to entangle itself once again with Harry Thaw in endless legal battles? Would it not be preferable to send him to an asylum in his native state, Pennsylvania?[4]

The Manhattan district attorney, Edward Swann, pressed his case nevertheless, saying that New York would ask for Thaw's extradition; but the Pennsylvania Commission on Lunacy determined on March 13 that Thaw was insane and that he was therefore a ward of the state. The governor of Pennsylvania, Martin Brumbaugh, promptly denied the extradition of Thaw back to New York, saying that it would be a travesty to prosecute an insane person. "For this state," Brumbaugh announced, "to surrender . . . one of its citizens declared by one of its courts to be insane and therefore unable to make his defense . . . [is] contrary to sound reason and justice."[5]

It was a decision that could find its justification independent of any political calculation. But it was also a predictable verdict: the Thaw family had long exerted great influence in western and central Pennsylvania, and Brumbaugh, whose support came mainly from the coal-mining districts, was mindful that a decision to send Thaw to New York would likely hurt his prospects for reelection.

The Court of Common Pleas committed Thaw indefinitely to the Pennsylvania Hospital for the Insane, a private asylum in West Philadelphia. Thaw lived a life of ease there, enjoying a privileged existence, even traveling on occasion with an attendant to visit relatives in Pittsburgh. Mary Thaw reached a financial settlement with the Gump family—some reports said that she paid $25,000 to put an end to the matter—and nothing more was said about the whipping.[6]

Evelyn Nesbit had first performed in vaudeville in 1913, dancing with Jack Clifford at the Victoria Theatre, an independent vaudeville house on Forty-second Street. It was a popular act—the theater was frequently sold out—and her booking agent, Eddie Darling, could guarantee her appearances months in advance. Each year, during the spring and summer, Evelyn and Jack went on tour under contract to the B. F. Keith Circuit, crisscrossing the United States, eventually reaching San Francisco and Los Angeles before traveling back to New York. On their return in the late summer, before the start of the fall season, they would go to the Adirondacks for several weeks, relaxing at the summer home that Jack owned on Lake Chateaugay, close to the border with Canada.[7]

It was welcome news to learn in April 1916, during an engagement in Memphis, that Harry Thaw had divorced her. Thaw had filed suit in the Court of Common Pleas in Pittsburgh, asking for a divorce on the grounds of his wife's infidelity. Evelyn Nesbit, according to Thaw's attorney William Stone, had begun an affair in New York in 1909 with John (Jack) Francis, a newspaper reporter. Francis had lived with Evelyn in Germany in 1910, and he was the father of her child.[8]

There was little point, Evelyn realized, in contesting the

suit. She had made her own way, earning her livelihood in vaudeville, settling into a relationship with Jack Clifford, and she was glad finally to be able to end her connection with Harry Thaw. Clifford also was pleased to hear the news; and the following month, on May 24, they married at the Emery Methodist Episcopal Church in Ellicott City, Maryland.[9]

But the relationship ended the next year. Jack Clifford had been unfaithful, initiating an affair with an actress, Juanita Hansen, and then seducing a second actress, Anna Luther. Their separation had little impact on Evelyn's career, and in October 1917 she appeared with a new dancing partner, Bobby O'Neill, at the Riverside Theatre on Ninety-sixth Street, subsequently appearing at the Palace Theatre that winter.[10]

But vaudeville was then in decline, fading away as the silent movies gained an audience. Evelyn followed the trend, shifting effortlessly from the stage to the silver screen. Her first film, *Threads of Destiny,* appeared in 1914; three years later she was the star of *Redemption.* Evelyn made three films in 1918 — *The Woman Who Gave, Her Mistake,* and *I Want to Forget* — and starred in five more before her movie career ended in 1922.[11]

Evelyn Nesbit had finally achieved the success that had always eluded her. She was a celebrity, a star whose name was invariably at the top of the bill, and her fame had little connection with a scandal that was already fading from memory. There were no longer any articles about Harry Thaw in the newspapers, and her success did not depend on the notoriety that had previously attached to her name because of Thaw. There were admittedly some stars who had more talent — Dorothy Gish, Mabel Normand, Marguerite Clark, and Anita Stewart were more accomplished actors—but in 1919, when she made four films for Fox Studios, Evelyn Nesbit had few rivals.[12]

But drug use was ubiquitous on Broadway, and few performers could resist the temptation. A dancer in the Ziegfeld Follies at the New Amsterdam Theatre introduced Evelyn to morphine in 1919, giving her an injection one evening at her apartment and subsequently arranging for Evelyn to receive a supply of morphine each week. Later that year, while making the film *My Little Sister* at the Fox Studios in Hollywood, Evelyn took cocaine for the first time.[13]

Her addictions effectively destroyed her career and wreaked havoc with her personal life. She had made a fortune on the stage and in the movies, often earning more than $3,000 each week, but her money quickly disappeared, consumed by her drug habit. She was in her mid-thirties, regularly taking four grains of morphine each day, and the film studios no longer had any interest in hiring an actress whose addiction had so obviously diminished her sex appeal.[14]

In 1922, in an interview with the *Washington Times,* Evelyn stated that she had finally beaten the drug habit; but almost all her money had disappeared. "I remember one party at Hollywood," Evelyn reminisced, "where cocaine was served in a big sugar bowl.... 'Pass the sugar, somebody,' would be the remark every few minutes, and all laughed at the joke....It cost me $100,000 to be a drug fiend, just in cash alone. And it cost me my friends, my self-respect, everything." Her mother, Florence, had threatened to take custody of her child, Russell, and Evelyn had eventually agreed to enter a sanatorium under a physician's care to cure her addiction.[15]

Evelyn Nesbit (right) opened a tearoom in 1921 in Manhattan on West Fifty-second Street, a few steps from Broadway. It was not a success, and the following year she began her career as a cabaret singer in nightclubs in Atlantic City. *(Library of Congress, LC-USZ62-78404)*

She moved back to New York and opened a tearoom at 235 West Fifty-second Street, close to Broadway, but it was not a success. Too many of Evelyn's former acquaintances, men and women who had fallen on hard times, came calling, asking for a loan, looking for a favor, and she was too kindhearted to turn them away. She had no experience in running a business; her kitchen staff stole whatever they could find—bottles of wine, tableware, even pots and pans—and her waiters cheated her, routinely submitting fraudulent receipts. She had put all her savings into the tearoom, even going into debt, and its failure left her penniless. There was only one way that she could make a living, and Evelyn moved to Atlantic City to perform in the resort's many nightclubs and cabarets.[16]

She first worked for Harry Katz as a singer at his nightclub, the Moulin Rouge; Henri Martin then engaged Evelyn for several weeks at Café Martin, a restaurant on the Boardwalk; and Max Williams, the owner of the Palais Royal, later employed her as a hostess. Her celebrity was still sufficiently potent to attract the crowds who flocked to Atlantic City every summer; but she was a single woman, alone and vulnerable, and the nightclub owners took advantage, cheating her at every opportunity, billing her for expenses, never paying her the money that they had promised.[17]

Evelyn continued to work in Atlantic City every summer, singing in the cabarets—Café Paris, El Prinkipo, Palais d'Or, and the Paradise Club—then going on tour in the fall and spring. She had long affected a brassy devil-may-care attitude, a flippant, happy-go-lucky exterior, but Evelyn lived a sad, lonely existence, and she was frequently depressed, often scared for her future, and in 1926, during an engagement in Chicago, she attempted suicide by drinking disinfectant.[18]

She recovered; but her moods often returned, frequently dragging her down. She could see no way out, no escape from her penury, condemned, night after night, to entertain the partygoers in the nightclubs, knowing all the while that the owners would soon find some other singer, someone younger, someone more attractive, to take her place. They would then pay her off, discard her, and think nothing of it, as they had discarded so many women before her.

It embittered Evelyn to know that Harry Thaw, after his release from the Pennsylvania Hospital for the Insane in 1924, continued to receive revenue generated by the family trust. The value of the Thaw estate had multiplied many times during the decade and, according to one estimate, was now worth more than $100 million. Harry received an annual income approaching $60,000, and the trustees frequently made special payments, often amounting to more than $100,000, to the heirs. Evelyn's son, Russell, was also Harry's child, Evelyn claimed, and Russell, she believed, was entitled to a share of the estate. But she had no ability to assert her son's claim, no means to challenge the Thaw lawyers in court, and she knew that the family would always deny the connection. Any lawsuit would be futile.[19]

Harry Thaw died of a coronary thrombosis on February 22, 1947, aged seventy-six, at his home in Miami Beach. He had inherited almost $3 million on the death of his mother in 1929, and he had spent the last two decades of his life in relative tranquility. In addition to his home in Florida, Thaw owned houses in Philadelphia, Pittsburgh, Manhattan, Saratoga Springs, California, and Virginia, and he traveled frequently, spending several weeks during the year in each location and occasionally sailing to Europe. He had many acquaintances but few friends, and his funeral in Pittsburgh was a lonely affair. His only surviving sibling, Alice, was too ill to attend, and only one relative, a nephew, Lawrence Thaw, attended the burial.[20]

He left an inheritance of $1,211,000, along with his various properties, but Evelyn received only $10,000 in the will. Her testimony in 1907, and again in 1908, had saved Harry from the electric chair, but there had never been any acknowledgment that she had sacrificed her reputation for his sake, never any gratitude for the courage and fortitude that she had displayed on the witness stand.[21]

She continued to work in New York, but she rarely appeared now in the glamorous nightclubs in the entertainment district around Times Square. She performed in out-of-the-way places, in saloons and dives in the working class neighborhoods, scratching out a living in the rough-and-tumble districts of the city. Her final performance was in March 1938 at Ye Old Tap Room, a saloon on the corner of Eighty-third Street and Columbus Avenue. She was fifty-three years old.[22]

Many movie stars of the silent era had met an early death, through either ill health or drug use, yet Evelyn Nesbit had somehow survived. Her son, Russell, earned his living as a commercial pilot, and he supported his mother, paying the rent on a small studio apartment in New York. After the war, Russell moved with his second wife to Los Angeles to work as a test pilot for the Douglas Aircraft Company, and Evelyn followed her son to California in 1952, renting an apartment on Figueroa Street in downtown Los Angeles. She passed her days quietly, doting on her young grandchildren, Teresa, Michael, and Russell, teaching sculpture classes at a nearby ceramics studio, fussing over her cats, attending mass at the Catholic church in her neighborhood.[23]

She had seemingly been forgotten; not even the gossip columnists could recall the details of the sensational murder that had gripped the nation so many decades before. But in 1955 she was again a celebrity, albeit briefly, when Twentieth Century–Fox produced *The Girl in the Red Velvet Swing,* with Joan Collins in the title role. Evelyn worked as a consultant on the film, receiving $30,000 for her trouble. She died, aged eighty-two, of natural causes in a nursing home in Santa Monica on January 17, 1967. A requiem mass was held in her memory three days later at St. Martin of Tours, a Roman Catholic church on Sunset Boulevard, and thirty acquaintances, many connected with the film industry, attended the burial at Holy Cross Cemetery in Culver City.[24]

AFTERWORD

ÉMILE ZOLA, IN HIS 1880 NOVEL, *NANA*, IMAGINED THE FICTIONAL
life of Anna (Nana) Coupeau, a courtesan living in Paris. Nana
first appears in the story as an actress in an operetta at the
Théâtre des Variétés who, despite her obvious lack of talent,
mesmerizes the audience with her physical beauty. Nana has a
series of lovers, abandoning each one as soon as he proves
unable to provide her with the luxuries that she has come to
expect. She is never satisfied, and her demands become increasingly outrageous, eventually leaving each of her lovers desti-
tute. Nana leaves a trail of devastation behind her, destroying
the careers and marriages of those men—representatives of
the Parisian bourgeoisie—who pursue her. Zola provided his
novel with a grim ending: Nana contracts smallpox and dies
alone, her beauty hideously destroyed by the disease.

It was no longer necessary, after the murder of Stanford
White, according to one New York writer, to read literature to
experience the passions unleashed by the beauty of a superbly
attractive woman. Evelyn Nesbit, who had first appeared on
the Broadway stage at sixteen, supposedly conquered Stanford
White and then a second man, Harry Thaw, and she provoked

the jealousy between her suitors that exploded in violence, Thaw killing his rival in a crowded theater in Madison Square Garden. Evelyn Nesbit, the writer concluded, was a latter-day version of Nana Coupeau, a woman who enslaved her lovers, coveting wealth and luxury and paying no heed to conventional morality.[1]

But the anonymous writer knew nothing of Evelyn Nesbit, and the remarks on her character could not have been further from the truth. Both Stanford White and Harry Thaw were too sophisticated and Evelyn Nesbit was too naïve for such a scenario to be plausible. White was immensely influential, one of the most prominent New Yorkers of his day; Thaw, wealthy beyond all measure, mingled easily with the social elite of two continents; so it was absurd to claim that a sixteen-year-old chorus girl with no experience of the world could have lured such men into the catastrophe that engulfed all three in 1906.

Stanford White revealed his true character when, shortly after meeting Evelyn Nesbit, he persuaded his friend Rudolf Eickemeyer to take a series of photographs of Evelyn, then sixteen years old. White, forty-seven, and Eickemeyer, thirty-nine, made all the arrangements, choosing the clothes that she wore for the session, and Evelyn Nesbit, unaware that the two men were deliberately manipulating her, posed for the camera in a way that suggested that she was sexually available. These photographs, taken sometime in the fall of 1901, have survived and now exist prominently on the Internet, reinforcing the impression that Evelyn's supposed promiscuity somehow contributed to the drama that played out between White and Harry Thaw.[2]

It is not easy to investigate the intimate life of an individual living a century ago, but the available evidence indicates that Evelyn Nesbit was never promiscuous, as legend would have it. She undoubtedly had opportunities for casual encounters — during the 1910s she made movies in Hollywood, and during the 1920s she sang in Atlantic City nightclubs — but she always sought security and permanence, marrying her second husband, Jack Clifford, shortly after her divorce from Harry Thaw in April 1916.

Thaw, like White, shamelessly manipulated Evelyn Nesbit for his own purposes. His attorneys in the first trial asserted that White had raped Evelyn as a young girl, and that Thaw therefore had reason to kill White. There was, however, only one person who could testify that the rape had occurred, and Evelyn was the principal witness at the trial, telling the court that White had lured her to his town house, subsequently drugging her and raping her while she lay unconscious. But on cross-examination Evelyn was required to provide details about her relationship with White, and during the interrogation by the district attorney, she revealed aspects of her life as an actress that were unacceptable in polite society. Evelyn, to save her husband, had humiliated herself, sacrificing her dignity and her reputation.

The tragedy of Evelyn Nesbit's life is that there had never been any necessity for her to testify. The district attorney, Travers Jerome, realizing that she did not understand the consequences that would follow from his cross-examination, offered at the outset to accept a plea of not guilty by reason of insanity. Harry Thaw, by accepting Jerome's offer, would have avoided the death penalty and would also have spared his wife her public humiliation; but Thaw's attorneys chose instead to put Evelyn on the witness stand in a futile attempt to prove his justification for the murder of White. Jerome's cross-examination of Evelyn Nesbit, moreover, raised doubts about the truthfulness of her testimony and questioned whether the rape had even occurred.

It does not frequently happen that an author is unsure that an event occurred; yet, surprisingly, it is impossible to know if the rape, as Evelyn Nesbit described it, did take place. One hesitates to throw doubt on her account, told with apparent sincerity, and recounted, moreover, two times without any contradiction between the first occasion and the second, but it would be foolish to ignore the questions that Jerome posed to his witness.

How is it possible, for example, to explain the interaction between Stanford White and Evelyn Nesbit after the rape if it had been as traumatic an event as Evelyn claimed? She admitted, on cross-examination, that she had seen White several times alone in his apartment after he had raped her, and she confessed also that she had subsequently written letters to White during her travels in Europe with Harry Thaw in 1903. Her testimony at the first trial was detailed and precise on some points but surprisingly vague on others. She could neither describe the weather on the day when she claimed the rape had occurred nor say, even to the month, when White had attacked her. The district attorney maintained, in conversations with reporters outside the courtroom, that Evelyn Nesbit had accidentally revealed the day of the rape as Tuesday, November 5, 1901, and Jerome stated that he could have established an alibi for Stanford White if the rules of the court-room had permitted him to do so.[3]

Did the rape happen? It will never be possible now to know the answer; but it is certainly the case that Thaw's lawyers, eager to justify their exorbitant fees, were determined to win an acquittal. It is at least feasible that they invented the entire episode and then successfully manipulated Evelyn Nesbit into testifying falsely in court that Stanford White had raped her. Thirty years later, writing in her autobiography, *Prodigal Days*, Evelyn recalled that evening very differently. White did not drug her, she wrote in *Prodigal Days;* she lost consciousness only because she had drunk too much champagne. She lost her virginity to White, she acknowledged, but in contrast to her courtroom testimony in 1907, the event here seems almost benign, not so much a rape as a sexual initiation. She was embarrassed and started to cry, but White, in her later account, behaved almost like a gentleman, speaking tenderly to her and soothing her so that she remained calm.[4]

Many historians have discussed the relationship between White and Evelyn Nesbit, usually as an aside in writing about White's architectural work, and some writers have repeated the claim that Nesbit had an abortion in January 1903 when she was a pupil at the DeMille school. But there is no evidence to support this assertion, and it appears likely that, as she wrote in her autobiography, she suffered an attack of appendicitis. It seems improbable that Nathaniel Bowditch Potter, the physician who attended Evelyn Nesbit at Pompton and subsequently cared for her in New York, would have associated himself with the felony crime of abortion. The New Jersey legislature had outlawed abortion in 1849 and New York State followed suit in 1869. Potter, professor of surgery at the College of Physicians and Surgeons, the medical school at Columbia University, was a leading member of the medical profession, and there is little reason to think that he would have jeopardized his career by performing an abortion.[5]

Several years later, in October 1910, Evelyn Nesbit did give birth to a boy. A newspaper reporter, Jack Francis, and not Harry Thaw, as Evelyn claimed, was the father. Francis had been close to Evelyn Nesbit in New York; they had lived together in Germany; and Evelyn, on returning to Manhattan, stayed in a house uptown that Francis rented. Several witnesses, including Jack Francis's brother Peter, testified in 1916, during Harry Thaw's divorce suit, that Jack Francis had admitted paternity of the child.[6]

The arc of Evelyn Nesbit's life bears testimony to her courage and fortitude. She had few resources as a young girl—her formal education at the DeMille school lasted only a few months—and her marriage to Harry Thaw became a heavy burden, a millstone that dragged her down even many years after their separation. She had done nothing to provoke Thaw's murder of Stanford White, yet she became tainted in the public eye through her association with the affair; and even now, more than a century later, some authors treat Evelyn Nesbit disparagingly, denying her dignity and respect. She eventually achieved a measure of independence and made her own way, earning her livelihood in the silent movies and then as a cabaret singer. It had been her misfortune to be caught, as a young girl, between two men, each of whom thought only of his own desires, but she eventually triumphed over her circumstances. Every life is a daily series of advances and retreats, intimate victories and private defeats, all measured not by grand events but by an awareness of the obstacles that have been overcome along the way. Evelyn Nesbit's life, in the end, was little different from the lives of millions of others, a story of perseverance and determination, of achievement and independence, that nothing could finally diminish.

Author's Note

"FOR HOW MANY MORE YEARS," THE *NEW YORK WORLD* ASKED IN 1909, three years after the murder of Stanford White, "must the case of Harry Thaw drag its slimy way through the courts of this State?" In June 1912, during the hearing on the third writ of habeas corpus, the same newspaper complained that Thaw's incessant appeals and motions, still clogging the courts six years after the murder, were bringing the law into disrepute. "This worthless youth has cost the State more and done more to discredit the administration of justice in New York than any other criminal ever brought before its courts.... Has there been in the entire history of American criminal procedure a worse scandal of justice than Thaw?"[1]

There is little doubt that the legal odyssey that wound its way through the courts after White's death constituted one of the most protracted and complex cases in American jurisprudence. The New York newspapers obsessively covered the twists and turns of the case, reporting each episode in all its details, gossiping breathlessly about the protagonists, and speculating endlessly about the most likely outcome. The transcripts of the courtroom proceedings have long since disappeared and it would have been impossible, therefore, to write this history without access to the accounts that appeared in the city's daily newspapers.

Two newspapers, Joseph Pulitzer's *World* and William Randolph Hearst's *New York Journal,* dominated New York City at the turn of the century. Hearst was the aggressive interloper, moving from California to New York, purchasing the *Journal* in 1895 and quickly boosting its circulation to 150,000 by dropping the price to one cent. Pulitzer followed suit shortly afterward, slashing the price of the *World* from two cents to one cent. The other morning newspapers desperately tried to keep pace: the *New York Sun,* the most conservative paper in the city; the *New York Herald,* one of the least reputable newspapers in existence; the *New-York Tribune,* still influential in national politics; and the *New York Times,* almost bankrupt in 1895 but saved from collapse the following year by its new owner, Adolph Ochs. These six newspapers constituted the principal sources for the account presented in this book. Other newspapers, most notably the *Evening Telegram* and the *Morning Telegraph,* were significant sources also, but neither paper was used consistently in my research.[2]

In the 1890s the morning newspapers, to capture a share of the evening readership, began to produce late editions, and eventually these editions became autonomous, employing distinct editorial and reporting staffs. The *New York World,* for example, produced several different editions each day, and early in the twentieth century the evening edition became an entirely separate newspaper, albeit still under the control of its owner, Joseph Pulitzer. The morning edition and its evening counterpart gradually adopted separate identities, sharing only an editorial viewpoint, one dictated by Pulitzer, but distinct in reporting the news. In writing this book I have usually relied upon the evening edition of the *New York World*.

It is also worth mentioning the *New York American* as an important source for the writing of this book. The Hearst newspapers had bitterly attacked William McKinley during and after the presidential campaign in 1900, and there had been editorial commentary in the *Journal* in April 1901 that the president's death would be no loss. A few months later, on September 6, an anarchist, Leon Czolgosz, shot and killed McKinley. Hearst had nothing to do with the assassination, but public outrage against the *Journal* was so intense that he changed the name of the newspaper to the *New York American* to avoid the obloquy that had attached itself to the *Journal*. The *New York American*, the beneficiary of Hearst's considerable fortune, was irrepressible in its reporting on Harry Thaw, ferreting out detail after detail, reprinting the dialogue of the protagonists, and even canvassing public opinion on its support for the murderer.[3]

Both Harry Thaw and Evelyn Nesbit wrote autobiographical accounts, and these also have been invaluable in reconstructing the sequence of events before and after the murder. The first half of Thaw's memoir, *The Traitor,* is a gossipy travelogue of his journeys through Europe; the second half is a detailed justification of his murder of Stanford White. Evelyn Nesbit's 1934 autobiography, *Prodigal Days,* combines a wistful account of her youthful experiences in New York with bitter regret that Thaw had so dramatically affected her later years.[4]

I have benefited enormously from reading the many books that other authors have written on Stanford White. Thirty years ago Leland Roth produced a magnificent account of the architectural work of McKim, Mead & White. The scope of the firm's work has never been so exhaustively detailed nor so carefully analyzed, and architectural historians are indebted to Roth for his superlative work. Mosette Broderick has written an insightful and perceptive account of the firm that focuses more closely on the cultural context provided by New York City, and she carefully limns the relationships between the coteries of artists, sculptors, writers, and illustrators, all of whom interacted, in one way or another, with the three partners. David Garrard Lowe has also focused on New York as the scene of White's greatest accomplishments, intertwining descriptions of his architecture with an engaging biography. Paula Uruburu is the author of an outstanding biography of Evelyn Nesbit that treats her as a cultural icon whose fame elevated her above her peers. Pictorial representations of Nesbit in the newspapers and magazines were ubiquitous both before and after the murder and transformed her into a celebrity who helped usher in the modern age. Finally, two magnificent books, lavishly illustrated, display the aesthetic qualities of White's many talents: Wayne Craven has written an erudite analysis of trends in Gilded Age architecture that influenced the styles adopted by McKim, Mead & White; and Samuel G. White and Elizabeth White have displayed their expert knowledge of Stanford White's architecture in their commentary on his masterworks.[5]

No one accomplishes anything alone and I have several debts to acknowledge. Yumiko Yamamori gave me her affection and support during the years that I spent writing this book, and her assistance was invaluable in bringing the project to its completion. The first draft of the manuscript was written during an extended stay in Tokyo, in Kichijōji, one of the few districts in the capital that retains an aura of prewar Japan. Kichijōji, with its endless maze of narrow alleyways, its innumerable cafes and tearooms, its cabaret clubs and pachinko parlors, jazz bars and izakaya, still has a slightly raffish reputation, and there could not have been a more pleasant place to live while writing the book. I was fortunate also, during my time in Japan, to have the institutional support of Meiji Gakuin University, one of the most prestigious universities in the Tokyo area.

Every author needs an agent to campaign on his or her behalf, and it has been my great fortune that Peter Steinberg at Foundry Media quickly recognized the merits of my proposal and almost immediately secured a contract. Peter has provided invaluable counsel at every stage, and his support has been crucial. My editor, Joshua Kendall, was enthusiastic from the outset, and he provided detailed notes on the manuscript that immensely improved the book. The staff at Little, Brown and Company—Peggy Freudenthal and Nicky Guerreiro, and freelance copyeditor Amanda Heller—have been outstanding in the care and consideration that they have given to the manuscript, and their meticulous attention to detail has gone a long way in ensuring its accuracy. Raveeta Jagnandan and Katelyn Kirk provided research assistance in locating elusive articles, and several colleagues and friends—Walter Hickel, Jeffrey Kroessler, Mark Swindle, Malcolm Tulloch, Nancy Unger—have all provided support in ways that have made my task less arduous. I presented versions of the book to audiences in the United States, at the University of Pennsylvania and Marymount Manhattan College; and in Britain, at the Rothermere American Institute at the University of Oxford. Each talk was the occasion for lively debate and discussion that helped inform my knowledge of New York City and its cultural and social history.

NOTES

Chapter 1 *First Encounter*

1. "Mrs. Harry Thaw Tells Jury of Her Relations with Stanford White," *New York World,* February 8, 1907; Evelyn Nesbit, *Prodigal Days: The Untold Story* (New York: Julian Messner, 1934), 2–3.
2. "Woman Coaxed Evelyn Nesbit to Meet Stanford White," *New York World,* June 29, 1906.
3. Nesbit, *Prodigal Days,* 1–2.
4. "The Story of Thaw's Wife," *New York Sun,* February 8, 1907.
5. "Mrs. Harry Thaw Tells Jury," *New York World,* February 8, 1907; Nesbit, *Prodigal Days,* 2–3, 25–26; "Evelyn Nesbit Thaw on Stand Says She Was Wronged at 16," *New York Evening Telegram,* February 7, 1907.
6. "Mrs. Harry Thaw Tells Jury," *New York World,* February 8, 1907; Nesbit, *Prodigal Days,* 2.
7. "With the Clubmen," *New York Times,* September 21, 1902; "Mrs. Reginald Ronalds Hints Paris Divorce," *New York Times,* May 3, 1924.
8. "The Story of Thaw's Wife," *New York Sun,* February 8, 1907; "Evelyn Nesbit Thaw, to Save Husband, Says Stanford White Caused Her Downfall When She Was Sixteen by Drugged Wine," *New York Herald,* February 8, 1907; Nesbit, *Prodigal Days,* 27; "Evelyn Thaw Collapses on Witness Stand," *New York Evening Journal,* February 7, 1907.
9. Nesbit, *Prodigal Days,* 8–10.
10. Ibid., 12–14.
11. Ibid., 15–16; "Evelyn Nesbit Thaw, to Save Husband," *New York Herald,* February 8, 1907; Barbara J. Mitnick and Thomas Folk, "The Artist and His Model: J. Carroll Beckwith and Evelyn Nesbit," *Arts & Crafts Quarterly* 5 (1992): 12–15.

12. Nesbit, *Prodigal Days,* 15–16, 18.

13. "Evelyn Florence Nesbit, a Beautiful Sixteen-Year-Old Model of the New York Studios," *Broadway Magazine,* March 1901.

14. Nesbit, *Prodigal Days,* 19–21; "Evelyn Thaw Tells Her Story," *New York Times,* February 8, 1907.

15. "'Floradora' a Success," *New York Times,* November 10, 1900; "Casino — Florodora," *New York Dramatic Mirror,* November 17, 1900.

16. "'Floradora' a Success," *New York Times,* November 10, 1900.

17. Nesbit, *Prodigal Days,* 1, 21–22.

18. Ibid., 28–29.

19. [Margaret Chanler], *Roman Spring: Memoirs* (Boston: Little, Brown & Co., 1935), 256; Elsie de Wolfe, *After All* (London: Heineman, 1935), 51–52; Nesbit, *Prodigal Days,* 29; Leland M. Roth, *McKim, Mead & White, Architects* (New York: Harper & Row, 1983), 62.

20. Edward Simmons, *From Seven to Seventy: Memories of a Painter and a Yankee* (New York: Harper & Brothers, 1922), 238–40.

21. Nesbit, *Prodigal Days,* 29–30.

22. Roth, *McKim, Mead & White,* 29–32.

23. Mosette Broderick, *Triumvirate: McKim, Mead & White* (New York: Alfred A. Knopf, 2010), 199–201.

24. Roth, *McKim, Mead & White,* 53–54, 56.

25. Ibid., 65–66, 83–88, 94–95.

26. Ibid., 115.

27. "Amended Plans for a Great Building," *New-York Tribune,* August 17, 1889; M. G. Van Rensselaer, "The Madison Square Garden," *Century Magazine* 47 (March 1894): 742–43; Roth, *McKim, Mead & White,* 161.

28. Roth, *McKim, Mead & White,* 159.

29. "Madison Square Garden," *New York Times,* January 21, 1893; Van Rensselaer, "The Madison Square Garden," 745.

30. "Among the Audience," *New York Press,* June 17, 1890; Editorial, "The Madison Square Garden," *New York Press,* June 17, 1890.

31. "A Brilliant Audience," *New York Times,* June 17, 1890.

32. "The Big Garden Opened," *New-York Tribune,* June 17, 1890.

33. Roth, *McKim, Mead & White,* 171–72; "Settled in Its New Home," *New-York Tribune,* August 21, 1893.

34. Nesbit, *Prodigal Days,* 37.

35. "Evelyn Nesbit Thaw on Stand," *New York Evening Telegram,* February 7, 1907.

36. Nesbit, *Prodigal Days,* 44–45; "Evelyn Nesbit Thaw on Stand," *New York Evening Telegram,* February 7, 1907.

Notes

Chapter 2 *Rape*

1. "Evelyn Nesbit Thaw on Stand Says She Was Wronged at 16," *New York Evening Telegram*, February 7, 1907; "Evelyn Thaw Collapses on Witness Stand," *New York Evening Journal*, February 7, 1907.

2. "Mrs. Harry Thaw Tells Jury of Her Relations with Stanford White," *New York World*, February 8, 1907.

3. "Evelyn Nesbit Thaw, to Save Husband, Says Stanford White Caused Her Downfall When She Was Sixteen by Drugged Wine," *New York Herald*, February 8, 1907.

4. Charles Somerville, "Young Wife's Awful Story Stuns Jurors," *New York Evening Journal*, February 7, 1907; "Evelyn Thaw Collapses," *New York Evening Journal*, February 7, 1907; Evelyn Nesbit, *Prodigal Days: The Untold Story* (New York: Julian Messner, 1934), 41.

5. Somerville, "Young Wife's Awful Story," *New York Evening Journal*, February 7, 1907.

6. "The Story of Thaw's Wife," *New York Sun*, February 8, 1907.

7. Nesbit, *Prodigal Days*, 33–34.

8. Ibid., 33–35; Ethel Barrymore, *Memories: An Autobiography* (New York: Harper & Brothers, 1955), 116–20; Isaac F. Marcosson and Daniel Frohman, *Charles Frohman: Manager and Man* (New York: Harper & Brothers, 1916), 216–17; Parker Morell, *Diamond Jim: The Life and Times of James Buchanan Brady* (New York: Simon and Schuster, 1934), 126–27.

9. Harry B. Smith, *First Nights and First Editions* (Boston: Little, Brown & Co., 1931), 212–13, 217–18; "Theatrical Gossip," *New York Times*, February 23, 1898; "George Lederer, Producer, Is Dead," *New York Times*, October 9, 1938.

10. Nesbit, *Prodigal Days*, 35; Mary Panzer, *In My Studio: Rudolf Eickemeyer, Jr., and the Art of the Camera, 1885–1930* (Yonkers, N.Y.: Hudson River Museum, 1986), 72–75.

11. Nesbit, *Prodigal Days*, 34.

12. Miriam Berman, *Madison Square: The Park and Its Celebrated Landmarks* (New York: Gibbs Smith, 2001), 130.

13. Nesbit, *Prodigal Days*, 47.

14. Ibid., 55–56, 77–78.

15. Ibid., 78; "Heads of Van Alen — Collier Houses Fail to Meet as Their Children Wed," *New York American Journal*, July 27, 1902; Caroline Seebohm, *The Man Who Was Vogue: The Life and Times of Condé Nast* (New York: Viking Press, 1982), 54.

16. Nesbit, *Prodigal Days*, 56–57, 59, 62.

17. John Kobler, *Damned in Paradise, The Life of John Barrymore* (New York: Atheneum, 1977), 41–42, 58–60.

18. "White Pursued Her after Marriage, Says Evelyn," *New York Evening Telegram,* February 8, 1907.

19. Kobler, *Damned in Paradise,* 69; Gene Fowler, *Good Night, Sweet Prince: The Life and Times of John Barrymore* (Philadelphia: Blakiston Co., 1943), 91.

20. Kobler, *Damned in Paradise,* 79–80; Lionel Barrymore, *We Barrymores* (New York: Appleton-Century-Crofts, 1951), 69–70, 88–90.

21. Samuel Hopkins Adams, "Mrs. Thaw Says White, Aided by Abe Hummel, Plotted against Harry," *New York World,* February 9, 1907.

22. Scott Eyman, *Empire of Dreams: The Epic Life of Cecil B. DeMille* (New York: Simon and Schuster, 2010), 30–33.

23. Jean L. De Forest, "School Life of Evelyn Nesbit Told by Teacher," *New York World,* February 11, 1907; "Evelyn Thaw's Life in School Described," *New York Evening Journal,* February 11, 1907; Nesbit, *Prodigal Days,* 68–71.

24. Nesbit, *Prodigal Days,* 73–74.

25. Ibid., 73–74.

26. Harry K. Thaw, *The Traitor* (Philadelphia: Dorrance & Co., 1926), 102–4.

27. "William Thaw Dead," *Pittsburg Dispatch,* August 18, 1889; "His Noble Charities," *Pittsburg Dispatch,* August 18, 1889; "Coke Trust Is Very Rich Part of Thaw Estate," *Pittsburg Dispatch,* April 30, 1903.

28. "Mrs. William Thaw Now Says There Is Insanity in Her Family," *New York Herald,* January 23, 1908.

29. Thaw, *The Traitor,* 23–30.

30. Nesbit, *Prodigal Days,* 75.

31. Ibid., 79–81.

32. Ibid., 80.

Chapter 3 *Marriage*

1. Evelyn Nesbit, *Prodigal Days: The Untold Story* (New York: Julian Messner, 1934), 80–81.

2. Ibid., 82.

3. Ibid.

4. Ibid.

5. Ibid., 115.

6. Ibid., 82, 117.

7. Elisabeth Marbury, *My Crystal Ball: Reminiscences* (New York: Boni & Liveright, 1923), 69–70, 111–15, 156; Alfred Allan Lewis, *Ladies and Not-So-Gentle Women: Elisabeth Marbury, Anne Morgan, Elsie de Wolfe, Anne Vanderbilt, and Their Times* (New York: Penguin, 2001), 134–35.

8. Nesbit, *Prodigal Days,* 86–87.

9. "Evelyn Thaw Collapses on Witness Stand," *New York Evening Journal,* February 7, 1907; "The Story of Thaw's Wife," *New York Sun,* February 8, 1907; Nesbit, *Prodigal Days,* 85–90.

10. "Evelyn Nesbit Thaw, to Save Husband, Says Stanford White Caused Her Downfall When She Was Sixteen by Drugged Wine," *New York Herald*, February 8, 1907; "Evelyn Nesbit Thaw on Stand Says She Was Wronged at 16," *New York Evening Telegram*, February 7, 1907.

11. Nesbit, *Prodigal Days*, 93.

12. "Evelyn Nesbit Thaw on Stand," *New York Evening Telegram*, February 7, 1907.

13. Harry K. Thaw, *The Traitor* (Philadelphia: Dorrance & Co., 1926), 108–9.

14. Nesbit, *Prodigal Days*, 101–2.

15. Thaw, *The Traitor*, 110.

16. Nesbit, *Prodigal Days*, 96.

17. Ibid., 119–20.

18. "Evelyn Nesbit Thaw, under Lash of Mr. Jerome's Cross Examination, Becomes a Stammering, Frightened, Faltering Witness," *New York Herald*, February 20, 1907.

19. "The Story of Thaw's Wife," *New York Sun*, February 8, 1907; "Evelyn Thaw, to Save Husband," *New York Herald*, February 8, 1907.

20. Nesbit, *Prodigal Days*, 123–24.

21. "White Pursued Her after Marriage," *New York Evening Telegram*, February 8, 1907; Samuel Hopkins Adams, "Mrs. Thaw Says White, Aided by Abe Hummel, Plotted against Harry," *New York World*, February 9, 1907.

22. "Evelyn Nesbit Thaw on Stand," *New York Evening Telegram*, February 7, 1907; "The Story of Thaw's Wife," *New York Sun*, February 8, 1907.

23. "Evelyn Nesbit Thaw on Stand," *New York Evening Telegram*, February 7, 1907; "The Story of Thaw's Wife," *New York Sun*, February 8, 1907.

24. Nesbit, *Prodigal Days*, 106–07.

25. "The 'Girl in the Pie' at the Three Thousand Five Hundred Dollar Dinner in Artist Breese's New York Studio," *New York World*, October 13, 1895.

26. Thaw, *The Traitor*, 129–31.

27. "Mrs. William Thaw Now Says There Is Insanity in Her Family," *New York Herald*, January 23, 1908; "Thaw's Mother Kills Defense of Hereditary Taint," *New York World*, January 23, 1908.

28. "Mrs. William Thaw," *New York Herald*, January 23, 1908; "Thaw's Mother," *New York World*, January 23, 1908.

29. "Football Echoes," *New York World*, November 18, 1889; "Football at Princeton," *New York Times*, November 5, 1891.

30. "The Marquess of Hertford," *The Times* (London), February 17, 1940.

31. "Ultimatum to Harry Thaw," *New York Times*, November 6, 1904; "Harry Thaw Is Hurrying Home to Be Spanked," *New York Morning Telegraph*, October 31, 1904.

32. "Millionaire Weds Actress," *Pittsburg Press*, April 5, 1905.

33. Nesbit, *Prodigal Days*, 153–57; "Thaw and Bride Talk Right Out," *New York Morning Telegraph*, April 7, 1905.

34. "Pittsburgh Balks at Evelyn Nesbit," *New York Morning Telegraph*, October 10, 1905; Nesbit, *Prodigal Days*, 163–64.

35. "Thaw's Artist-Model Bride to Leave Him, Friends Say," *New York World*, December 6, 1905; "Wife Who Posed May Quit Thaw," *New York Evening Journal*, December 6, 1905.

36. "Evelyn Nesbit as Sausage Ad," *New York Morning Telegraph*, December 26, 1905; "Picture on Sausage 'Ad,' Mrs. Harry Thaw Angry," *New York Evening Telegram*, December 26, 1905.

37. "Evelyn Nesbit Again on View," *New York Morning Telegraph*, January 13, 1906; "The Thaws Annoyed Again," *New York Times*, January 13, 1906.

Chapter 4 *Murder*

1. "White Wanted to Meet a Show Girl," *New York World*, June 29, 1906.

2. "Roof Garden Attractions—Seaside Amusements—Vaudeville," *New York Herald*, June 24, 1906; "Another Roof Garden," *New-York Daily Tribune*, June 24, 1906; "New Musical Play Opens Roof Garden," *New York Herald*, June 26, 1906.

3. "White Wanted to Meet a Show Girl," *New York World*, June 29, 1906; "The Wages of Sin Paid in the Death of White," *New York American*, June 27, 1906; "Harry Thaw Is Indicted for the Murder of White; Scandal Stories Loosed," *New York Herald*, June 29, 1906.

4. "White Borrowed Big Sum, but Left Little," *New York American*, June 30, 1906; Mosette Broderick, *Triumvirate: McKim, Mead & White* (New York: Alfred A. Knopf, 2010), 489–90.

5. "May Not Sell the Garden," *New York Times*, May 12, 1897; "Madison Square Garden for Sale," *New York Times*, November 12, 1908; Leland M. Roth, *McKim, Mead & White, Architects* (New York: Harper & Row, 1983), 164.

6. "Stanford White Loses Art Objects in Fire," *New York Times*, February 14, 1905; "Fire Darkened Broadway," *New York Sun*, February 14, 1905; "A Bad Tenderloin Blaze," *New-York Tribune*, February 14, 1905; "Pictures a Total Loss," *New York Sun*, February 15, 1905.

7. "White Was Dying Slowly, When Shot," *New York American*, June 29, 1906.

8. "White Knew That Thaw Had Threatened Him," *New York World*, June 27, 1906; "White Tracked by Thaw's Sleuths for a Whole Year, Says Victim's Bodyguard," *New York World*, July 1, 1906.

9. "Evelyn Nesbit Thaw on Stand Says She Was Wronged at 16," *New York Evening Telegram*, February 7, 1907; "Evelyn Thaw Collapses on Witness Stand," *New York Evening Journal*, February 7, 1907.

10. "Truxtun Beale Went to War," *New York Sun*, July 1, 1906.

11. "Saw Thaw, Lucid, Scan the Garden for His Victim," *New York Herald*, March 13, 1907; Samuel Hopkins Adams, "Portrays Thaw Cool, Watchful and Calculating," *New York World*, March 13, 1907.

12. "Saw Thaw," *New York Herald*, March 13, 1907; Adams, "Portrays Thaw Cool," *New York World*, March 13, 1907.

13. "Autopsy Shows One Bullet Was Fatal," *New York World*, June 27, 1906; "Three Bullets Found," *New-York Tribune*, June 27, 1906; "Autopsy on White Shows Where the 3 Bullets Hit Him," *New York American*, June 27, 1906.

14. "Thaw Kills Stanford White," *New-York Tribune*, June 26, 1906.

15. "Harry Thaw Kills Stanford White on Roof Garden!" *New York American*, June 26, 1906; "Stanford White Murdered," *New York Sun*, June 26, 1906.

16. "Harry Thaw Kills Stanford White on Roof Garden!" *New York American*, June 26, 1906.

17. Samuel Hopkins Adams, "State Quickly Puts in Its Case against Thaw: Defense Has Many Forms," *New York World*, February 5, 1907.

18. "Evelyn Nesbit Thaw on Stand Says She Was Wronged at 16," *New York Evening Telegram*, February 7, 1907; "Thaw Murders Stanford White," *New York Times*, June 26, 1906; "Harry Thaw Kills Stanford White on Roof Garden!" *New York American*, June 26, 1906.

19. "Stanford White Murdered," *New York Sun*, June 26, 1906; "Murderers' Row Gets Harry Thaw," *New York Times*, June 27, 1906.

20. "Thaw Lodged in Tombs," *New-York Tribune*, June 27, 1906.

21. "Insults Goaded Thaw to Kill; Millions Ready for Defence," *New York American*, June 27, 1906.

22. Bertram Reinitz, "The Old Tombs Prison under Criticism Again," *New York Times*, June 30, 1929.

23. "Thaw Declared Sane," *New-York Tribune*, June 28, 1906; "Thaw May Plead He Was Justified," *New York Times*, June 28, 1906.

24. "Thaw Indictment In," *New-York Tribune*, June 29, 1906; "Insane When He Shot White but Sane Now, Will Be Thaw's Plea," *New York World*, June 29, 1906; "Harry Thaw Is Indicted for the Murder of White; Scandal Stories Loosed," *New York Herald*, June 29, 1906.

25. "Emotional Insanity," *New York Sun*, June 29, 1906.

26. "Pleads Not Guilty," *New-York Tribune*, June 30, 1906; "Wife Comes to Thaw's Aid," *New York Sun*, June 30, 1906.

27. "Mrs. White Calm at News of Death," *New York American*, June 27, 1906; "Stanford White Stretched at the Feet of Venus," *New York World*, June 27, 1906.

28. "Thaw's Victim, Stanford White, Is in His Grave," *New York World*, June 29, 1906; "Stanford White Buried," *New York Sun*, June 29, 1906; "Harry Thaw Is Indicted," *New York Herald*, June 29, 1906.

29. "No Funeral Service Here," *New York Times*, June 28, 1906; "White's Aged Mother Not at His Funeral," *New York American*, June 29, 1906.

30. "White's Alleged Victims Come to Thaw's Defense," *New York World*, June 30, 1906.

31. "'The Rich Moral Pervert Must Go,' Says Anthony Comstock," *New York American*, June 28, 1906.

32. "Comstock Starts Crusade on White's Companions," *New York American*, July 1, 1906.

33. "'White Tragedy a Warning to the Nation,'" *New York American*, July 2, 1906.

34. "Evangelist R. A. Torrey Sees Good in Tragedy," *New York American*, July 2, 1906; "'Thaw Fulfilled a Law as Old as the World,' Says Dr. Gregory," *New York American*, July 3, 1906.

35. "Thaw Put Comstock on White's Trail," *New York World*, June 29, 1906; "Charges Untrue, Says a Friend," *New York World*, June 30, 1906.

36. "Stanford White Stretched at the Feet of Venus," *New York World*, June 27, 1906.

37. "Pays Tribute to White," *New-York Tribune*, June 29, 1906; "Mr. White as an Architect," *New York Times*, June 27, 1906.

38. "School Girls Alleged to Be His Victims," *New York World*, July 2, 1906; "Rich Clubman Arrested on Little Girls' Charges," *New York American*, July 2, 1906; "Henry Short Held, Accused by Girls," *New York Herald*, July 2, 1906.

39. "'Transients Taken': A 'Red-Light' Guide," *New York American*, July 4, 1906.

40. "The Herald Summoned to Court," *New York American*, July 8, 1906.

41. "Say White Drugged Thaw's Wife," *New York American*, June 29, 1906.

42. "Harry Thaw in Anger Turns Off His Counsel," *New York Times*, July 15, 1906.

43. "Was Thaw Justified?" *New York Evening Journal*, July 27, 1906.

44. "Asylum or Trial; Mrs. Thaw to Say!" *New York American*, July 10, 1906.

45. "Thaw Changes Lawyers on Short Notice," *New York World*, July 15, 1906; "Thaw Bars Great Law Firm Out of Case," *New York American*, July 15, 1906.

46. "Thaw Changes His Lawyers," *New York Sun*, July 15, 1906; "Long Wireless Quest for Thaw's Mother," *New York American*, June 27, 1906.

47. "Mrs. Thaw Sticks to Olcott," *New York Sun*, July 17, 1906; "Cell's Gate Flies Open for Thaw's Mother," *New York American*, July 17, 1906; "Thaw's Mother to Decide on Son's Defense," *New York World*, July 17, 1906.

48. "Mother Yields to Thaw!" *New York Evening Journal*, July 21, 1906.

Chapter 5 *First Trial*

1. Charles Somerville, "Thaw's Face Softens with Pity as White's Young Son Testifies," *New York Evening Journal*, February 4, 1907; "Hereditary Insanity, with Epilepsy, Is the Defence Set Up for Harry Thaw," *New York Herald*, February 5, 1907.

2. Samuel Hopkins Adams, "State Quickly Puts in Its Case against Thaw; Defense Has Many Forms," *New York World*, February 5, 1907.

3. Emma H. de Zouche, "Prosecution Play Young White as a Trump Card," *New York World*, February 5, 1907; "Thaw's Defence Is Insanity," *New York Sun*, February 5, 1907.

4. "State Rests!" *New York Evening Journal*, February 4, 1907; Adams, "State Quickly Puts in Its Case," *New York World*, February 5, 1907.

5. "Hereditary Insanity," *New York Herald*, February 5, 1907.

6. Adams, "State Quickly Puts in Its Case," *New York World*, February 5, 1907.

7. Charles Somerville, "Young Wife's Awful Story Stuns Jurors," *New York Evening Journal*, February 7, 1907; "Evelyn Thaw Tells Her Story," *New York Times*, February 8, 1907.

8. "Evelyn Nesbit Thaw, to Save Husband, Says Stanford White Caused Her Downfall When She Was Sixteen by Drugged Wine," *New York Herald*, February 8, 1907.

9. Irwin Cobb, *Exit Laughing* (New York: Bobbs-Merrill, 1941), 233–34.

10. Somerville, "Young Wife's Awful Story Stuns Jurors," *New York Evening Journal*, February 7, 1907; "Mrs. Harry Thaw Tells Jury of Her Relations with Stanford White," *New York World*, February 8, 1907; "The Story of Thaw's Wife," *New York Sun*, February 8, 1907, "Evelyn Thaw Tells Her Story," *New York Times*, February 8, 1907.

11. "White Pursued Her after Marriage, Says Evelyn," *New York Evening Telegram*, February 8, 1907.

12. Ibid.

13. "City Plans to Keep Thaw Testimony Out of Print," *New York Evening Telegram*, February 9, 1907; "Would Keep Thaw Case from Public," *New York World*, February 11, 1907; "Chicago Opinion Divided upon It," *New York World*, February 12, 1907; "Pittsburgh W.C.T.U. Opposes Printing Details of Thaw Trial," *New York World*, February 14, 1907.

14. "Thaw Indictments for Four Editors," *New York Evening Telegram*, February 14, 1907; "Asks House to Keep Thaw Trial Out of the Mails," *New York Evening Telegram*, February 14, 1907.

15. "Roosevelt Aims at Censorship of Newspapers," *New York World*, February 12, 1907; "President Would Bar Some Newspapers," *New York Herald*, February 12, 1907.

16. "Canada's Mails Bar Thaw Revelations," *New York Evening Telegram*, February 9, 1907; "Roosevelt Plans Thaw Censorship," *New York Times*, February 12, 1907.

17. "Attorney-General on the Thaw Case," *New York World*, February 14, 1907.

18. "Says Thaw Was Insane When He Shot Mr. White," *New York Herald*, February 13, 1907.

19. "Say Harry Thaw Was Insane on Wedding Day," *New York Herald*, February 19, 1907.

20. "Says Thaw Was Insane When He Shot Mr. White," *New York Herald*, February 13, 1907; "Thaw Paranoiac Expert Swears," *New York Evening Journal*, February 12, 1907.

21. "Says Thaw Was Insane When He Shot Mr. White," *New York Herald*, February 13, 1907.

22. "Thaw's Wife Ends Her Story," *New York Sun*, February 20, 1907; "Evelyn Nesbit Thaw, under Lash of Mr. Jerome's Cross-Examination, Becomes a Stammering, Frightened, Shrinking, Faltering Witness," *New York Herald*, February 20, 1907.

23. Richard O'Connor, *Courtroom Warrior: The Combative Career of William Travers Jerome* (Boston: Little, Brown & Co., 1963), 46–48, 60, 74–82.

24. Ibid., 55–56; Cobb, *Exit Laughing*, 234.

25. "Mr. White Not in Studio on Night Evelyn Charges," *New York Herald*, February 27, 1907; "Evelyn Thaw Lied on Stand, Jerome Believes," *New York World*, April 14, 1907.

26. "Evelyn Nesbit Thaw, under Lash of Mr. Jerome's Cross-Examination," *New York Herald*, February 20, 1907; "Evelyn Nesbit Admits Accepting $25 a Week from Stanford White Long after Time She Told Husband That Her Life Was Wrecked," *New York Herald*, February 21, 1907.

27. "Evelyn Nesbit Admits Accepting $25 a Week," *New York Herald*, February 21, 1907.

28. "Evelyn Nesbit Thaw, under Lash of Mr. Jerome's Cross-Examination," *New York Herald*, February 20, 1907.

29. "Evelyn Nesbit Admits Accepting $25 a Week," *New York Herald*, February 21, 1907.

30. "Love Secrets," *New York Evening Journal*, February 25, 1907.

31. "Mrs. Thaw All Day under Fire," *New York Sun*, February 21, 1907; "Evelyn Nesbit Admits Accepting $25 a Week," *New York Herald*, February 21, 1907.

32. Charles Somerville, "Days of Rest Do Much for All Principals," *New York Evening Journal*, February 25, 1907.

33. "Evelyn Thaw Sheds Tears as Mr. Jerome's Questions Bare Her Life's Secrets," *New York Herald*, February 22, 1907.

34. "Mrs. Holman Puts the Blame on Thaw for Girl's Sacrifice," *New York Evening Journal*, February 25, 1907.

35. Samuel Hopkins Adams, "Mrs. Thaw Paints Her Own Picture in Darker Tints," *New York World*, February 22, 1907; Samuel Hopkins Adams, "Crisis To-Day in Wife's Story and Thaw's Defense," *New York World*, February 26, 1907.

36. "Evelyn Thaw Sheds Tears," *New York Herald*, February 22, 1907; "Her Life with White and Thaw," *New York Sun*, February 22, 1907; Charles Somerville, "Prisoner's Wife Sobs on Stand as Jerome Drags Out Her Heart Secrets," *New York Evening Journal*, February 21, 1907.

37. Arthur Train, *True Stories of Crime: From the District Attorney's Office* (New York: Charles Scribner's Sons, 1922), 283–313; Richard H. Rovere, *Howe & Hummel: Their True and Scandalous History* (New York: Farrar, Straus and Giroux, 1985), 134–62; Cait Murphy, *Scoundrels in Law: The Trials of Howe & Hummel* (New York: HarperCollins, 2010), 244–48.

38. Somerville, "Days of Rest," *New York Evening Journal*, February 25, 1907.

39. "Says Thaw Beat, Throttled and Cowhided Her," *New York Herald*, February 26, 1907.

40. Adams, "Crisis To-Day in Wife's Story," *New York World*, February 26, 1907.

41. "Says Thaw Beat, Throttled and Cowhided Her," *New York Herald*, February 26, 1907.

42. "Saw Thaw, Lucid, Scan the Garden for His Victim," *New York Herald*, March 13, 1907.

43. "Hummel, Whom Jerome Punished, Testifies for Him," *New York World*, March 16, 1907.

44. "In Beginning His Pleas for the Life of Harry K. Thaw, Mr. Delmas Eloquently Asks Belief in Evelyn's Story," *New York Herald*, April 9, 1907; "Delmas at Last Gives a Name to Thaw's Insanity," *New York World*, April 10, 1907.

45. "Thaw Jury Is Locked Up for the Night after Hearing Mr. Jerome Demand Death in the Electric Chair for Slayer of Stanford White," *New York Herald*, April 11, 1907.

46. Instructions of the Judge to the Jury, Box 131.1 (Thaw Murder Trial), fol. 4705, New York State Historical Association.

47. Instructions of the Judge to the Jury, Box 131.1 (Thaw Murder Trial), fols. 4708, 4711, New York State Historical Association.

48. "Thaw to Be Tried Again; Jury Disagrees, Seven Voting for Conviction," *New York World*, April 13, 1907.

49. "Thaw Jury, Unable to Reach Verdict, Again Locked Up for the Night," *New York Herald*, April 12, 1907.

50. "Jurors Did Their Best, They Say, to Reach an Agreement, *New York World*, April 13, 1907.

51. "Thaw to Be Tried Again," *New York World*, April 13, 1907; "Standing Seven for Murder in First Degree and Five for Acquittal," *New York Herald*, April 13, 1907.

Chapter 6 *Second Trial*

1. "One Crushed by Grief and Illness, the Other Radiant, Thaw's Mother and His Wife Seek to Save His Life," *New York Herald*, January 18, 1908.

2. "Mrs. William Thaw Now Says There Is Insanity in Her Family," *New York Herald*, January 23, 1908.

3. "Martin Littleton Dies at 62; Noted Orator, Lawyer," *New York Herald Tribune*, December 20, 1934; "M. W. Littleton Sr., Lawyer, Dies at 62," *New York Times*, December 20, 1934; "Martin W. Littleton Sr. Dies," *New York Sun*, December 24, 1934.

4. "Martin Littleton Dies at 62," *New York Herald Tribune*, December 20, 1934; "M. W. Littleton Sr.," *New York Times*, December 20, 1934.

5. "Mrs. William Thaw Now Says," *New York Herald*, January 23, 1908; "Thaw's Mother Kills Defense of Hereditary Taint," *New York World*, January 23, 1908.

6. "Mrs. William Thaw Now Says," *New York Herald,* January 23, 1908.

7. Ibid.

8. "Tell of Thaw's Odd Behavior," *New York World,* January 18, 1908; "Evelyn Thaw on the Stand," *New York Evening Journal,* January 17, 1908.

9. "White Threatened Thaw's Life," *New York Evening Journal,* January 16, 1908; "Jerome May Admit Insanity of Thaw," *New York Times,* January 17, 1908.

10. "Thaw Insane at School," *New York Evening Journal,* January 14, 1908; "Insanity Secrets of Thaw Family Held Inviolate," *New York Herald,* January 15, 1908.

11. "Insanity Secrets," *New York Herald,* January 15, 1908.

12. "Harry Thaw Ordered 20 Tons of Ice," *New York Evening Journal,* January 27, 1908; "Defence Says Thaw Has 'Manic-Depressive' Insanity and Rests Its Case," *New York Herald,* January 28, 1908.

13. "Harry Thaw Ordered 20 Tons of Ice," *New York Evening Journal,* January 27, 1908; "Defence Says Thaw Has 'Manic-Depressive' Insanity," *New York Herald,* January 28, 1908.

14. "Thaw's Wife Says Husband Planned Death in Waldorf," *New York Herald,* January 21, 1908.

15. "Thaw Twice Was Bent on Suicide, His Wife Swears," *New York World,* January 21, 1908.

16. "Evelyn Thaw Tells Life Story Again," *New York Times,* January 21, 1908.

17. "Thaw's Wife Says Husband Planned Death in Waldorf," *New York Herald,* January 21, 1908.

18. "Defence Says Thaw Has 'Manic-Depressive' Insanity," *New York Herald,* January 28, 1908.

19. "Thaw's Defense In: Alienists Have Bad Hour," *New York World,* January 28, 1908; "Defence Says Thaw Has 'Manic-Depressive' Insanity," *New York Herald,* January 28, 1908.

20. "Calling Thaw a Maniac, Pleads for His Life," *New York Herald,* January 30, 1908; "Littleton Begs for Thaw's Life," *New York Evening Journal,* January 29, 1908.

21. "Littleton in Plea for Thaw Assails Jerome," *New York World,* January 30, 1908; "Calling Thaw a Maniac," *New York Herald,* January 30, 1908; "Littleton Begs for Thaw's Life," *New York Evening Journal,* January 29, 1908.

22. "Jerome, in Summing Up, Acts Thaw Tragedy!" *New York Evening Journal,* January 30, 1908; "Calling Him Sane, Mr. Jerome Demands Death for Harry Thaw, but Emphasizes Second Degree," *New York Herald,* January 31, 1908.

23. "Two Girls Tell of Thaw's Insanity," *New York Evening Journal,* January 15, 1908; "Thaw a Coward First and Last, Says Jerome," *New York World,* January 31, 1908.

24. "Jerome, in Summing Up, Acts Thaw Tragedy!" *New York Evening Journal,* January 30, 1908.

25. Ibid.

26. "Calling Him Sane, Mr. Jerome Demands Death," *New York Herald,* January 31, 1908.

27. Charles Somerville, "Thaw Jury Foreman a Fine American Type," *New York Evening Journal*, January 8, 1908; "Thaw Jury Ready, First Witnesses Called Monday," *New York Herald*, January 11, 1908.

28. "Harry Thaw, Not Guilty on Ground of Insanity, Locked Up in Matteawan," *New York Herald*, February 2, 1908.

29. Charles Somerville, " 'Jury Will Acquit Me,' Says Thaw," *New York Evening Journal*, February 1, 1908.

30. "For 25 Hours Jurors Disputed before Reaching Their Verdict," *New York World*, February 2, 1908.

31. Ibid.

32. "Harry Thaw, Not Guilty on Ground of Insanity," *New York Herald*, February 2, 1908.

33. Ibid.

34. Ibid.; "Thaw Acquitted Because Insane, Sent to Asylum," *New York World*, February 2, 1908.

35. "Harry Thaw, Not Guilty," *New York Herald*, February 2, 1908; "Thaw Acquitted Because Insane," *New York World*, February 2, 1908.

Chapter 7 *Asylum*

1. Henry M. Hurd, ed., *The Institutional Care of the Insane in the United States and Canada*, 4 vols. (Baltimore: Johns Hopkins Press, 1916), 3:243.

2. *Fifty-First Annual Report of the Medical Superintendent of the Matteawan State Hospital* (Matteawan, N.Y., 1910), 8, 14–16.

3. "Harry Thaw, Not Guilty on Ground of Insanity, Locked Up in Matteawan," *New York Herald*, February 2, 1908.

4. "What Thaw's New Prison Is Like," *New York World*, February 2, 1908; "He's No. 719 at the Asylum," *New York Times*, February 2, 1908.

5. "Thaw Sulks in His Asylum Uniform," *New York Times*, February 3, 1908; "Say Maniacs Are Menace to Thaw," *New York Herald*, February 4, 1908; "Matteawan Askew in Thaw's Opinion," *New York Times*, February 4, 1908; "Thaw Predicts He Will Go Free in Week," *New York Herald*, February 3, 1908.

6. "Myles M'Donnell Shot Dead in Albany," *New York Times*, June 8, 1904; "Preusser Verdict Insanity," *New York Times*, June 24, 1906; "McDonnell's Slayer Now Sane," *New York Times*, August 2, 1906.

7. "Setback for Thaw," *New York Evening Journal*, February 5, 1908.

8. Evelyn Nesbit, *Prodigal Days: The Untold Story* (New York: Julian Messner, 1934), 213.

9. Ibid., 213–14.

10. "Matteawan Askew in Thaw's Opinion," *New York Times*, February 4, 1908; Charles Somerville, "Will Invoke Law to a Sensational Degree for Thaw," *New York Evening Journal*, February 4, 1908.

11. "Setback for Thaw," *New York Evening Journal*, February 5, 1908.

12. "Robert Brockway Lamb, M.D.," *New York State Journal of Medicine* 52 (1952): 1685–86; *Fifty-Second Annual Report of the Medical Superintendent of the Matteawan State Hospital* (Matteawan, N.Y., 1911), 7–8.

13. "First Step to Free Thaw," *New York Sun*, April 21, 1908; "Thaw Lawyers Attack Law," *New York Sun*, May 14, 1908.

14. "Thaw's Fate Is Now in Hands of Dutchess Judge," *New York World*, May 5, 1908.

15. "Thaw Declared to Be Insane," *New York Sun*, May 26, 1908; Editorial, "The Insanity of Thaw," *New York Times*, May 26, 1908.

16. "Thaw Attacks Wife after Learning of Detectives' Report," *New York World*, March 9, 1908.

17. "Thaw's Wife Testifies She Began Action to Annul Her Marriage," *New York Herald*, August 27, 1913; Nesbit, *Prodigal Days*, 216; "$1,000 a Month to Mrs. Thaw," *New York Sun*, May 27, 1908.

18. Nesbit, *Prodigal Days*, 208–10, 216–17, 218, 230.

19. "Law Seals Lips of Mrs. Thaw on Threat to Kill," *New York World*, July 14, 1909.

20. Ibid.

21. "Thaw's Threat to Kill Her Wrung from His Wife," *New York World*, July 16, 1909; "Mrs. Thaw Tells of Threat," *New York Sun*, July 16, 1909; "Thaw Threat Let In; Said He'd Kill Wife," *New York Times*, July 16, 1909.

22. " 'I Threaten Evelyn? Absurd,' Says Thaw," *New York World*, July 16, 1909.

23. "Thaw Evidence to Show Him Insane," *New York World*, August 3, 1909; "Thaw Insane and Menace If Free, Assert Alienists at Sanity Hearing," *New York Herald*, August 4, 1909.

24. "Thaw with Whip Beat Many Girls, Woman Testifies," *New York World*, July 28, 1909; "Thaw, Shown His Foolish Writings, Loses His Bravado," *New York World*, July 30, 1909.

25. "Thaw with Whip Beat Many Girls," *New York World*, July 28, 1909.

26. "Pistol with Which Thaw Slew Mr. White Stolen," *New York Herald*, August 3, 1909; "Thaw Evidence to Show Him Insane," *New York World*, August 3, 1909.

27. "Thaw, Free, Would Menace Public, Says Dr. Baker," *New York World*, August 4, 1909; "Thaw Insane and Menace If Free," *New York Herald*, August 4, 1909.

28. "Thaw a Lunatic; Liberty Is Denied; He Will Try Again," *New York Herald*, August 13, 1909.

29. "Lees Accuses Himself of Being Incendiary," *Brooklyn Daily Eagle*, February 23, 1910.

30. "Once in Asylum Now Fighting to Have Girl Freed," *New York World*, January 17, 1911.

31. "Girl of 17 among Convicts," *New York Sun*, February 19, 1911.

32. Marguerite Mooers Marshall, "Dora Schram Tells of the Torture She Suffered While in Matteawan," *New York World*, February 28, 1911.

33. "Another Woman Seeks Liberty in Thaw's Campaign," *New York World*, February 28, 1911; "Woman Convict Charges Cruelty in Matteawan," *New York Evening Telegram*, March 17, 1911.

34. "To Leave Matteawan," *New-York Tribune*, February 19, 1911.

35. "Calls Matteawan Worse Than State Prison," *New York World*, February 18, 1911.

36. "Say Insane Man Died of Beating," *New York American*, February 9, 1911; "Brutality in Matteawan to Be Revealed," *New York American*, February 10, 1911.

37. "Asylum Inmate Fell in Attempt to Make Escape," *New York World*, February 8, 1911.

38. "Differ on Nugent's Death," *New-York Tribune*, February 24, 1911; "Galbraith Now Accused," *New-York Tribune*, February 28, 1911.

39. "Matteawan Investigation," *New-York Tribune*, February 11, 1911; "Gov. Dix Orders Probe of Abuses at Matteawan," *New York World*, March 4, 1911.

40. "Saxe Bill Unopposed," *New-York Tribune*, April 19, 1911; "The Legislature at Work," *New York Sun*, April 20, 1911.

41. "Matteawan Asylum Inquiry," *New York Sun*, February 19, 1911; "Supt. Collins, Head of Prisons, Resigns Office," *New York World*, April 26, 1911.

42. "Made a Bogus Court Order," *New York Sun*, June 4, 1911; "Dr. Lamb Explains," *New York Sun*, June 18, 1911.

43. "Dr. Lamb Out," *New York Sun*, July 8, 1911; "Dr. R. B. Lamb Resigns," *New-York Tribune*, July 8, 1911.

44. "Dr. Amos Baker Resigns," *New-York Tribune*, August 15, 1911; "Glad That Dr. Lamb Resigned," *New York Sun*, August 20, 1911.

45. "Mrs. Edward R. Thomas Sues for Divorce," *New-York Tribune*, March 20, 1912.

46. "Mrs. Evelyn Thaw in New Fight for Her Baby's Sake," *New York Herald*, May 13, 1912; Nesbit, *Prodigal Days*, 239–44.

47. Nesbit, *Prodigal Days*, 244–47.

48. "Evelyn Thaw Says Husband Is Father of Her Young Son," *New York Evening Journal*, May 9, 1913.

49. "Thaw Letter Fake, Says C. J. Shearn," *New York Sun*, May 17, 1912.

50. "Wife Who Saved Him on Stand against Thaw in Fight for Liberty," *New York World*, June 19, 1912; "Thaw's 'Silence Money' Paid to Over 200 Girls, Swears Susan Merrill," *New York World*, June 20, 1912.

51. "Thaw's Wife as Witness Tells of His Crazy Acts," *New York World*, June 20, 1912; "Evelyn Thaw Again on Witness Stand," *New York Sun*, June 20, 1912.

52. "Mrs. Thaw in Rage Shouts She Won't Tell of Her Ruin," *New York World*, June 22, 1912.

53. Ibid.

54. "Thaw Still Mad, Release a Peril, Justice Decides," *New York World*, July 27, 1912.

55. "Anhut's Denial of Thaw-Russell Deal His Defense," *New York Morning Telegraph*, May 17, 1913.

56. Matthew L. Lifflander, *The Impeachment of Governor Sulzer: A Story of American Politics* (Albany: State University of New York Press, 2012), 123–27, 183–88.

57. "Sulzer Drops Mills from Prison Employ," *New York Times*, March 1, 1913; "Sulzer Dismisses Col. Scott, Senate Rejects Gibbs," *New York Morning Telegraph*, March 14, 1913.

58. "Anhut to Prison in Bribe Case," *New York Evening Journal*, May 23, 1913.

59. "Thaw Rejected Plan to Escape, Alienist Says," *New York Evening Journal*, March 14, 1913.

Chapter 8 *Escape*

1. "Harry Thaw Flees Matteawan," *New York World*, August 18, 1913; "H. K. Thaw Escapes from Asylum," *New York Herald*, August 18, 1913; "Thaw Escapes in Auto from Matteawan," *New York Times*, August 18, 1913.

2. "Harry Thaw Flees Matteawan," *New York World*, August 18, 1913; "H. K. Thaw Escapes," *New York Herald*, August 18, 1913; "Thaw Escapes," *New York Times*, August 18, 1913; Richard J. Butler, *Dock Walloper: The Story of "Big Dick" Butler* (New York: G. P. Putnam's Sons, 1933), 159–61.

3. "Butler Is a Chum of Bill Devery," *New York World*, August 19, 1913.

4. "$25,000 Paid Band Men Who Aided Thaw's Escape, Police Are Informed," *New York Herald*, August 20, 1913.

5. "Thaw, Caught in Canada, Begins Fight against Return," *New York Herald*, August 20, 1913; "He Engages Counsel and Will Seek to Raise Extradition Issue," *New York Times*, August 20, 1913; "Thaw Arrested in Canada, May Be Sent Back," *New York World*, August 20, 1913.

6. "Thaw's Mother Glad He Escaped," *New York Times*, August 18, 1913; "Asylum Fugitive Believed to Be Seeking Safety on Water," *New York Herald*, August 18, 1913.

7. "Evelyn Thaw Fears Death for Herself and Baby Boy," *New York Herald*, August 18, 1913.

8. "Thaw Dangerous Says Dr. Flint," *New York Times*, August 18, 1913; "Will Revert to Old Habits," *New York Times*, August 18, 1913.

9. "Harry Thaw Flees Matteawan," *New York World*, August 18, 1913.

10. "Thaw Escapes in Auto," *New York Times*, August 18, 1913; "Thought Thaw Was in Lenox," *New York Times*, August 19, 1913; "Two Automobiles Are Reported Speeding for Canadian Border," *New York Herald*, August 19, 1913.

11. "Thaw Declared Safe from Extradition by Legal Experts Here and Elsewhere," *New York Herald*, August 19, 1913; "Thaw Cannot Be Extradited, Legal Authorities Agree," *New York Herald*, August 19, 1913.

12. "Thaw Declared Safe," *New York Herald*, August 19, 1913.

13. "Harry Thaw Flees Matteawan," *New York World*, August 18, 1913.
14. Ibid.
15. "Mr. Glynn Asks Details of Harry Thaw's Escape," *New York Herald*, August 18, 1913.
16. "He Engages Counsel," *New York Times*, August 20, 1913; "Thaw, Caught in Canada," *New York Herald*, August 20, 1913.
17. Mabel F. Timlin, "Canada's Immigration Policy, 1896–1910," *Canadian Journal of Economics and Political Science* 26 (1960): 517–32.
18. "Inspectors Sent Ready to Deport," *New York World*, August 20, 1913; "Dominion Law Provides for the Exclusion of Thaw," *New York Herald*, August 20, 1913.
19. "Mr. Conger Goes to Coaticook to Demand Thaw's Deportation," *New York Herald*, August 20, 1913.
20. "Evelyn Returned to 'Old Life,' So He Fled, Says Thaw," *New York World*, August 21, 1913.
21. "Thaw Wins Point; Cheers in Court, Ovation Outside," *New York Herald*, August 28, 1913.
22. "Thaw Wins First Skirmish; Crowds Wildly Cheer Him," *New York World*, August 28, 1913.
23. "Thaw Will Be Deported Today; New Judge to Act," *New York World*, August 30, 1913; "New Move To-Day to Deport Thaw; Driver Gets Bail," *New York Herald*, August 30, 1913.
24. "New Writ Issued to Deport Thaw; Decision Tuesday," *New York Herald*, August 31, 1913; "Coup Puts Thaw in Jerome's Reach," *New York Times*, August 31, 1913.
25. "Thaw's Hearing Will Be Held in Judge's Chambers," *New York Herald*, September 2, 1913; "Court to Exclude Mr. Jerome To-Day," *New York Herald*, September 2, 1913.
26. "Premier Rules That Thaw Cannot Hide in Jail," *New York Herald*, September 3, 1913.
27. "Jerome Said to Plan Auto Dash Back with Thaw," *New York World*, September 3, 1913.
28. "Thaw, a Nervous Wreck, Freed, Seized Again and Faces Deportation To-Day," *New York Herald*, September 4, 1913; "Thaw at Border on His Way Back," *New York Times*, September 4, 1913.
29. "Thaw, a Nervous Wreck, Freed," *New York Herald*, September 4, 1913; "Thaw at Border," *New York Times*, September 4, 1913; "I'll Never Go Back to Asylum! Sobs Thaw, Losing Fight," *New York World*, September 4, 1913.
30. "Will Rush Thaw into U.S. To-Day, It Seems Sure," *New York World*, September 5, 1913; "Thaw to Be Sent to Vermont To-Day," *New York Times*, September 5, 1913.
31. "Will Rush Thaw into U.S.," *New York World*, September 5, 1913
32. "Thaw Is Saved for Time; Jerome Put under Arrest," *New York World*, September 6, 1913.

33. Ibid.

34. Ibid.

35. "Thaw, Serenaded by Village Band, Starts a Speech," *New York World*, September 7, 1913.

36. "Show Girls Cheer Thaw in Prison," *New York Herald*, September 10, 1913; "Weary of Roses, Thaw Picks Wild Flowers in Field," *New York World*, September 10, 1913.

37. "Ask High Court to Let Jerome Address It in Person," *New York World*, September 9, 1913.

38. "Thaw Deported in Spite of Writ," *New York Times*, September 11, 1913; "Canada Throws Out Thaw, Despite High Court Order," *New York Herald*, September 11, 1913; "Thaw, Flung Back into U.S., Is Now a Hotel Prisoner," *New York World*, September 11, 1913.

39. "Thaw, Flung Back into U.S.," *New York World*, September 11, 1913; "Canada Throws Out Thaw," *New York Herald*, September 11, 1913.

Chapter 9 *Final Verdict*

1. "Thaw Deported in Spite of Writ," *New York Times*, September 11, 1913; "Canada Throws Out Thaw, Despite High Court Order," *New York Herald*, September 11, 1913; "Thaw, Flung Back into U.S., Is Now a Hotel Prisoner," *New York World*, September 11, 1913.

2. "Warrant for Thaw Charges Conspiracy," *New York World*, September 12, 1913; "New Warrant for Thaw," *New York Times*, September 12, 1913.

3. "New Hampshire Doesn't Want Thaw," *New York World*, August 21, 1913; "'Human Hyena' Is Name Mrs. Thaw Gives to Jerome," *New York World*, September 25, 1913.

4. "Grand Jury Fails to Indict Thaw," *New York Times*, September 20, 1913; "Seesaw on Thaw by a Grand Jury," *New York World*, September 25, 1913.

5. "Thaw Enthusiasts in Fight on Jerome," *New York Times*, October 5, 1913.

6. "Thaw Like Hero to Crowds along His Day's Route," *New York World*, September 18, 1913; "Mayor Begs Thaw for Brief Speech, Also Autograph," *New York World*, September 19, 1913.

7. "Jerome Departs to Ask Instant Return of Thaw," *New York World*, October 24, 1913; "Thaw Is Indicted in Rapid Transit Fashion," *New-York Tribune*, October 24, 1913; "Jerome on His Way to Get Harry Thaw," *New York Times*, October 25, 1913.

8. "Thaw Requisition Signed by Felker," *New York Sun*, November 9, 1913.

9. "Thaw's Sanity Up to U.S. Court," *New-York Tribune*, December 10, 1913.

10. "Thaw Wins Writ, but Not Freedom," *New-York Tribune*, April 15, 1914.

11. "Thaw Wins Writ of Habeas Corpus but Is Still Held," *New York World*, April 14, 1914.

12. Sheldon M. Novick, *Honorable Justice: The Life of Oliver Wendell Holmes* (Boston: Little, Brown & Co., 1989), 310.

13. Oliver Wendell Holmes Jr. to Charlotte Moncheur, December 19, 1914, Mark DeWolfe Howe Research Materials Relating to Life of Oliver Wendell Holmes, Harvard Law School Library.

14. *Holman A. Drew v. Harry K. Thaw*, 235 U.S. 432 (1914).

15. "Thaw Cheerful as Sheriff Puts Him on Train for Trip Back to New York Prison," *New York World*, January 23, 1915.

16. "Thaw Back in Tombs To-Day; 'Shame!' Cry Mobs on Way," *New York Sun*, January 24, 1915.

17. "Thaw on Last Lap to Tombs; Due at 8 A.M.," *New-York Tribune*, January 24, 1915.

18. "Back in Tombs, Thaw Says 'Out Soon,'" *New York Evening Telegram*, January 24, 1915.

19. Ibid

20. "Thaw as Witness Testifies He Paid $7,025 for Escape," *New York World*, March 12, 1915.

21. "Thaw Jury Fails to Agree; Locked Up for the Night," *New York World*, March 13, 1915.

22. "Thaw Acquitted; Fight to Set Him at Liberty Is On," *New York World*, March 14, 1915.

23. "Thaw Defeated, Gets a New Writ," *New York Times*, March 17, 1915.

24. "Thaw Gets a Jury Trial, but Verdict Will Not Be Final," *New York World*, April 24, 1915.

25. "Thaw Is Sanest Fisherman That Undertaker Met," *New York World*, June 25, 1915; "Looks for Evelyn Thaw to Appear and Fight Harry," *New York World*, June 26, 1915.

26. "Evelyn Thaw May Flee into Canada to Escape Court," *New York World*, July 8, 1915.

27. "To Seize Thaw's Wife and Make Her Testify," *New York Evening Telegram*, July 7, 1915.

28. "Mrs. Thaw's Testimony Read to Jury," *New York Evening Telegram*, July 9, 1915; "Harry Thaw Has Dinner at Biltmore," *New York Morning Telegraph*, July 10, 1915; "Thaw Mistrial Is Refused to State; Wife Out of Case," *New York World*, July 10, 1915.

29. "Harry Thaw Has Dinner at Biltmore," *New York Morning Telegraph*, July 10, 1915; "Mrs. Thaw's Testimony Read to Jury," *New York Evening Telegram*, July 9, 1915.

30. "Thaw Mistrial Is Refused," *New York World*, July 10, 1915; "Thaw Finishes His Story, Then Dines in Luxury," *New York Sun*, July 10, 1915; "Harry Thaw Has Dinner at Biltmore," *New York Morning Telegraph*, July 10, 1915.

31. "Thaw Six Hours under Fire of State's Lawyer," *New York Morning Telegraph*, July 9, 1915; "Wife's Story of White Meeting," *New York Evening Telegram*, July 8, 1915.

32. "Wife's Story of White Meeting," *New York Evening Telegram*, July 8, 1915; "Mrs. Thaw's Testimony Read to Jury," *New York Evening Telegram*, July 9, 1915.
33. "State Will Appeal as Court Reserves Thaw Sanity Ruling," *New York Evening Telegram*, July 14, 1915; "Thaw Sane, Jury Finds; Thousands Cheer Slayer Who Now Asks Freedom," *New York World*, July 15, 1915.
34. "Harry K. Thaw Now Sane, Jury's Verdict on Second Ballot," *New York Morning Telegraph*, July 15, 1915.
35. Ibid.
36. "State Will Appeal," *New York Evening Telegram*, July 14, 1915.
37. "Thaw, Freed, Starts Home," *New York Evening Telegram*, July 16, 1915; "Judge Scorns Alienists as He Frees Thaw on Bail," *New-York Tribune*, July 17, 1915.
38. "Thaw's Nine-Year Legal Fight Cost Him More Than $1,000,000," *New-York Tribune*, July 15, 1915.
39. Editorial, "The Thaw Verdict Will Meet with General Approval, We Believe," *New York Morning Telegraph*, July 15, 1915.
40. Editorial, "Thaw Sane and Insane," *New York World*, July 17, 1915.
41. Editorial, "Thaw Sane," *New York Press*, July 17, 1915.
42. "'Thaw Still Cad,' Wife's Comment," *New-York Tribune*, July 17, 1915.

Chapter 10 *Epilogue*

1. "Thaw Indicted on Boy's Charge He Was Lashed," *New York World*, January 10, 1917.
2. "Gump's Story of the Way He Was Lashed by Thaw," *New York World*, January 12, 1917.
3. "Thaw Fails to End Life," *New-York Tribune*, January 12, 1917.
4. "Thaw a Lunatic, Mother Concedes," *Philadelphia Evening Ledger*, February 26, 1917; "Insanity Hearing Sought for Thaw," *New York Sun*, January 16, 1917.
5. "New York's Request for Thaw Denied," *New-York Tribune*, May 10, 1917.
6. "Thaw Found Sane; Is Not Yet Free; Retrial Is Asked," *New York World*, April 23, 1924.
7. Evelyn Nesbit, *Prodigal Days: The Untold Story* (New York: Julian Messner, 1934), 264, 276–78, 280.
8. "Thaw Riches May Go to Evelyn's Boy," *New York Sun*, April 23, 1916.
9. "Evelyn Nesbit Thaw Weds Dancing Partner," *New-York Tribune*, May 25, 1916; "Didn't Know It Was Evelyn," *New York Sun*, May 26, 1916.
10. Nesbit, *Prodigal Days*, 280–81; "Evelyn Nesbit at the Palace," *New-York Tribune*, November 6, 1917; "Film Girls Named by Evelyn Nesbit," *Sun and New York Herald*, June 18, 1920.
11. "On the Screen," *New-York Tribune*, May 22, 1917.
12. "New Era Finds Film Stars Leaning on Playwrights as Never Before," *New York Sun*, April 6, 1919; "William Fox to Film Novels with All-Star Casts," *New-York Tribune*, June 8, 1919.

13. Nesbit, *Prodigal Days,* 281–83, 290–91; "Evelyn Nesbit Tells How She Won Over Drug Habit," *Washington Times,* December 18, 1922.

14. Nesbit, *Prodigal Days,* 264; "Evelyn Nesbit Tells," *Washington Times,* December 18, 1922.

15. "Evelyn Nesbit Tells," *Washington Times,* December 18, 1922.

16. Nesbit, *Prodigal Days,* 286–88; "Evelyn Nesbit Wins Bout with the Law," *New York Herald,* September 21, 1921.

17. Nesbit, *Prodigal Days,* 292–93, 296–97; "Evelyn Nesbit Thaw Faces Jail Sentence," *New York Herald,* November 10, 1922.

18. Nesbit, *Prodigal Days,* 301–2.

19. "Thaw Might Get $5,000,000," *New York Times,* April 14, 1924; "Harry Thaw Income Is $60,000 Yearly," *Chicago Herald and Examiner,* July 10, 1924; "$152,645 for Harry Thaw," *New York Times,* October 13, 1927.

20. "Harry K. Thaw, 76, Is Dead in Florida," *New York Times,* February 23, 1947; "Funeral Held for Thaw," *New York Times,* February 27, 1947.

21. "Thaw Left $10,000 to Evelyn Nesbit," *New York Times,* March 30, 1947; "Harry K. Thaw Left Estate of $1,211,094," *New York Times,* July 23, 1948.

22. Jack Gould, "News and Gossip of Night Clubs," *New York Times,* March 27, 1938.

23. Seymour Korman, "The Girl in the Scandal of the Century!" *Chicago Sunday Tribune Magazine,* September 5, 1954.

24. Bosley Crowther, "Screen: Musty Scandal," *New York Times,* October 20, 1955; "Evelyn Nesbit, 82, Dies in California," *New York Times,* January 19, 1967; "Evelyn Nesbit Buried," *New York Times,* January 21, 1967.

Afterword

1. "Brief Whirl of Gayety Is Ended by Pistol Shots," *New York World,* June 26, 1906.

2. Ruthie Dennis, seventeen when she met White, had a similar experience. White introduced her to the photographer James Breese, who persuaded Dennis to pose nude. Breese later gave White a set of the photographs. See M. H. Dunlop, *Gilded City: Scandal and Sensation in Turn-of-the-Century New York* (New York: HarperCollins, 2000), 157.

3. "Mr. White Not in Studio on Night Evelyn Charges," *New York Herald,* February 27, 1907.

4. Evelyn Nesbit, *Prodigal Days: The Untold Story* (New York: Julian Messner, 1934), 41–42.

5. James C. Mohr, *Abortion in America: The Origins and Evolution of National Policy, 1800–1900* (New York: Oxford University Press, 1978), 136, 215–19.

6. Nesbit, *Prodigal Days,* 236, 242–43, 246; "Thaw's Riches May Go to Evelyn's Boy," *New York Sun,* April 23, 1916.

Author's Note

1. Editorial, "How Long, O Lord?" *New York World,* July 29, 1909; Editorial, "Thaw," *New York World,* June 18, 1912.
2. David Nasaw, *The Chief: The Life of William Randolph Hearst* (New York: Houghton Mifflin Co., 2000), 96–101, 104; James McGrath Morris, *Pulitzer: A Life in Politics, Print, and Power* (New York: HarperCollins, 2010), 321.
3. Nasaw, *The Chief,* 156–58.
4. Harry Thaw, *The Traitor* (Philadelphia: Dorrance & Co., 1926); Evelyn Nesbit, *Prodigal Days: The Untold Story* (New York: Julian Messner, 1934).
5. Leland M. Roth, *McKim, Mead & White, Architects* (New York: Harper & Row, 1983); Mosette Broderick, *Triumvirate: McKim, Mead & White* (New York: Alfred A. Knopf, 2010); Paula Uruburu, *American Eve: Evelyn Nesbit, Stanford White and the Crime of the Century* (New York: Riverhead Books, 2008); David Garrard Lowe, *Stanford White's New York* (New York: Doubleday, 1992); Wayne Craven, *Gilded Mansions: Grand Architecture and High Society* (New York: W. W. Norton & Co., 2009); Samuel G. White and Elizabeth White, *Stanford White, Architect* (New York: Rizzoli, 2008).

INDEX

Index

Index

Index

Index

Index

Index

ABOUT THE AUTHOR

SIMON BAATZ is a *New York Times* bestselling author and award-winning historian. He has graduate degrees in history from the University of Pennsylvania and Imperial College London, and he currently teaches United States history and American legal history at John Jay College, City University of New York. Simon grew up in London and has lived in Philadelphia, Washington, D.C., and Frankfurt am Main, Germany.

MULHOLLAND BOOKS

You won't be able to put down these Mulholland books.

BLUEBIRD, BLUEBIRD *by Attica Locke*

RIGHTEOUS *by Joe Ide*

A MAP OF THE DARK *by Karen Ellis*

THE GIRL ON THE VELVET SWING *by Simon Baatz*

THE TAKE *by Christopher Reich*

DOWN THE RIVER UNTO THE SEA *by Walter Mosley*

GREEN SUN *by Kent Anderson*

Visit mulhollandbooks.com for
your daily suspense fix.